DISCIPLINE,
ACHIEVEMENT,
AND
MENTAL HEALTH

2ND EDITION

E. Lakin Phillips
George Washington University

Daniel N. Wiener
Veterans Administration and University of Minnesota

Prentice-Hall, Inc., Englewood Cliffs, New Jersey

13-215798-5

Library of Congress Catalog Card Number: 78-151666

PRINTED IN THE UNITED STATES OF AMERICA

Current printing (last digit):

10 9 8 7 6 5 4 3 2

PRENTICE-HALL INTERNATIONAL, INC., *London*
PRENTICE-HALL OF AUSTRALIA, PTY. LTD., *Sydney*
PRENTICE-HALL OF CANADA, LTD., *Toronto*
PRENTICE-HALL OF INDIA PRIVATE LIMITED, *New Delhi*
PRENTICE-HALL OF JAPAN, INC., *Tokyo*

2/22/73 Robert Taylor 8.50

To GLP and our children
who have taught me more about learning
than have any schools
or classes

CONTENTS

PREFACE

The Preface to our 1960 edition opened with an overview of changes being proposed for classroom content and administration, but we wrote that the "worst neglect . . . lies in our too lightly passing over the details of how the child learns," and referred to the "central issue with education in any curriculum" being that of "How does one best structure, guide, and reinforce (reward) learning so that the child can continue to develop effectively on his own?"

A revolution has begun in American classrooms in the more than ten years since we wrote the first edition. Human and social values have been given renewed priority over administrative convenience, local customs, and social class habits. Slowly a more sensitive and democratic attitude toward students and their parents has intruded to change school administration.

Basic changes are occurring and new programs find far more favorable reception than perhaps since the twenties and thirties when professional educators, not nonprofessionals (as now) tended to initiate them. Whether the changes are happening too fast or too slowly, they are occurring much faster and deeper than for several decades; the educational system can never return to its structure and processes of the fifties and sixties. Opportunities to learn must be as equal and rich as they can be for all children. Relationships among children must be as democratic as possible. Teachers must be as sensitive and responsive to their students' needs and differences as they can be. The *momentum for change* today is in all of these directions.

But the *process* and *structure* for learning does not change so fast. Sorrowfully, many hopeful researchers are having to conclude from their data that none of these changes by itself or in combination is sufficient to produce and sustain catch-up learning in those who have not learned well in the past, nor to sustain it in new students. These changes may well be *necessary* but not *sufficient* conditions for optimal learning.

What remains to be done, when the best possible environmental conditions are obtained in the classroom—or in the home, or at work, or wherever—is to "structure, guide, and reinforce (reward) learning...." And this is our purpose today, in this edition. Even the home where all conditions for learning are made very favorable, with plenty of money, love, understanding, intelligence, and equality, will be capable of completely thwarting—or not developing—the learning of its children, if the learning process is not directed well.

We repeat here from the earlier edition that "The whole matter is one of promoting the *total process* of classroom learning. It is an organizational matter—it is a matter of planning and rewarding the learner's efforts so that he does not learn the wrong things, become bored, or just drift.

"Effective learning requires good discipline in the external process of education, and in the learner. It is hard work. It requires effort and sustained application. No device will substitute for these requirements, although it may help to implement learning activities.

"Good discipline promotes achievement. Good discipline and achievement promote mental health; one's view of oneself hinges to a great extent upon how one meets the demands and expectations of daily living.

"The association of good discipline and achievement is obvious. The ties of both to mental health can, we think, be easily perceived. The teacher can enhance all three of these vital links in the educational process by the means that we will discuss."

We have recast large chunks of the previous edition, particularly to incorporate some findings from behavior modification, which is pointing to new and more effective ways of changing behavior. We have also given more systematic consideration to ways that changes in the school environment can enhance classroom learning, changes such as increasing flexibility in student transfers, and classroom arrangements. There is, in addition, an effort to make our writing on concepts and practices more rigorous and concise.

In a personal way, we have gained more confidence in this intervening decade in the effectiveness of our views and methods. One of us has been counseling students and their parents in how to improve learning conditions and habits; the other of us has founded a school to teach severely disturbed and mentally retarded children what they need to know to handle themselves as well as what they are capable of, in the outside world.

We remain as optimistic as before that methods of training children well in the classroom are sufficiently known to us today so that teachers can with confidence learn them and, having learned them, can then practice their skills with a sure hand and quiet success.

E. LAKIN PHILLIPS
DANIEL N. WIENER

1

INTRODUCTION

The problems associated with discipline, achievement, and the mental health of children are among the most prevalent and serious of any problems found in the school system today.

Knock on any classroom door and ask the teacher what her biggest problems with children are. Ask a new teacher, one who is in her first or second year. Ask a seasoned teacher. Consult a principal who has taught classes and who has also handled students and their problems from an administrative standpoint.

To illustrate, a supervisor from Missouri writes:

> In the nine years I have served as a supervisor, the one single thing most frequently associated with teaching inadequacies and problems with children has been the need for better discipline.

A superintendent from New Hampshire writes:

> I think the joint problems of discipline and getting the best achievement out of children are the two biggest problems we face in our schools.

A teacher from California agrees and adds to the above statements:

> If the mental health of children—and I mean by "mental health" not only psychological well-being but efficient use of one's self and the capacity for

fruitful achievement—could be our principal effort in the schools, then I think society would profit and individuals would be happier and more useful citizens.

What do these statements imply? They say that teachers and administrators can benefit from more thought and training in the areas of discipline, achievement, and mental health to enable them to handle behavior problems better, cope with the able but unwilling learner, and direct the bully and the unhappy child effectively. Can one spend less time punishing and more time motivating children for solid achievement? Can one perform these important educational and mental health services without fostering false or unachievable goals and without neglecting other vital ones?

One may not need to knock on any classroom door, but simply view the school as a whole, or look to reports of a general nature on disciplinary problems. Some of these problems are obvious. For example:

1. Too large classes, making for classroom disciplinary as well as general school problems; usually, the larger the school and/or classroom, the more pressing the disciplinary problems.
2. Problems of discipline in classes that seem to be least popular—for example, science and math—and in classes required of all, such as English.
3. The tendency for home-based problems to spill over into the school and classroom. It is well known that delinquency and other social offenses rates have increased in the past decade or two, resulting not only in more community and home problems, but in many additional ones at school. The school is often blamed for disciplinary troubles at large in society.
4. An increase in acts of physical violence to persons (teachers and peers) at the junior and senior high school levels, and increased acts of vandalism.

One unfortunate consequence of these problems is that other troubles are multiplied. Schools have even had to close for short periods of time because they cannot cope with violence; teachers and principals have resigned or refused to work in troubled locations; and parents have descended upon school personnel to implore them to improve conditions. Social unrest, or at least acute dissatisfaction about disciplinary methods, broadly viewed, is widespread in our society. While the solution to these problems is now not wholly one of "tightening the reins" at school, this kind of structuring help, as well as community support, is sorely needed if the disciplinary problems are to end.

PROBLEMS WITH DISCIPLINE

How many times a day have you said or heard others say:
"This room is too noisy. You will have to settle down."

"Please do not force me to send you out of the room to the office."

"You will have to stop this fighting on the playground if you don't want to lose your recess period."

"When the class has come to order we can begin to work" (which this teacher had already said four times with a still unruly class.)

And so on, far into the school day. How many teachers do you know who spend more time scolding their students than they do teaching?

In one study of over 14,000 student misbehavior citations reported, 12,000 fell into a dozen categories of which the following were the most common: disturbance, disobedience, disrespect, and misrepresentation. Other disciplinary infractions included ignoring health and safety factors, smoking on school premises, fighting, doing property damage, using profane or obscene language, gambling, theft, and cheating. Over three-quarters of the infractions were included in the first three categories. In the past decade the more violent infractions have been found to be on the increase.

Time is spent on these disciplinary problems not because teachers want to spend time on them, but because there seems to be no way to avoid them. How many genuinely agreeable and interesting teachers do you know who are completely exhausted when the day is over?

What is the problem? In a word, DISCIPLINE. *What is the answer?* Better discipline on a preventive basis. And with this preventive effort, comes increased achievement and the better mental health of students and teachers. There are many answers to the need for better education, for more solid achievement, and for improved attitudes and mental health, and discipline figures in all of them.

THE BASIC IMPORTANCE OF DISCIPLINE

Why is discipline so important? Why stress it so much?

Simply because no group of people can share or work together without the presence of rules and regulations. This is true whether they are working as individuals or as members of a group.

But why are there rules and regulations? Are they imposed arbitrarily from outside by someone who doesn't know the needs of the group or the individuals?

No. Rules and regulations are necessary for the group to function well through its individual members or through its combined effort. They sometimes may be arbitrary or irrelevant, but some order is necessary for effective effort.

Good discipline is a way of achieving *team work toward goals.* It is a way of helping the individual to rise to his potential. Without good discipline, baseball teams, factories, and governments cannot function successfully. They might exist without disciplined organization, but they would not work well. An effective classroom full of students also is preposterous without good discipline. A team cannot play without effort, without coordination, without sharing goals. Who would know what to do—when, where, how—without rules and regulations, or without disciplined arrangements of players, rules, and goals?

Nor can a classroom teacher function without good discipline. Students cannot *learn* without purposeful application to the tasks at hand. Teachers cannot *teach* unless they have the students' attention, their interest, their application. The student has to be *involved* in the subject matter in order to learn.

Without good discipline then, the team is chaotic. Without good discipline, the schoolroom is a waste of people's time. No wonder the teacher who has to spend most of his time on behavior problems cannot teach the youngster what he should learn. No wonder the teacher is worn out from daily tugs-of-war—back and forth, forth and back—between himself and the students. It is not puzzling that achievement is impaired. Mental health problems arise in undisciplined atmospheres! Undisciplined atmospheres mean that goals are not shared, that procedures are not reliably pointed to achieving goals, that discouragement is common and that people become impatient or hostile with one another. Here "undisciplined" means "disordered," or without long-range purpose or structure leading to goals. If one purposefully wants to defeat the enemy, he plans how he can throw the adversary's plans into disorder, how the goals the opponent pursues can be disorganized. Sometimes these changes happen without an explicit enemy or adversary—they happen owing to poor planning, to disorder, and to the lack of appreciation of what discipline is needed if order is to be maintained.

THE PURPOSE OF THIS BOOK

In this book we will discuss with you—teacher, principal, guidance counselor, social worker, visiting teacher—these commonly shared problems. All who work with youth encounter discipline problems at one time or another—even the best of teachers. All teachers have students with achievement problems. It is not necessarily a reflection on the student or the teacher, if the problems are not ignored, but any professional involved should take responsibility to help overcome them.

It is important also to relate discipline to general mental health and achievement. Metal health problems are not seen or felt in isolation. They face the good teacher in the classroom and in the management of the child's learning just as they face the parent or any other person who is involved in child-rearing problems. The teacher and the school administrator need to relate discipline *and* achievement, and to relate both of these to the child's *mental health*.

Although many suggestions and much advice are given about discipline, this is not a look backward. It is not recommended that we return to the "good old days" of woodshed discipline, the razor strap or the paddle. We are attempting to deal in a more scientific and functionally adequate way with *current* problems that are often neglected in the classroom and in the school. Some of us may have assumed that if we push the right educational "button" all children would want to learn. A very unproductive search often results when we try to find a single correct way to motivate children. Some children do come to the teacher ready, motivated, eager to learn, easily reinforced for their efforts. But most children come to the school situation with scattered interests—some in learning, some in diversionary activities, and many in sports and other play activities. Children come eager to learn some things but not necessarily all things, and certainly not always the matters we as adults feel it important for them to learn. Most children do not give direction to their own learning by themselves. Society has always recognized this, otherwise we would not need schools.

Almost all children like to play ball games, but it takes the efforts of a persistent and patient coach to whip their scattered interests into disciplined, well-coordinated play. Children like to learn; at least they like to learn *something*. They are open to stimulation. By this we mean that they have a general curiosity, though it is often poorly coordinated, poorly directed, and may produce poor results. If left alone, natural curiosity would not necessarily direct the children in underprivileged areas of our own country; often many grow up lacking the ability to cope with our adult society.

A team could not achieve much if it were not well coordinated, even if it were composed of individually skilled players. In all-star games, stars are brought together temporarily to play a more seasoned and experienced group of players. Generally, if the leagues in which these teams play are evenly matched, the well-coordinated, experienced team wins over the all-stars, even though as individuals the all-stars may be superior. What the loser lacks is the coordinated, well-disciplined team work that the seasoned team has achieved.

A student does not achieve his best level of work if he is not well coordinated in his methods of study. If a student learns only "by ear"—that is, without some reliable learning guides and study skills—his likelihood of efficient achievement is precarious, at the least. He is not likely to last long with the rigors of higher education or professional life, or in skilled trades if his knowledge rests on what he can pick up here and there.

Not only is good discipline important in achievement, it is equally important in affecting the way we feel about ourselves and, indirectly, the way we feel about others. Our morale, our confidence, our self-esteem are all affected by the manner in which we achieve what we set out to achieve.

By the way we handle the tasks of everyday life, we evaluate ourselves either in positive or negative terms. We tend to reinforce ourselves positively or to condemn or dislike ourselves for our failures.

Take the child who is able but who never gets around to doing his assignments:

"Billy, I know you can do that if you will just try."

"Come Susan, give it your best effort, and we will see how well you *can* do it."

"I can't get Henry to make an effort—no wonder he can't handle his arithmetic assignment."

"They told me that my child does not apply himself, but I wasn't told how to help him improve this situation." (a mother's report from a teacher conference)

Mothers, fathers, teachers, principals—everyone who works with children is perplexed by the student who will not try. How can anyone learn successful habits if he does not make the effort?

Many teachers and parents are looking for an "open sesame" to the child's educational problems; thus, they may emphasize finding a simple key to get the child to *like* his learning task.

Perhaps most of us have at some time stretched our imagination to its limits in order to appeal to the child, to his wanting to learn. We serve up a delicious educational menu, and then if the child does not partake, we do not know what to do except to try to serve the same educational menu even more delightfully. Our intentions to educate are good, but they often miss the mark.

Teachers attribute too many of their educational, disciplinary, and related problems to *motivation*. We feel that much effort is wasted in this direction. We may be inadvertently teaching the child to expect his tutors to jump through educational hoops in order to please (or to motivate) the child. At the extreme, such a student could sit back with his arms folded and his eyes half closed, as if to say, "Try it again—you don't please me yet!"

But we shouldn't try to cram the material down the students' throats either. What then, shall we do? If we cannot *appeal* to them, and if we cannot *force* them, *what can we do?*

THE EDUCATIONAL DILEMMA

This is the dilemma in which we place ourselves. We try too hard to please; we try too hard to "sell" our educational wares to the child. We need not compete with Madison Avenue marketing experts; however, we certainly can learn from what other experienced groups—educators, classroom teachers, school systems, even nations—have been able to accomplish.

We need to take a careful look at our children, at our ways of teaching them, at our past and current deemphasis on discipline. If we do this, we will observe that we have been neglecting the very *core* of the problem. We have been neglecting what is needed in order to bring any complex pursuit involving people into a reasonable, productive course.

We have to set goals; we have to keep them clear; we have to let children know what is expected of them. We have to begin our teaching with a quiet, orderly (i.e., well-disciplined) class. We have to move through small steps to our goals to encourage even the slightest movement toward these goals. We must be more ready to reinforce small efforts toward acceptable goals than to punish failures or false starts.

In the well-ordered class there will be less wear and tear on the teacher and on the children; there will be less necessity for repeating assignments. Furthermore, orderliness is contagious, and when the child understands that the class lesson does not begin until order is established, it will be easier to maintain good discipline in the classroom.

We should not wait until the child goes astray educationally, loses interest, or fights against pressure before we attempt remedial effort. We should catch him on the bounce, as soon as his deflection is apparent. Catching him early is important.

IS DISCIPLINE OLD-FASHIONED?

"Isn't all this very old-fashioned, very dry, and really not very close to the child's needs?" a critic asks. Some people take this attitude toward discipline, saying that it is unimportant in achievement and in mental health. Some people look upon discipline as anathema to good education and mental health. This objection misses the real point about good discipline. Discipline has been misunderstood and certainly understressed until very recently. Discipline has been wrongly criticized as being injurious to learning, to the mental health of the child, and to the development of motivation for learning.

In this book we emphasize the role of discipline. It is important to differentiate more clearly between good and bad discipline. We want to assist teachers and others who are trying to help children to differentiate between old-fashioned "woodshed" discipline and discipline as "ordered learning."

Many of the problems of modern education will not be remedied by the discovery of new and fascinating methods of teaching or new mechanical devices. This is not to belittle new efforts or devices, but it is to caution against considering them as a substitute for, or at the expense of, better disciplined teaching and learning.

It also seems unlikely that the problems of education will be resolved by help from some as-yet hidden facts about motivation, which would unleash a learning spree in the average child. True, learning devices and increased motivation can be helpful (and we will discuss them later), *but they do not go to the root of the problem.* When such devices are helpful, they obtain their value through assisting the student to progress through meaningful steps to a goal and through certain reinforcement of effort. No device attempting to motivate through enticing presentation is likely to be very beneficial for long in the absence of disciplined habits.

We believe that a strong case can be made for that most maligned and poorly understood factor in learning: discipline. We feel that it is intimately related to achievement and to the student's psychological well-being, hence the title of this book: *Discipline, Achievement, and Mental Health.*

These three cornerstones to education are vital to learning any subject, be it first aid, metal shop, or calculus.

A BRIEF VIEW OF GOOD DISCIPLINE

Good discipline, like most good habits, should be unobtrusive. A teacher who acts and talks "tough" or only permissively is impaired as a good disciplinarian and as an effective teacher. A musician who is forever trying to get back on pitch or to retune his instrument is not in a favorable position to play; likewise, a teacher who is always having to try to discipline an unruly class is wasting much of his time and that of the students. Good discipline should be based upon a firm, quiet, fair, and reasonable program of order and learning, integrated with the student's activities and his level of competence.

In short, good discipline is composed of orderly presentation, orderly effort, and orderly use of the materials that have been learned, as well as dependable rewards or reinforcements.

Discipline has had its day before; it has been subject to changing whims and styles. It has been part of educational and child-rearing fads over decades and centuries, but something can be extracted and distilled from the past and current knowledge of discipline that is *modern, germane,* and that can *meet the child's needs* educationally and psychologically. The development, clarification, and application of this viewpoint are the aims of this book.

SELECTED READINGS

BENEDICT, R., "Child rearing in certain European countries." *Amer. J. Orthopsychiat.*, 1949, *19*, 342–50.

BLOM, G. E., "Psychoeducational aspects of classroom management." *Exceptional Children*, 1966, *32*, 377–83.

HURLOCK, E. B., *Child Development*. New York: McGraw-Hill, 1964.

PHILLIPS, E., D. N. WIENER, and N. G. HARING, *Discipline, Achievement, and Mental Health*. Englewood Cliffs, N.J.: Prentice-Hall, 1960.

ROBERTS, J. I., *School Children in the Urban Slum*. New York: The Free Press, 1967.

SPOCK, B., "What we know about the development of healthy personalities in children," *Understanding the Child*, 1951, *20*, 2–9.

SYMONDS, P. M., *What Education Has to Learn from Psychology*. New York: Bureau of Publications, Teachers College, Columbia University, 1958.

TYLER, R. W., "The behavioral sciences and the schools," 65th Yearbook of the National Society for the Study of Education, Part II, 1966, 200–14.

2

CHANGING
STYLES AND VALUES
IN DISCIPLINE

Classroom teachers tend to be practical people. Although attitudes toward discipline as well as philosophies of education have changed from time to time, classroom teachers have tended to be conservative, to know the value of discipline, and to try to maintain it. It may be true, as some have stated, that there is a considerable discrepancy between theoretical beliefs and actual classroom practices, yet discipline has always held at least an unofficial position of great importance with the classroom teacher. Also, many who have given up teaching or who have moved from one age group to another have frequently done so because of the problem of discipline with the group they have left.

Teachers have been sensitive to various aspects of discipline and mental health. Research over the past 40 or 50 years suggests that teachers tend to use disciplinary methods (discipline in the old-fashioned sense) most frequently with recalcitrant and overtly aggressive youngsters. They have thought of discipline as punitive. They have also tended to overlook the problem of the withdrawn child in favor of the child who has forced himself upon the teacher's attention because of the overt problems he has created. Teachers have felt that the withdrawn child needed no discipline in the old sense of the term (punishment), but that the obstreperous child did need it ("We've got to discipline him").

Perhaps this discrepancy between theory and practice touches not only the teacher but the parent, and all of society, as well. We tend to "punish" to try to get someone to stop doing something. Fines, sentences, beatings, cursing, threats, admonitions, all fall into this punitive category. Yet, against this punitiveness, we talk about how good it is to encourage, to reinforce, to set valid and viable examples, to work for alternatives. There has been little or no systematic realignment to reduce discrepancies between theory and practice in this large area of educational psychology. The teacher has been confused by this discrepancy.

To many, the dropping of old-fashioned punitiveness (discipline in the older sense) has left a void; too few are able to put the positive alternatives into effect here, or they are too impatient to work for long-range results. What is called for is a more creative, ingenious, *positive* approach to disciplinary problems. Instead of the parent saying, "If you don't stop that drumming on the table, you'll drive me crazy," he or she might say, "You know, Bill, you forgot to empty the trash this morning; *now* is a good time." This is avoiding punitiveness (harsh words), and finding a creative, positive alternative; it is especially good because, in this example, Bill had not done his assigned work. After all, isn't this what we want him to learn to do? Should we not, then, concentrate on this positive goal? And should we not use the same general approach if Bill were simply sitting, passively daydreaming, wandering from reality? The positive alternative here is to get the trash box emptied, but it belongs to a very large class of events which make up our day-to-day world most of the time.

DISCIPLINE OF THE WITHDRAWN CHILD

In the past decade or two teachers have been taught to look for the withdrawn child as well as the overly assertive or aggressive child. If education is to be effective, it has to reach each child. If education is to reach each child, the teacher has to know about the problems of the withdrawn child. The withdrawn child needs good discipline in the broad sense of the word as much as the overactive child needs it.

Thus the emphasis moves away from associating discipline only with the woodshed, the back of the hand, or the strap, and from the application of these measures to the recalcitrant and overactive child. An appreciation has grown of the mental health problems and disciplinary needs of the withdrawn child as well. The practical difficulty lies in how to apply discipline to the problem of the shy or withdrawn child. The authors' feeling is that in many ways the problems of the shy child are very similar to the problems of his opposite, and that the same general techniques of discipline apply.

The shy or withdrawn child tends not to make the initial effort. The overaggressive or overassertive child tends to make an effort but usually in a distracted or poorly directed way or in a manner not compatible with the learning task at hand. Both types of children need an orderly, disciplined *beginning point*. It is important in the case of the shy child to give very small assignments, perhaps one arithmetic problem at a time or three or four spelling words at a time, in order to give him confidence in achievement.

It is also important to build confidence in the shy child through small incremental steps in social participation. For example, the shy child can be asked to check the classroom register of attendance for the day and report to the teacher. This does not involve much interaction with the other children and shyness is usually not challenged severely by this kind of classroom participation. After a while the shy child can be asked to give brief reports on some subject that interests him. As a further step, this child can participate with two or three other children on a committee, in preparing some skit for the classroom, or in explaining a chart or map which might hang from the wall. The shy child needs special attention until his first feeble efforts are reliably encouraged and educational and social development momentum is established. From this point on, it is a matter of directing small changes through efforts and reinforcements, permitting the child to form a general pattern of achievement and social confidence.

REASONING: A SUBSTITUTE FOR DISCIPLINE?

As the mental hygiene movement and Freudian views began to take hold, great emphasis was placed on "understanding" the child. "Understanding" meant to probe the "deep" urges, drives, and early traumas which were presumably at the roots of many problems of conduct. If a child failed to obey, it was thought that it was because he did not feel understood and loved by the adult. Getting the child to sit down with the adult and sympathetically talk over the whole matter was supposed to settle most of the problems.

This book in no way speaks against "understanding" the child. The reader must, however, be cautioned that understanding is not the final answer to solving problems. Certainly proper discipline requires understanding; and it also requires understanding to know when to let the child work out his own solutions. But we need to ask, "Understanding for what purpose?"

If it is understanding in order to better motivate the child—to help him achieve better discipline, to get him to follow through with assignments, to learn to handle his efforts at social exchange with his peers—well and good. The understanding has to be made specific in terms of goals and concrete situations, and not left to stand by itself, for then it solves nothing.

Concomitantly, *reasoning* has been and often still is thought to be very important in solving behavior problems. When does the child reach the age of reason? At what time does the child become responsive to reason? How is reasoning made effective? These and many more problems arise with the emphasis on reasoning.

At what age does the child become responsive to reason? Estimates vary from about age three up to age twelve. Today we realize that there is no precise "age of reason," no precise time in which a child becomes and remains susceptible to reason. Amenability to reasoning depends upon many conditions such as a child's emotional state at the time, the issues involved in conduct, the attitude and the manner of the adult, and the presence or absence of social pressures from fellow students. Also, a child may reason very clearly in one situation and very poorly in another one, when there is no basic difference in the reasoning or intellectual power involved. Ability to reason depends upon what is at stake as well as upon intellectual ability or willingness to face the facts.

Of course reasoning is important in conduct and in the self-control that an individual has to acquire progressively if he is to take his place in society. But it is not a technique that can be directly taught and depended upon in the classroom. The emphasis on reason arose, in part, out of a growing revulsion against corporal punishment. Perhaps all styles in behavior as in dress reach a point of excess and then slowly recede or are modified with a countertrend.

Reasoning, we believe, has been an overworked concept in the past; its value today in education and in child rearing is related to its use in the context of meaning given the child by responsible adults. We reason with the child that he must get his work done before he can play, but if we only reason with him and fail to *support* this logic with clear follow-through on our part, then we have misused reasoning and overlooked other crucial considerations.

Some would say *empathy* plays a big role here. Empathic reasoning would be better than nonempathic reasoning. That is, taking the child's feelings and point of view into consideration is important. Empathy, here, means that the *approach* to the child is in terms of his values and his perspective, but this emphasis on empathic *means* does not, of course, change the ends we have in mind. That is, the ends are to get some behavior to change (such as to get work done, or to be more considerate of others) ; we approach the child empathically in order to appeal to him or to get into his behavior or psychological economy, to facilitate the change we have in mind.

Piaget's work helps us with the empathic understanding of the child. In turn, this capacity depends upon knowing the individual child, or upon knowing some important things about how children look at the world, how they reason with facts, and how they are able to draw conclusions and act on the basis of evidence at hand. We should avoid imposing solutions on the child wholly from the "outside," as we would mold concrete to a given shape. Children do not harden and stay in place; we always have to take their feelings and condition into prime consideration. This is the *means* part of the issue of changing behavior—understanding children and reaching desired goals with them. The *ends*, of course, are equally important and help us to focus on how well we reach our goals and whether correction—which may involve rearranging the means—is indicated.

SOCIAL CHANGE ALSO AFFECTS DISCIPLINE

In the frontier days of our country, discipline was probably more rigorous than it is today. The very lives of the pioneers depended on the maintenance of good discipline, for there were many dangers lurking which could readily destroy them. It was not only the destruction of the individual that was involved; the entire community might be destroyed because of the undisciplined ones.

There was apparently little interest in "permissiveness" during our frontier period. "Spare the rod and spoil the child" seems to have been a tacit if not an explicit slogan. Life was too earnest and too demanding for parents to allow their child to sulk when he should be watering the chickens or taking fodder to the horses. There was too much urgency in daily living to allow much time for the luxuries of self-commiseration or self-indulgence about the wrongs one suffered from others. When people acquired more leisure time, however, more choices were available. With more choices available, there were more opportunities for differences of opinion. The structure of social demands and of work for the necessities of life has receded and allows for many more individual choices in our present world. The survival value of certain standards of conduct is no longer as clear; additional problems in discipline have resulted.

Some sociologists today discuss discipline problems in terms of the variety of social roles people are asked to play. A child may climb on the furniture at home, but not at his neighbor's house. The child may "talk back" to his older brother and sister or to younger aunts and uncles, but he cannot get by with this conduct at school. A child may be rewarded unwittingly by his parents after taking unfair advantage of smaller children, but this code may not hold up when he participates with Boy Scouts, with those stronger than himself, or in school competition.

Social roles have also changed with the times. There are more social roles today and they are generally more complex than ever before. A child today has more to learn about social proprieties than he had to two or three generations ago.

Even the word "discipline" has had different connotations over time. Though it has been in poor repute, this situation is changing, and there is considerably more respect for the importance of discipline today than there was a decade ago. If we add the prefix "self" and make the word "self-discipline," it is even more acceptable. Today the word still has a connotation from the permissive era, referring to woodshed tactics more than to guiding, supervising, and directing the child's opportunities and choices.

WHAT IS THE RELATIONSHIP
BETWEEN PUNISHMENT AND DISCIPLINE?

The further one goes back in time—at least within the confines of the last two centuries in our country—the more "discipline" tends to connote punishment. "To discipline" has meant to punish, often physically—spanking, smacking, strapping, switching.

It is easy to see how a revulsion to these tactics grew as the urgency for control lessened. Corporal punishment was a privilege which parents, teachers, and other adults could easily overdo. The child was the greatest immediate loser in such a program; the adults and society in general were the indirect losers, feeling the effects of the child's resentment in being so summarily or brutally treated.

The reaction against physical punishment became so great that now most states have passed laws against the "laying of hands" on the child at school. Only recently, with the revival of interest in firmer discipline in the school and with concern over the growth of many assaults against persons and school property, has repeal of this type of law been considered in some states. Some schools today will administer corporal punishment if the individual parent signs a form stating that he will allow it and stand behind the teacher's corrective efforts, or if a chaotic situation calls for an immediate show of strength by adults against gangs or crowds.

Punishment has several meanings. First, it is meant to correct an infraction—the individual who is punished is expected not to recommit the offense; he is supposed to learn a lesson from his punishment. Another use of punishment is to serve as an example to other people. Society says in effect, "See, you cannot get by with this kind of behavior." A third function is to assuage the conscience of society, by taking its "vengeance" on the individual for the harm done to society.

We know today that punishment as such is not a very effective way of controlling behavior. The number of people who have been executed, put in jail, or confined in penitentiaries for long sentences has not in any discernible way reduced crime. So the preventive value of punishment certainly can be questioned.

The corrective value of punishment can also be questioned. Many offenders are repeaters who get into further difficulty after their original offense. The punishment they suffered has not deterred them nor directed them into more productive social living. Similarly with vengeance; most people are not interested in the social offender after he has been apprehended and confined. In fact, this very disinterest has limited rehabilitative efforts and led to an overemphasis on punishment.

In summary, then, punishment is ineffectual in rehabilitation, it is often unfair to its victims, and it does not function in the misguided ways it is intended for.

It is important for the reader to realize that there is no identity in this book of discipline with punishment. Discipline has an entirely different meaning and should not in any way be confused with punishment.

THE NEWER MEANING OF DISCIPLINE

It is a curious twist of usage that has allowed so many connotations of the word "discipline" to develop. If one consults a dictionary, the most likely definition of "discipline" will have to do with being taught, with subordinating oneself to the demands of learning. The word "discipline" is related to the word "disciple," which means to learn or to be a student, to submit oneself to some master or some task. We are returning now to this definition, completely away from any punitive connotation.

The older meaning of discipline is reemerging, then, as we strip away the obscuring layers and connotations of the word. One can recognize that discipline meant regulated scholarship, learning, organized activity; that various intervening philosophies of education and child rearing which played on man's values had imposed connotations which distorted the original view of discipline. It is the revival of this earlier notion, refined by modern science, in the study of child rearing and behavior that is needed for the success of both education and child rearing.

The new dress which we propose for the old form is one woven from the best information from modern sciences having to do with man and his development, man and his problems of living in social groups. As we have indicated in the first chapter, undisciplined social living is anathema to the effective educational process. It is, in effect, a kind of anarchy in education. Good discipline, on the other hand, is a basic and necessary condition for social living and for education. Creating interest and using modern educational tools are, of course, other important considerations.

In summary, then, we hope to be able now to build upon a system of disciplined learning which can utilize all scientific findings to produce well-educated students. How can this be done?

SELECTED READINGS

CLIFFORD, E., "Discipline in the home: A controlled observational study of parental practices." *J. Genet. Psychol.*, 1959, *95*, 45–82.

FLAVELL, JOHN H., *The Developmental Psychology of Jean Piaget*. New York: Van Nostrand Reinhold, 1963.

HARING, NORRIS G., and E. LAKIN PHILLIPS, *Educating Emotionally Disturbed Children*. New York: McGraw-Hill, 1962.

JOHNSON, DONALD M., *The Psychology of Thought and Judgment*. New York: Harper and Row, 1955.

KAPLAN, BERNARD, and HEINZ WERNER, eds., *Perspectives in Psychological Theory*. New York: International Universities Press, 1960.

PIAGET, JEAN, *The Child's Conception of the World*. New York: Harcourt Brace, 1929.

WERTHEIMER, MAX, *Productive Thinking* (revised ed.). New York: Harper and Row, 1959.

3

FEATURES
OF GOOD AND BAD
DISCIPLINE

Discipline of some sort is necessary in the classroom. Even those who appear to oppose it or to minimize its importance know that sooner or later they will have to employ discipline in some form. One problem is that those who fail to accept discipline as *integral* to the school and classroom find it difficult to use it effectively when they are faced with crises. This poor use of discipline tends to lead to punitive or placating methods which give discipline a bad name.

By "bad" discipline we mean discipline that is too harsh, too quickly administered, too negative, overgeneralized—and self-defeating, emphasizing the person rather than his deed. Good discipline should have positive and trouble-preventive characteristics.

BAD DISCIPLINE:
TOO HARSH AND TOO QUICK

Discipline that is too harsh is, by definition, disproportionate to the act that it seeks to correct. If you park your car overtime on the street and are fined $1,000, the penalty is too harsh. Similarly, if you take away a child's recess time for one month because he is caught whispering when he should have been quiet, the penalty is too harsh. The corrective measure should fit the infraction in a meaningful way.

Discipline that is too quickly administered is undesirable. It is important for the adult to wait to see if the child is going to follow through on his request. We do not want to "jump the gun" on the child. Some children move slowly; some of them know they will follow through on your orders but first they want to make you doubt it or want to take their time. If you wait them out, you and the child will be spared unnecessary conflict. Ordinarily we should not expect children to "jump" when spoken to, but we do not want to wait indefinitely either. It should suffice that the teacher can see some evidence that the child is beginning to move toward compliance; small efforts toward the goal should be encouraged.

Children will sometimes resist by being slow, obstinate or negative. If we know this is true of a certain child, we can expect it as part of his expression of his feelings, and we will not act upon his recalcitrance. With the passage of time the child tends to "cool off" and often changes in a favorable direction. Our present purpose is not to delineate all possibilities in a child's reaction but simply to suggest that the child has a kind of time schedule on which he operates—it is best to know this and to accept it.

BAD DISCIPLINE: TOO NEGATIVE

Sometimes discipline is too negative in its effects. Since discipline should serve to *correct* an error, misapprehension, or misdemeanor, it should indicate the *positive alternatives* that are available to the person. It is better to illustrate what is wrong and to suggest positive alternatives rather than leave the learner with no guidance. For example, in telling a child that he cannot draw during arithmetic class, it is more effective to say that drawing can be resumed when the arithmetic lesson is finished. This does not eliminate drawing altogether—an act that might irritate or depress the child and produce inertia in arithmetic—but allows it at its proper time. The use of No should be accompanied, whenever possible, by the conditions under which Yes would be possible. Room should be left for reasonable adjustment.

The controversy over whether a child learns better through punishment or reward is involved here. Punishment does more harm than good in the sense in which we have discussed it above. But the restatement of punishment in the terms of corrective discipline leading to positive alternatives can be useful. Commonly, negative discipline and punishment do not lead to alternatives—they deprive the child of his freedom and allow him little recourse for improvement. Such a procedure puts the child in a state of frustration and conflict. "No, you cannot do this, but you *may* do that," can be a helpful approach.

Reward and reinforcement do lead to alternatives. Reward indicates what is acceptable and is most easily applied when the child picks or approximates the right alternative. You may have to work extensively with him, you may have to be patient almost to the breaking point, but once the child is moving in the right direction, the rewards can follow naturally. There is nothing more powerful for learning than a reward or reinforcement. The child simply has to learn how the rewards are obtained in his environment, particularly with regard to educational matters and conduct, and then he can be on his way to constructive endeavor.

BAD DISCIPLINE:
OVERGENERALIZED AND SELF-DEFEATING

Poor discipline is self-defeating, especially when the teacher tries to get the child to behave more congenially or to see through a problem, and then becomes overcritical of the child if he fails. If he is admonished too much, if he is accused of being "dumb" or "stubborn," if his whole personality is included in the accusation, he may be overwhelmed.

This is damaging to the child's self-respect, causing him to wonder why he should try at all if he is so bad. The teacher may mean well in such instances, but *the strategy needs correction.* The teacher wants to lead the child to positive, rewardable alternatives but may lose his patience, impairing his normal skillfulness. As a result, the teacher may concentrate on the child's shortcomings, overgeneralizing to the whole personality of the child instead of keeping corrections within the confines of the problem at hand. If a child is slow in learning important behavior, it does not follow that he is "dumb" (we can learn from objective tests if the child is a slow learner, and if so, we need to make proper allowances for his rate of learning), but it does follow that *our* techniques may need changing.

Self-defeating, overgeneralizing discipline also appears when adults take children's mischief too seriously and act as if *any* deviation needs immediate correction. A group of youngsters in the upper elementary grades sang the following song just below their principal's window:

> Mine eyes have seen the glory of the burning of the school; We have tortured every teacher, and we have broken every rule; We have ransacked the office and we have killed the principal; As we go marching on.

To the surprise of the children and many of the other faculty members, the song brought down the wrath of the principal on the children. He made several attempts to get the names of those who had sung the "impudent and disrespectful" song and to have them suspended from school. Applying such serious consequences to harmless childhood behavior backfired and caused the principal embarrassment. He might have laughed with the children, or ignored them with better effect.

Well-intended corrective measures may suffer because of misapplication. A teacher who asks the student to write 500 times "I must not chew gum in class" is not utilizing corrective measures. This type of discipline fails to provide an alternative to what the child has done and centers too much attention on the infraction itself. We ordinarily gain more from corrective measures which skip over the wrong behavior and emphasize positive alternatives.

BAD DISCIPLINE:
MIXING CORRECTION AND EDUCATION

One should not mix educational requirements with corrective disciplinary measures. A child does not profit from being made to study as punishment for misbehavior. Such a procedure impairs both the studying and the punishment.

Consider the common practice of keeping children after school because of misbehavior, and expecting them to study during this time. "Which is which?" we might ask. Which is supposed to be the more important, the punishment of staying after school as a correction for misbehavior, or the staying after school for the purpose of studying?

A better way to handle this type of problem is to have the child immediately finish his incomplete schoolwork, rather than have him stay after school. Thus, if he has taken another child's pencil, returning it is the first order of business, or perhaps bringing in a new pencil to replace the stolen one. Keeping him after school to study is a penalty which may well contribute to poor study attitudes and habits and increased resentment of school, rather than correction of the misconduct. We do not disagree with the corrective intent on the teacher's part, but correction should hit the mark.

Teachers have been known to limit the activities and privileges of a whole class because of the failure to identify a particular child who was an offender. This is even worse than having a child stay after school and study for some infraction because it is an accusation against innocent children—it is punitive and negative. It is also self-defeating and makes the teacher appear both helpless and wrong.

Nor should low grades be given for misdemeanors. Able and achieving students may also show behavior problems, and sometimes school authorities reduce their grades to try to correct their misbehavior. Grades and conduct should be kept separate. It is not fair to the child and not representative of the learning facts to cut his "A" in arithmetic back to a "B" because he misbehaves in the arithmetic class. Mixing correction and education is injurious to both efforts.

BAD DISCIPLINE: OVERDOING CORRECTION

Sometimes teachers with good intentions and good aims overdiscipline the child, applying too much confusing correction. If you were learning to drive a car and your tutor corrected every little mistake you made, you might become so upset that you would give up in anger or despair. The teacher may merely be overly cautious, even if corrections are given in good spirit.

A child or an adult learning a complex skill needs to get a feeling for the whole action sequence. The teacher should break the sequence into manageable parts, without destroying the child's understanding of the whole activity (the gestalt). Ball players and other athletes are sometimes "tightened up" or "overdisciplined," meaning that they are so afraid of making errors that they fail to take reasonable chances and lose the aggressiveness and skill which they normally possess.

A critic can always pick out minutia to ridicule, but the criticism has no corrective or disciplinary effect whatsoever if it simply confuses or angers. Teachers who mean to instruct the student would do well to consider the frequency with which they risk being overmeticulous and self-defeating.

Meticulous criticism and guidance should usually be reserved for the "spit and polish" stages of a performance. If you were helping students with a play, you would not expect them to have proper inflections and interpretations with the first reading; you would be willing to let that develop with time. Likewise in the acquisition of classroom skills or in the remedying of misconduct, the big ruffles have to be ironed out first, with the details being attended to later.

But might not a little mistake or act of dishonesty be overlooked and lead to others? In time, several small errors, added together, may require the special attention given a major mistake. Elsewhere we note that errors should be corrected as immediately as possible. We comment here only on situations where numerous errors cannot be attended to right away without disrupting the larger purpose.

Sometimes the mistakes a child makes carry with them sufficient corrections. It is of no value to add criticism when he already knows that he has erred or misbehaved. If the consequences of the child's action are clear to him, this is the best lesson he can learn. For example, a child who leaves his bicycle unattached or unlocked at the side of the school building during an evening scout meeting comes out to find the bicycle stolen. The error and its consequence are clear to the child. To scold or admonish will only add guilt and resentment to the child's feelings. Let the reality of the situation stand for itself as admonition, if possible. Better yet, try to go on to a more constructive alternative, such as what it would cost to buy the proper lock for the next bicycle. Or how the child can earn money to buy a replacement bicycle, with the proper facilities for its security.

Consider also the cancellation of an examination for cheating. If the paper is destroyed and the child is given a zero for that test, with no chance to recoup, you need not lecture him or warn him at the beginning of all future examinations. The penalty is sufficient and complete. Keeping the issue alive simply adds to the child's guilt and does not facilitate the development of alternatives (e.g., better studying for exams and reading the entire examination over before he begins writing).

Teachers may let correctible episodes go by without attention, hoping that the child will correct himself. When the child's behavior continues, the teacher may experience a "summation effect." That is, he will punish the child all at once—too strongly to be effective. Like learning, correction proceeds more successfully by small increments and early application.

CORRECTION VERSUS PUNISHMENT

A common cause of poor discipline comes from the teacher's tendency to take the child's threats of retaliation too seriously. If you give children a chance, they will often "defend" themselves. That is, they will hold a point of view or a course of action under criticism which seems unrealistic to an adult. This tendency on the part of the child—and indeed on the part of all of us sometimes—must be accepted as natural. This is especially true with youth since they are not fully socialized and often take a narrow view of matters affecting them. If we take seriously their lying or stubborn refusal to face the facts, they may be driven into taking a course that is momentarily logical to them but harmful in the long run. In such instances, the child sees no other way out without losing face.

In approaching a child whom you suspect of lying, you will do best to avoid referring to the lie itself; rather, you should place emphasis on the acts or conditions about which the dispute arises. Frequently statements like "Don't lie to me" or "I'll get the truth out of you if it is the last thing I do" are unnecessary and do not uncover the facts.

If there is sufficient evidence to indicate the child's guilt, do not try to "break him down" or demand a confession. This will worsen his attitude, narrow his viewpoint, humiliate him, or prejudice him toward you as a teacher and friend. Children may be very loyal to themselves, to a code, and to a friend, and often will stand against adults against all odds. One such child was Ralph.

Ralph was the only child in the room during a break at a scout meeting. He had to stay in because of some earlier misconduct. When the scoutmaster and children returned after the break, one child discovered that he had lost his new fountain pen, which he had just been using at the meeting. He immediately turned to Ralph, the boy sitting behind him who had to stay behind, and accused him. Ralph denied the charge. The scoutmaster, seeing the likely correctness of the charges against Ralph began to cross-examine the boy: "Did you see this pen on William's desk?" "Did you know it was his pen?" "Did you use it?" "Did you borrow it perhaps?" and so on for several minutes of fruitless probing.

The evidence in such a case might permit the scoutmaster (or teacher) to call the boy before him and to ask him quietly and unobtrusively to turn in the pen. The adult might give him some words of caution or suggest he discuss with his parents the buying of a new pen and then let the matter drop. But by giving the child the "third degree" the adult does not enhance morality, self-discipline, or a sense of fair play in the boy. The confrontation is too blunt and humiliating to be likely to succeed.

As with any punishment-reward considerations, the remedy here is to point the way to the remedial response or attitude (i.e., returning the pen) rather than dwelling on the errors themselves. Taking the child's lying at face value, assuming that this is the way he really wants to look at the matter, is too harsh and rigid a punishment. It is better to touch lightly on the misconduct and to put emphasis on the solution.

Fear, also, is a poor disciplinary method. Occasionally one encounters a teacher or parent who tries to frighten the child as much as possible to get compliance. "If you do not do your work, I will call the principal and he will spank you." "If you do not study, God will not like it and he will punish you." Children often use drastic threats to control one another. "You play with me or I will strike a match and burn your fingers," was the control one child tried to use on a playmate. The operation of bullies is generally based on fear-ridden control.

Fear is an example of bad discipline because the threats are usually fantastically unreal and will not be implemented. The accuser is thereby likely to lose status as well as the respect of the one he is trying to control. The threatening one is seen as the weak person he indeed is, in calling upon fear. The alternative to invoking fear as a method of discipline is obviously that of finding realistic consequences and then seeing that the consequences come true.

IS PUNISHMENT REALLY NECESSARY?

Punishment, we believe, is usually an ineffectual or harmful form of discipline; good discipline should point the way to *alternative* ways of behaving. We should not, from a modern scientific viewpoint, equate discipline with punishment. *We should equate discipline with learning, guidance, control, direction and purpose, and reinforcement of the desired behavior.*

The reader may protest: "Positive action is of course best, but how can you always get to it?" "Is it not necessary to meet misconduct and unwanted behavior 'head on' in some cases?" "Don't you actually need to punish the offensive behavior?"

The issue can be solved by referring not to punishment, with all of its negative connotations, but to the importance of levying *consequences* for behavior that is undesirable. Take, for example, a common household situation. If you do not pay your telephone bills, the company disconnects your telephone. Are they punishing you for not paying your bill? Hardly. At least it is not calculated as punishment per se; it is simply a necessary concomitant of the service agreement. Suppose also that a girl leaves her new doll out in the rain and discovers in a few days that the doll has become disfigured and is beginning to disintegrate. Is nature punishing her for her careless actions with the doll? There are cases where nature may seem to "punish," without calculation; this is a mystical interpretation of the facts.

THE NEED FOR CONSEQUENCES AND ALTERNATIVES

Our point is simply this: Let the deed carry its own automatic consequences and we need not punish the doer. In place of punishment one can think in terms of natural or logical consequences that follow an action—or that you would want to follow any action—and see that these consequences do follow whenever possible. Consequences should be stated in advance. Then when the consequences do befall the child, they will not be viewed as punishment but rather as the end result of a course of action, which the child could anticipate. The teacher in such cases may well be tested to see if he means what he says.

The consequences of actions that the child may take can be spelled out in positive terms: "When you have completed your seat work, you may help Suzie make a castle in the playhouse." "All children who have finished the arithmetic assignment may begin their art work in the next room." "You may go out to play when you have done your spelling lesson accurately." There are countless possibilities.

In this manner of levying consequences, then, these are the major steps:

1. First, set some positive, agreeable alternatives (rewards) for the child by telling him he may engage in the desired activity after he has acceptably completed the job at hand. This is a matter of settling a contingency. You may have 'A" after you have performed "B."

2. He must first complete an assignment which is already before him or which he knows about.
3. No punishment is suggested; work is related to a reward that is built into the child's activity.
4. All relevant matters are stated in advance. One does not pop up at the last minute with some punishment or unexpected condidition that sets the child against you or his work.

In these ways the child learns to respect the adult's requirements. He knows that the teacher's word will be backed up with clear-cut action that is well mapped out in advance. What better way is there to train children to make good choices and develop self-discipline?

This procedure precludes the use of punishment in the negative, blocking, accusative, personality-damaging sense of the word. It does not however, naively assume that if you do the right thing all the time, you will automatically elicit the desired behavior from the child. It does take into account that the child may be very reluctant to do as asked but that, with the presentation of clear-cut alternatives, the child knows what will happen to him with either course of action. He may wish to test the teacher to see if he means business. But the course of what happens will be the best teaching condition. The child will see and will learn that the alternatives are present; that they are being firmly held; that they are followed by known consequences; and that the courses of action are thereby open for him to see and to judge.

If a child continues to create problems and to make poor choices, the teacher may ask himself if he has been following his own words, if he has been acting instead of just talking, and if he may have done things which have offset or undercut the natural consequences which he has been trying to employ. It will be unusual if the child does not learn in a short time that his efforts belong on one side of the fence and not on the other. An extremely disturbed child may contend with teachers, but as fair and firm tests of the child's amenability to change are observed and assessed in the manner suggested, we will have our best measure of when the child is beyond teaching in the regular classroom. He may then have to be placed in a different environment—perhaps in some specially arranged class—but probably on the same general consequences basis.

SELECTED READINGS

AMSTERDAM, RUTH, *Constructive Classroom Discipline and Practice.* New York: Comet Press Books, 1957.

BENNETT, E. M., "A socio-cultural interpretation of maladjustive behavior." *J. Soc. Psychol.*, 1953, *37*, 19–26.

BOWMAN, HERMAN J., "A review of discipline." *National Assn. of Secondary School Principals Bull.*, 1959, *43*, 147–56.

CHRISTENSEN, C. M., "Relationships between pupil achievement, pupil affect-need, teacher warmth, and teacher permissiveness." *J. Educ. Psychol.*, 1960, *51*, 169–74.

CUTTS, NORMA E., and NICHOLAS MOSLEY, "Four schools of school discipline— A synthesis." *School and Society*, 1959, *87*, 87.

GESELL, A., F. L. ILG, and L. B. AMES, *Youth: The Years from Ten to Sixteen.* New York: Harper and Row, 1956.

HYMES, JAMES L., Jr., *Behavior and Misbehavior.* Englewood Cliffs, N.J.: Prentice-Hall, 1955.

KRALL, GEORGE M., "What about discipline?" *The Clearing House*, 1960, *34*, 534–36.

McGUIRE, C., and G. D. WHITE, "Social-class influences on discipline at school." *Educ. Leadership*, 1957, *14*, 229–31, 234–36.

SEARS, R. R., E. E. MACCOBY, and H. LEVIN, *Patterns of Child Rearing.* New York: Harper and Row, 1957.

WATSON, G., "Some personality differences in children related to strict or permissive parental discipline." *J. Psychol.*, 1957, *44*, 227–49.

WHITLEY, H. E., "Mental health problems in the classroom." *Understanding the Child*, 1954, *23*, 98–103.

4

HOW
GOOD DISCIPLINE
IS DEVELOPED
AND MAINTAINED

Techniques for influencing behavior are as old as mankind's social relationships. Probably no one era has had a monopoly on effective disciplinary techniques. In fact, some ages have been known for their lack of discipline. Historians have remarked that a measure of the disintegration of a nation is a people who were undisciplined and self-indulging.

In some ways today we are only slightly wiser than people of past generations. If we are wiser, it is because we can stand on the shoulders of these others and, with the aid of science, test the usefulness of knowledge more readily and more accurately and communicate knowledge more widely. Thus, if new or revised techniques of discipline are proposed, we can study them today more systematically and determine their effectiveness or the limits of their applicability.

It is important to realize that good discipline must not only be effective at the moment but it must build long-range habits and supporting attitudes. It is one thing to influence a person on a momentary basis, and another matter to have this influence built into the integrity of the individual's behavioral economy. One can clap one's hands loudly and frighten another person, draw another's attention, or abruptly cause someone to stop doing whatever he is doing. In a sense this is a momentary external disciplinary measure, and it might be useful in calling somebody back from slipping into deep water or walking thoughtlessly into heavy traffic. But such an alert does not in itself teach a person always to be careful while swimming or cautious when crossing the street.

As previously discussed, there are two general approaches to discipline which have not been effective, at least on a long-term basis. The first is the kind that is too abrupt or harsh or that is disproportionate to the situation it seeks to correct. The second is that which is too weak or equivocal. While used throughout the ages, both these extremes of disciplinary control have suffered from lack of self-conscious and deliberate direction as to how discipline can be made effective. Insofar as discipline differs today from what it has been in the past, it may lie in our seeking a middle ground that attempts to avoid the extremes of harshness, with its lack of resilience, and of permissiveness, with its excessive resilience.

In the previous chapter we began to put some flesh of meaning on our skeleton of good discipline, and its relation to the classroom situation. Throughout the remainder of this book we will attempt to fill out the picture and to consider discipline in the perspective of our present scientific knowledge and in relation to achievement and mental health.

GOOD DISCIPLINE IS PLANNED

We should know as well as we can the child's present level of achievement, his abilities, and his interests. On the basis of knowledge about his achievement in comparison with his ability, we can infer his past and present motivation. If he has achieved up to or near his capacity, then there is no gap to close between what he is capable of doing and what he in fact does. If, however, he has performed very poorly in comparison with his ability, we have good reason to infer that he lacks motivation, has poor work habits, does not know how to concentrate, or fails to receive proper encouragement (reinforcement) from his environment. This is where good discipline can be of considerable help.

Psychological tests and careful supplemental observations are useful ways of learning about the child's achievement, his interests, and his ability. Test use has to be left mainly to the school or child psychologists, or to guidance counselors who have sufficient training and knowledge to interpret their meaning. This is not the place to enter into a detailed discussion of tests and measurements, but sound information in this area is a sine qua non if the suggestions which follow are to be effectively used.

Other information that is useful comes from conferences with, or reports from, previous teachers, especially if they have collected good concrete data on the child's behavior and achievement. Sometimes a change of teachers helps a child achieve more if the new teacher lets the child start afresh and does not hold a bias against him for his previous lack of achievement. Moreover some recent research has shown that when teachers were told that children were more able than they in fact were shown to be on tests, that these children actually achieved better than the test would have predicted. This is to say that when a situation is created in which more is expected of the child, he tends to rise to the occasion and to perform as is expected of him.

Planning for achievement based on better disciplinary effort can utilize the results of such a study. First, environment can set the stage for the child to perform more adequately by diligently reinforcing his efforts. Also, the teacher can continue to support movement in the direction of self-discipline in the child through a well-structured plan.

The study of achievement that is better than predicted suggests that teachers, like other people, may have their prejudices. They may have simply had a wrong view of the child in the past, and if they can be persuaded that the child is capable of more, and can support this persuasion factually by eliciting better performance from him on a daily basis, there is little doubt that the child can learn to sustain achievement over time.

A word of caution must be added, however, for there are cases where teachers may err in the opposite direction. They may have the wrong slant on the child by virtue of the child's superficial cooperativeness and pleasant attitude and, thereby, because of his social competency, think the child is "brighter" for academic purposes than he, indeed is. Even in this case, however, it is likely that the child will perform more adequately than if the teacher underestimates him.

You should also remember that children do respond differently to different adults and to different approaches. From his childhood experiences, every adult knows how avidly he responded to some teachers and other adults and how clearly others "turned him off." Apparently no one teacher and no one kind of teaching is best for all children. Therefore, some skepticism should be attached to most former teachers' reports on a child. Regardless of whether the past teachers were right or wrong, the child and you, the present teacher, will have to make out together somehow. The child should be able to prove himself to you, and you will have to show him that. You will also have to show him that you feel it is important for him to produce on a daily basis.

YOUR PERSONALITY IS IMPORTANT ALSO

The effectiveness of your personality on the child is important. While we speak of firmness, fairness, consistency and follow-through, we do not want to lose sight of the fact some persons can promote these desirable ends better than others can. Teachers differ in their makeup as much as children do. And even though they may modify or suppress some features of their personality in the classroom, many subtleties are sensed by the children, such as whether the teacher likes them, whether the teacher has confidence in them, and whether the teacher will ignore infractions of rules.

Because teacher personalities differ, no one set of procedures is likely to be implemented equally well by all of them. If a teacher finds that, despite a fair trial, he cannot readily follow the suggestions we are making here, it may be that these suggestions are not for him. Most teachers, however, in their interactions with children, will tend to become better teachers as they become firmer ones. Such firmness is just as important in teaching, it would appear, as clarity of directions is in helping one find his way about or clear instructions are in aiding one to assemble some object. There can, of course, be exceptions and the use of firmness should not be misconstrued to mean a display of power demanding unfair obedience or subservience. Again, the teacher behavior characteristics that seem most desirable are *firmness, fairness,* and *consistency.* Teachers have been admonished to offer tender, loving care as if school were a major nurturing source for the child. One cannot object to loving care, but that alone, while desirable in some contexts, will not necessarily foster the growth of self-discipline and achievement commensurate with the child's ability or generally good mental health, which we take to be the school's major mission.

GROWTH PATTERNS DIFFER

Even though a general curve of development may look like a straight line which gently slopes upward as a result of averaging the performance of many children, we know that individual children differ greatly in their particular patterns. The growth curve in reading, for example, may vary considerably between any two children in a class. The teacher should consider these differences, knowing each child well in terms of his achievement and present progress. One child may show a spurt in reading in the second and third grades, whereas another child may not pick up momentum until he is in the fourth or fifth grade. We cannot therefore, expect the same amount or quality of work from each child. Each child's particular assets and weaknesses must be taken into account. As these matters are realized, the discipline of classroom learning can be more judiciously developed. Discipline alone will not do much to accelerate or slow some major growth tendencies; these appear to be somewhat independent of momentary classroom activities. However, the teacher can teach more judiciously and constructively if he knows the idiosyncrasies of each child, if he knows approximately where each child stands in his own growth momentum, and if he knows how most appropriately to offer reinforcement or encouragement.

EARLY CONTACTS SET THE STAGE

First contacts with the child should be made as effective as possible. It does not hurt to appear somewhat on the firm and detached side in initial contacts. Ordinarily, adults try to impress the child with friendliness; this can be easily overdone, and the child in the classroom may look upon the teacher as too eager or as *primarily* concerned about obtaining his friendship. Even though they may be corrected later, first impressions are unfortunately often the most vivid and lasting. We can take advantage of this common psychological phenomenon to get off to a good, firm start—keeping our attention on our primary purpose with each new child and each new class.

A middle-aged woman went back to teaching after her family had grown and left home. Having had the experience of rearing children and teaching Sunday school, she thought that her initial teaching experience some 20 years earlier was too flabby and unstructured. She resolved, therefore, to begin with a very firm attitude the first day of school, and to sustain it. By Thanksgiving day, her class had settled into very productive activity. There were no disciplinary problems, and the children were friendly, respectful, and hardworking. Another teacher also returned after a period of absence from teaching, she began with an attitude of "just loving the children to death." By Thanksgiving time the second teacher was in trouble in many respects: her children were not doing the work requested; there were many behavior problems; and complaints flowed from parents. The teacher's good intentions had been dashed in about three months! Both these teachers were conscientious, well trained, and able. One displayed an attitude of "business first, pleasure later," while the second started with the opposite viewpoint. In the second case, the children gained the impression that the classroom was a place where they were to be pleased, rather than a place to learn to enjoy doing what was required of them.

The first teacher was using a contingency management tactic—holding up reinforcement until she got what she wanted. The second teacher held no apparent contingency strategy and, in effect, reinforced the children with attention and laxity *before* they performed educationally.

From the first day of school onward, teachers should conduct business. The sooner and the more effectively they start a regimen, the less disciplinary trouble they will have and the more teaching they will be able to do in the following months. Effective teachers may begin the school year with a statement like the following:

> "We are here to work and play; there will be time for both. We will work before we play, however. I want to be your friend, to make learning as appealing as possible, and to get you interested in many things, but I also want you to remember that I am here to teach and you are here to learn. This is our business.

The teacher can say things like this and follow through on them without being mean or unfair. Firmness is not unfairness. The teacher must realize this and carry the meaning to the children through words and deeds. It does no good to make a pronouncement like the one above and then fail to follow through on it. The purpose is not to threaten the children but to let them know the main business of school work, and to clarify their role in it. The same kind of structure and firmness might profitably apply to boy scout leaders, to recreation leaders, to Sunday school teachers. Every parent has observed scout troops, Sunday schools, and recreational groups, that have lacked discipline and have failed to bring the child the kinds of experiences and learning intended. Every adult has observed that children soon tire of these too loose group structures and, having engaged in some misbehavior themselves, either feel guilty about returning to the group or lose interest because "nothing happens" at the meetings. Children's disenchantment with group activities is often caused by the group's lacking firmness, clarity, purpose, and consistency.

Perhaps more important than words are the actions of the teacher; they often impress his students more than anything he can say. Some youngsters will probably try to test the teacher's words to discover whether real firmness is present. If the teacher does mean business and can stand by his pronouncements, both he and the children will gain because a precedent of consequences will have been established.

The teacher might well begin by giving each child a small amount of work to do, commensurate with the child's ability, interest, and present level of achievement. Giving small amounts of work first and expecting the child to complete them satisfactorily provides both encouragement to the child and a feedback of information to the teacher. If the child is unable or unwilling to complete the work, then it should be broken down into smaller or simpler detail, but the requirement of finishing it in a satisfactory manner should be held until the child produces some kind of acceptable performance. When the teacher assigns a task, it is important for him to require its completion, unless he discovers he has made an error. If he has erred in estimating the child's capacity, this should be admitted openly and readily. The mistake should be corrected, and new and more realistic tasks set. The teacher should not apologize profusely for the mistake, nor should he permit the child to challenge him all the time. Admitting the mistake provides a constructive basis for rebuilding a relationship. It should not provide an excuse for weakening the structure for teaching.

ADDING TASKS ON AN INCREMENTAL BASIS

Having given the child work to do commensurate with his ability, achievement, and interests, the teacher may then note the child's strong and weak points in doing the assignment and proceed to build from there. Once the child is moving in this modest way, the teacher can continue feeding him work so that a pattern of successful completion on a small incremental basis begins to be established. In this way a pattern of success is shaped. The child is continually forming habits contributing either to success or failure with respect to his work. As a teacher, by breaking down the requirements into easily attainable units, you can help him toward this success pattern.

Many times children will at first be lost or call for help in the midst of an assignment, even a simple one. At such time the teacher should hold firmly to a reasonable expectation and not let the child pass back the responsibility. The teacher can encourage the child to stay with the work, reminding him that when his work is done, he may draw, paint, or engage in some other activity he may prefer. This is not to cajole the child but to spell out consequences. It is to let him know that he will be kept at his work until he is able to finish it, and in the meantime he may miss out on some more enjoyable or recreational activity.

The teacher should realize that our comments here are to be applied on a minute-to-minute, task-by-task, and hour-by-hour basis. An active, attentive, firm attitude on the teacher's part usually spells the difference between poor and acceptable work. Often teachers are firm enough on a week-to-week, or month-to-month, or semester-to-semester basis, particularly at the end of a grading period, but such units of firmness, are too far spaced for the child to comprehend well, too remote for him to follow as a guide to his *daily* work. Some teachers are particularly firm about turning in low grades, marking papers severely, refusing to let the child make up incomplete or missed work. If the tough grading is fair, then this is an acceptable practice. But on the other hand, if the only time a teacher is firm is at the end of the task, after having neglected the interim steps, then the firmness may not be fair and may represent a kind of inconsistency. Many times teachers fail to feed back information on tests or on the assignments that children have completed, but they dispense low grades at the end of a six- or nine-week grading period without the children or the parents being forewarned that the performance was poor. Six- or nine-week grading periods are really too long for effective guidance. Administratively, it may be a convenience to pass out grades four to six times a year, but psychologically, it is certainly not a useful practice for directing the activities of the child. His grades should be passed out each day in each subject, or perhaps even several times a day. Immediate reinforcement and correction are imperative in good learning and self-discipline.

The teacher, however, may object to supervising the children's work on a daily or hourly basis. A teacher recently remarked about an eight-year old girl who was not doing her arithmetic properly, "Oh, she knows she is supposed to do the work." When asked what the teacher meant by this, she added, "Well, if she doesn't know now, she will find out when she gets a failing grade at the end of the six-week period." Although such a failing grade might have some influence on the child, we need to emphasize what her obligations are on a day-to-day basis. The punitiveness implied in this teacher's remarks and the remoteness of the consequences (six weeks off) are of very little use and may actually be harmful in the day-to-day and hour-to-hour relationship between the child and her teacher. If the child has practiced poor work habits for six weeks, how can a low final grade operate effectively against her habits and offset her poor progress and the attitudes toward herself and her work which have been developing? And what about practices of this sort which extend over a semester or a year, or perhaps throughout the entire schooling?

We are aware that many parents and teachers say to their children "You'd better get good grades now (while you are in the eighth or ninth grade) because your College Boards won't get you into college if your grades don't improve." Motivating a child at the eighth or ninth grade level or perhaps even through the tenth or eleventh grades, in terms of the demands of college acceptance is an extremely remote and unfair type of practice. The child should do his work today and tomorrow and this coming weekend (and be reinforced for these efforts) because the assignments are relevant to his learning and because it is important for him to understand and practice fulfilling his obligations—not because he might not get into college four, five, or six years hence.

HANDLING RECALCITRANTS

Accept the fact that the child may not take readily to a structured program at all times. He may be accustomed to kicking up a fuss at home, protesting, sulking, or resorting to a host of other techniques calculated to either get the teacher to do the work for him or to relieve him of his responsibility. The teacher should not naively assume that just because he is doing the "right thing" the child will respond correctly all of the time. It would be nice if children did thus respond, but in all probability it will not happen in this simple way. Often the child will protest carrying out the assignment and will try many circumventing tactics. The teacher should be prepared to cope with these delaying tactics.

Our outline of acceptable procedures is designed to help the teacher obtain optimum ends, but it carries no guarantee of this achievement. In a sense we act as architects drawing the blueprints, but the teacher must be the builder who executes the plans.

A good way of being prepared for the negative child is to understand that there will always be some children who are hard to manage. If you know and accept this fact at the outset, you are better equipped to follow through. When you run into extremely difficult children, you should realize that the individual differences in students and teachers may necessitate extraordinary persistence and vigilance in some cases. Most children will respond with a fair amount of effort within a reasonable period of time without adamant resistance. But with an extremely refractory student, the question of special education will probably have to be considered.

NEED FOR FOLLOW-THROUGH

Be prepared to follow through indefinitely with the procedure of setting requirements and giving attention (reinforcement) to the child's responses. It is pleasant that some children do not need more than a slight push of encouragement to be able to navigate on their own. There are not, however, many children with so delightful an attitude: Estimates at the college level indicate that about 15 or 20 percent of the students are effectively self-motivated, self-directed, and highly energetic in their programs. In the secondary and elementary school probably the percentage is not any higher. As children get older, it is easier to recognize those who are interested in schoolwork and who see it as relevant to their goals, contrasted with those who tend to split off from schoolwork and think in terms of activities outside of school.

At any rate, most children must have a general structure that sustains attention and rewards effort for the school to succeed. Otherwise, they feel that the teacher does not care. The teacher's viewpoint and his expectations as to what the student should do must be periodically reaffirmed to the student. A pronouncement at the beginning of the school term, while useful as a starter, will not sustain the teacher nor the child throughout the year. Indeed, most adults need some prompting each day to sustain many of our own activities, which are vital to our welfare, our economy, and our relationships with others.

We often err by assuming that if we explain to someone—the reason for an action—he will carry on without further attention. This places an inordinate burden on reasoning. However, modern science tells us there is a tendency in both living and nonliving systems to "run down" or to show "entropy." This generalization seems to apply to various human skills, attitudes, efforts, and behavior in general. We all need support (continuous or with at least periodic reinforcement) for our attitudes, skills, and knowledge, and periodically, we need help from others to sustain them. It is logical, then, to expect that it will be necessary to replenish or support the child's efforts at learning and at self-control on a periodic and well-structured basis.

Numerous studies of learning and memory suggest that most forgetting of skills and knowledge takes place soon after practice has stopped, or soon after the exposure has terminated. The child who has just learned a new set of skills is most likely to show some decrement in his accomplishments before the next practice periods. These facts indicate the necessity of viewing all accomplishments as requiring support or continued effort if they are to be maintained at a high level. The child in the classroom will deteriorate in his attitudes, knowledge, and skills if the teacher and his lifestyle do not reinforce actively his use of these skills and attitudes.

In this connection, most teachers note how children show some decrement in their knowledge over the summer vacation. Children may sometimes lose between one-quarter and one-half of a year in level of reading, word knowledge, and arithmetic skill. A three-month vacation in the summer, was instituted for economic reasons, but the need has changed, and so long a lay off can no longer be considered desirable. Therefore, it would be useful for some kind of summer schooling or some kind of replenishment or updating of the child's skills to go on during the summer. At the very least, even if no new gains were made, summer practice would offset the decrement, thus allowing the child to resume school in September at a point very close to where he left off in May or June, rather than perhaps a half grade below his former level.

We recently heard a teacher remark, "You know, Billy was doing so well for a while—now look at him, he hardly opens a book." Left alone most children will not automatically refurbish their skills and achievements. Some will, but we should not assume that all or most of them will, and we must not fail to recognize that most children need prompting and encouragement. Those who do tend to keep themselves advancing generally do not reflect complete self-sufficiency so much as the active approval of family or friends. Often they are from families that place a high value on studiousness and scholarship. In subtle ways these children are probably finding much reinforcement in their environment.

Not only do average children and adults need practice and support for their accomplishments, so do gifted individuals. There is a story that a famous violinist remarked, when asked about his practicing activities, that if he missed one day, he could notice it, if he missed two days of practice his accompanist and close friends noticed it; if by chance he missed a whole week, his audiences noticed it. Even the most highly practiced skills decline.

Very important to this sustaining of activity on a daily or interim basis is the continued encouragement by teachers and families in a way that becomes more or less automatic as natural reinforcement for the child's activities.

A word must be said about the "culture of nonachievement," which seems to be more prevalant especially in high ability students than was true a few years ago. Many high school students in all eras have said, "If you get good grades, you are just a brain and a grind." Scholarship or interest in learning has been equated with dullness in other areas of life. Factually, these are incorrect generalizations, often voiced by the young person who simply wants to avoid the self-discipline of studying. However, there is a kind of culture of nonachievement now, and school personnel should be aware of its growing prevalence among the brighter and more thoughtful students as well as among those of marginal ability and achievement. Because of national efforts and values, which may be askew, they say, they should not develop themselves in conventional school programs. We believe, however, that there should always be a wide enough range of learning materials and an obvious enough use of self-discipline and achievement goals to appeal to any student—if the teacher remains flexible and broadly interested in education.

SELF-DIRECTION

As time passes the student will, with the teacher's continued support —which becomes less obtrusive and obvious as the child matures—begin to regulate himself to get his work done with less outside prompting. Just as he learns to adapt emotionally to his parents' standards and values, he should begin to take over his own discipline in education. After all, what is learning but the acquisition of behavior that was once foreign to us?

There is a logical and progressive relationship between the previous section on follow-through and the present one on self-direction. In follow-through the emphasis is on the need for persistence and consistency. As these conditions are maintained in the child's social and educational environment, he begins to learn for himself, and finally the child is on the road to becoming self-directed, self-activated, reasonably self-governing, and self-rewarding. The completely achieved state of affairs is seldom wholly achieved or seldom covers all of life, but any movement toward such goals is desirable. To the extent that they are achieved, the person has at his disposal many reinforcing elements which formerly were not available to him. He is able to respond to cues that are minimal compared to what was originally the case. The knowledge he acquires in this way gives him an ever-increasing facility for dealing with his environment.

OVERTALKING

Many times we talk too much to accomplish our ends efficiently. To the child, a lot of talk is negatively correlated with effective guidance: the more one talks beyond a minimal point in the process of discipline, the less he generally transmits to the child. The child becomes inured to excessive adult talk. A man was putting a screen door in his front door frame, and the family's eight-year-old boy was present. The boy kept playing with the tools, trying to get in and out of the house through the door being worked on, begging his mother and father for the special privilege. An observer noted that the father ordered the boy away eight times over a period of about three or four minutes before he finally resolved the situation by pulling the child inside until he could decide what to do. Each time the parent threatened the child, the child was not encouraged to accept the order but was really encouraged to "test" the parent all the more. The words served not as a cue to disciplinary control but as a cue to contesting what the parent wanted. As a result, both the child and the parent were caught in a criss-cross of threats and infractions, where words came to mean nothing more than the continuation of the battle.

Frequently, teachers have such problems. One teacher in a workshop on discipline said, "I just talk and talk to those youngsters—tell me where I go wrong." Typical of many, this teacher needed to talk less and become more efficient in other ways.

A loquacious teacher noticed that a child who wore a hearing aid turned down the aid whenever the teacher began to raise her voice or talk too much. An interview with the child verified the teacher's observation and revealed more about his attitude toward the teacher. "She talks too much; and when she does, I just turn down my aid so I won't hear her, and I go on and do my work." Too much talking impairs whatever effectiveness oral instruction may have.

ENCOURAGING THE SENSE OF WELL-BEING

A sense of well-being, of accomplishment, of success arises from the ability to accomplish one's tasks and solve one's problems. How else can a person measure his success in life or in a particular undertaking unless he sees himself overcoming the many hurdles he meets and accomplishing his ends? The unhappy or unsuccessful person is one who characteristically does not feel up to the problems that beset him or feels that his efforts to work them out are continuously a failure. The happy and successful person gets his daily jobs done well enough to satisfy himself. There is a kind of behavioral economy that operates somewhat parallel to a financial economy. A person who can never meet his financial obligations is always in trouble and is always being downed. A person who is psychologically behind in his achievements and accomplishments, according to his own objectives or commitments, discomfits himself in addition to inviting penalties from his environment.

Children also learn to measure themselves against how they discharge their obligations. They arrive at generalizations about themselves, "I am no good," "I can't do it," or "I like my work," "I am up to the job." As teachers and monitoring adults, we can provide not only incentives and challenges but a workable plan of action which children can employ to meet their daily obligations. By their experiences they judge themselves. We judge ourselves this way also. People arrive at generalizations about themselves: "self-images" and these self-images guide them in new activities, to either success or failure.

It seems to us, therefore, that if we blame a child's lack of success or his faulty attitudes on emotional factors and act as if these factors were totally beyond our control as teachers or parents, we overlook the crucial issue of mental health in the classroom. Teachers can go far in helping the child remove inadequate feelings and, what is more important, *replace* them with successful habits for daily living.

EMOTIONS—STAMP OF APPROVAL OR DISAPPROVAL ON EXPERIENCE

Emotions are not something apart from the way life is lived. They are not separate characteristics of the child that have to be ferreted out and worked on. Emotions are the felt evaluations of one's life; they are by-products, so to speak, of one's successes and failures in living. If there are ways to encourage more successful living—in the classroom, at home, elsewhere—then these are ways to encourage satisfying emotional development. We would emphasize emotional development in school in terms of successful classroom living. We are stressing the child's development through proper classroom discipline in the largest sense of the term. Almost all children can achieve success when their experiences are arranged so that they can note the accomplishments which eventuate if the task is accomplished and if the teacher provides firm support and reinforcement.

SECURITY—WHAT DOES IT MEAN?

"Security" is a word in wide use today. Children who are disturbed or who do not accomplish are diagnosed as being "insecure" or as having a "false self-image." These two terms are frequently used interchangably, as if they were a clear pathology.

But is not security a feeling of consonance between one's self and one's surroundings? It is not a mystical state nor some disembodied psychological condition; rather, security is also a by-product of successful living. Security cannot be successfully pursued as an end in itself.

The child in the classroom, insofar as the classroom experiences are constructive, feels secure with himself and his teacher, as he continues to meet his daily obligations in a reasonably adequate manner. If he feels insecure, this is the signal that his activities are not commensurate with the goals. It is not a sign that something mysterious is wrong with him or that the causes lie in the past and are therefore beyond the realm of control in the present classroom situation. When insecurity persists in the face of well-structured and accomplished learning, it is time to look for more complex causes and cures, but such a condition will characterize a small number of the students now labeled "insecure" or "emotionally disturbed."

CONCLUSIONS

Classroom requirements are simply ways in which we teach the child how to live effectively and with satisfaction.

We can use such courses as arithmetic and reading as *materials* out of which the student fashions not only his understanding of the world around him but also his self-knowledge, which is his knowledge of himself *in relation* to his environment.

The subject matter fields are important as instruments for knowledge and as materials about the world, but frequently overlooked is the fact that they are equally important as instruments for knowledge about one's self.

As we handle the subjects of living, we learn how to live. No evaluations of self or of subject matter can arise without the child having *contact with his tasks*. Without obligations, without problems, without contacts, how is one to know how to live, to evaluate himself, and to change?

Thus we emphasize the *fusing* of discipline with mental health and with achievement. Discipline is a way of working, the use of a behavioral repertoire, by and through which we learn subject matter (achievement) and from the applied result, judge our success (mental health).

In turn, our success in handling our problems gives rise to our emotional evaluations, our self-image, our feelings of security, which is but another way of putting the problem of mental health.

SELECTED READINGS

BALDWIN, A. L., *Theories of Child Development*. New York: John Wiley, 1967.

BANDURA, A., and R. H. WALTERS, *Social Learning and Personality Development*. New York: Holt, Rinehart and Winston, 1963.

Becker, W. C., C. H. Madsen, C. R. Arnold, and D. R. Thomas, "The contingent use of teacher attention and praise in reducing classroom behavior problems." *J. Special Educ.*, 1967, *1*, 287–307.

Carlin, S., and E. Armstrong, "Rewarding social responsibility in disturbed children: A group play technique." *Psychotherapy*, 1968, *5*, 169–74.

Clifford, E., "Discipline in the home: A controlled observational study of parental practices." *J. Genet. Psychol.*, 1959, *95*, 45–82.

Davis, A., and R. J. Havinghurst, *Father of the Man*. Boston: Houghton Mifflin, 1947.

Krumboltz, J. D., "Parable of the good counselor." *Personnel and Guidance J.*, 1961, *43*, 118–24.

Madsen, C. H., "Positive reinforcement in the toilet training of a normal child," in L. P. Ullmann, and L. Krasner, eds., *Case Studies In Behavior Modification*. New York: Holt, Rinehart and Winston, 1965, pp. 305–7.

5

FACILITATING ACHIEVEMENT

In the previous chapters we have considered how certain attitudes and practices can facilitate learning. The relationship stems from a refined and extended use of the modern concept of discipline. We have touched briefly on the connection between discipline and mental health and how both relate to achievement. Our purpose in this chapter is to deal more specifically with achievement and to show how it is facilitated by good discipline in the learning situations presented to the child.

UTILIZING THE LEARNING PROCESS

For the child the learning process begins at birth (perhaps even sooner, some scientists think). Every stimulus, each new situation, affects the child in one way or another. The child is bound to learn *something* in school, as he is in his environment generally. No child remains a blank, even though it may appear to some teachers that children come to them unmarked and also leave unmarked. If the child is certain to learn *something,* then we, as mentors, must arrange for and direct what he learns according to our assigned mission.

The child's neurological equipment and his psychology both can be utilized on our side; that is, the child is adaptable. He is open to stimulation. And as a result of the stimulation, his behavior is subject to modification. *In short, the child is always capable of learning.*

If this learning can be made systematic with respect to given problems, if we can *arrange the child's environment* so that he learns what we wish him to learn and what he holds important, then we have well utilized his potential. We can then say that he achieves satisfactorily—that he is moving toward important goals.

The task is to bring his modifiability—his capacity to achieve—under some deliberate direction. And direction means discipline. It means acting on the belief that if we do such and such the child will respond within limits in such-and-such a way. It means that once we have arranged the environment and presented material effectively, learning should proceed with economy and reliability. We have to know what we want, however, and how to go about obtaining it if we are to direct effectively. If we wish to foster achievement in a given area, we are obliged to set out in this direction and keep our course as straight as possible.

ABSORBING KNOWLEDGE

Assuming that the ability to learn is present, probably the most common cause of poor achievement is the failure to *take in* knowledge. There is the failure to discriminate between what is important and what is not important. There is the failure to set out to learn, with a plan or purpose in mind, which permits discrimination on the basis of some learning criteria. Numerous experiments detail the ineffectiveness of just throwing stimuli at the child. The child who is motivated to learn will, when confronted with a specified learning task, separate it from what is not to be learned. If, however, he is confronted with indistinguishable masses of stimulation, he may not follow any path consistently.

In order to absorb knowledge, there has to be some separation of what is to be learned from what is neutral or useless. The mind, in a sense, is like a radar screen; it selects certain types of stimulation from the environment. We are not concerned here (but will be later) with what is done with the knowledge obtained. The child has to learn to distinguish what he is to do in a learning task. This is what we mean by "set" or "preparatory set" in learning. This is also what some people have called a "direction" or "instructional set," or, in a more complex sense, "the curriculum." A radar screen does not detect odors, the camera does not detect sound, each has its domain; in a sense, what the child has to learn is based on analogous discrimination. The mind is broader and infinitely more flexible than the radar screen or the camera, although in some ways it works as these instruments do.

Breadth and flexibility can be man's weaknesses as well as his strengths. How so? Our flexibility and malleability may be put to such use that we fail to discriminate. We may let every stimulation fall on us with equal effect; we are then too readily diverted. Consider the inattentive student in class; he is likely to wool-gather about how nice it would be to go fishing or play ball instead of being in class, or to roam over such a wide set of thoughts that none prevails. He is not tuned in to his classroom stimulation. The brain-damaged person also is often like the "untuned" radio set or the radar screen that is picking up random stimulation; he lacks adaptability and selective power. Sometimes the average student acts this way but from a lack of discipline rather than from faulty neurological equipment.

WAYS TO IMPROVE THE LEARNING ENVIRONMENT

Classes for brain-damaged children help them to select stimuli appropriately from the environment by simplifying the environment. Specifically, we cut down on the range of stimulation. We soften the play of physical forces on their eyes, ears, and other senses. We enable them to relate to their environment by having it come to them in smaller and less complex doses. For example, in a school for brain-damaged children the walls may be painted a drab color, pictures may be omitted from the walls, artificial light in any obtrusive manner may be avoided, and even the teacher's dress may be purposely plain. Likewise, the sound environment and the social movement of other children may be controlled because both these factors tend to increase the stimulus complex.

Should we do the same kind of thing with the normal child in a classroom to enhance learning? Within limits, such a course seems likely to enhance learning of relevant material. In teaching arithmetic, for example, one would not introduce long division first. One would begin with the simple arithmetic functions of adding, dividing, subtracting, multiplying on a one- or two-digit basis and then move on to short division. It is not our point here to equate the brain-damaged with the normal child, but simply to illustrate how the same learning principle applies (at a different level) and how control of the environment can facilitate learning.

With the typical child we do not alter the environment as much as with the brain-damaged, but we try to get him to take in the parts of the environment we wish him to discriminate. Sometimes this can involve altering the environment, but, mainly, we are trying efficiently to gain and hold his attention for the tasks at hand.

As a teacher, you are the most significant person in the child's environment during the week days. You want him to tune to your signals. You want him to get on your "beam." You are asking him to register what you are saying, not to just pass it over or to consider it casually.

The common failing in the learning process, it would appear, the weakest link in the series of habits that constitute effective studying, concerns taking in the proper environmental stimulation. If the prescribed stimulation has little or no impact, then behavior that it is supposed to follow will not occur or is likely to be weak and transitory. If the child does not pay close attention, or if his attention wanders, his learning will be haphazard. He learns some facts, confuses others, and relates them poorly. To a great extent, he learns almost by chance, with some bias in favor of the proper direction, but not very much.

One might also say that the child discriminates among environmental opportunities. Thus, if he is told that he has a nickel to spend, he immediately concentrates on the candy counter and more specifically on articles that can be bought for five cents or less. He does not try to buy paper clips, clothes, or tools with the money. He discriminates between what is within his province at the moment, meaning within his behavioral capacity given the five cents to spend. Thus, when we speak to a child he will be "taking in" our words, and also discriminating between what we are saying at the moment and what somebody else is saying or has said—or simply his own thoughts. Both "taking in" and "discriminating" concepts encompass the same kind of behavior, namely, the way that the person learns to attend to that part of the environment that is relevant or should be most relevant for him.

PROGRESSIVE STEPS IN LEARNING

The failure to attend to stimulation properly can usually be overcome by the teacher if he can set up the learning situation according to the principles that we are emphasizing. He begins with knowledge of the child's strengths and weaknesses and his psychological habits (such as wandering off or paying attention for only brief periods).

Perhaps some learning takes place on the first exposure. Psychologists do not agree on the extent to which learning depends on repetition. Maybe some simple situations are learned in one trial, but complex or extended tasks need repetition, even if *some* learning takes place on each separate trial. The most reasonable assumption is that some learning takes place on *each* exposure, such as a class period and study hour, therefore, we should try to use each such period to its fullest extent. Drill and future exposure will, if the initial learning is progressing well, take care of the more complex aspects. For example, if the child is learning to type, it is absurd to think of his learning to do so in one trial; however, he is learning *something*, such as where the letter f or the letter k is placed on the typewriter. On the other hand, he might learn where downtown is in a new community with one exposure because of the presence of environmental cues, and his ability to discriminate between left and right turns.

Efficiency of learning in the classroom depends upon a disciplined routine. Each exposure should count for something. One should not assume that what is not learned now will inevitably be acquired in time if the reason for not learning something now is lack of attention to the task at hand.

Nor will repetition alone insure success. Repetition may allow the student to practice inattention. He may be learning to ignore the lesson or the teacher, or he may be in the process of becoming inured to the task.

The first presentation should be made especially efficient and effective. Get the child's attention right away, which means get him to discriminate between what you want done and the rest of the environment. The first impression can count heavily. Preparation is important. As you grow in ability to gain the child's attention at the beginning of new tasks, you will find it easier to teach, and the child will develop a pattern of success correspondingly faster. Much of the time the teacher wastes stems from having to repeat material that should have been learned sooner. The student's radar-like mind has been wandering unselectively over the terrain. Much drill—though certainly not all of it—could be eliminated if the first impressions and the first efforts at discrimination were gainful.

A case in point might be the effort to teach a ten-year-old child about classical music. The child was not particularly interested in Tschaikowsky, nor in Tschaikowsky's *1812 Overture*. However, when the boy learned that the orchestra was going to shoot off cannons at the end of the selection, he sat with rapt attention, watching the musicians in the television presentation, periodically asking what the instruments were that were being shown, and maintaining his attention throughout the overture, which culminated in the blast of cannons at the end. Unfortunately, all music appreciation cannot be taught by such a fascinating adjunct. On the other hand, children have varied interests; if we capitalize on them, they can help us hold the children's attention while threading our way through complex material. The ten-year-old boy learned something about the *1812 Overture*, how to pronounce the name of the composer, and variations among the instruments in the orchestra. He may always associate this knowledge with the cannon blast, the environmental event which helped him "take in" or "discriminate" a very complex set of environmental factors and, therefore, learn something of a constructive nature.

Once the child has been led to take in an impression or, as we prefer to say, make a discrimination, it is much easier to stimulate and to teach him. The foundation has been laid. If subsequent presentations are worked out carefully also, they will likewise be successful. In teaching the child cited above more about music appreciation, it might be well to go from Tschaikowsky's *1812 Overture* to other examples of music which have interesting tidbits likely to appeal to his interests and attention. With the beachhead secured, learning steps can be longer and fewer in the acquisition of complex behavior. Much of the drudgery of teaching *and* learning arises from insufficient presentation, with aimlessness of purpose and early discouraging results.

ELIMINATING DISTRACTIONS

Eliminating distractions or screening out interference is important in making first impressions effective. If a child is not attending to the matter at hand—spelling, mathematics, reading, music appreciation—he is doing something else. Something is *interfering* with his concentration or his discriminatory response to the environment.

> Susan, a third grader, was given some arithmetic problems to do. When she was asked to add such combinations as 15 and 5, and 25 and 15, she would say, "Five and five, hummmm; I like reading better than arithmetic. You know our teacher lets us go to the library and pick out our own reading books to take home." At this point the instructor returned Susan's attention to the arithmetic problem at hand. Susan said again, "Five and five, hummm; that is ten." She put down ten as the answer, ignoring the numeral in the ten's column.

It is plain that this child needs to be kept at the task, needs to be brought back from her wanderings, and needs the encouragement of reinforcement for her successful efforts. Successfully adding 5 and 5 and other single digit pairs may be the basis for reinforcement that encourages her to move on to more complex additions. As this effort increases efficiency, we will know more about what Susan is capable of doing and we will also know better how to get a reasonable performance from her each day. As interfering ideas and distracting stimuli are screened out by the teacher's actions, helping Susan to discriminate and be reinforced, Susan's real ability will be brought to bear on the problem.

Walking around, doodling, talking to one's neighbor at will—all these militate against concentration and effective study. Freedom in the classroom has probably gone too far when the children spend a large part of their time in nonproductive pursuits. The schoolroom can become like an inefficient office where the workers are socializing instead of doing their work. When the "coffee break"—or the occasional respite in the classroom—extends to 30 minutes or more and then trails into more nonbusiness conversation, too much time is being spent unproductively. A respite is intended to replenish energy, not to give rise to a whole new pattern of behavior.

ENCOURAGING CONCENTRATION

Concentration "games" may be employed to help the child focus on the problem at hand, reason out what is required, devise an appropriate answer, and obtain social reinforcement. Such games also provide a working model which the child often grasps more quickly than other approaches. One such game is to have a teacher or child say:

> I am going on a trip, and I am going to take along some *salt*. The next person might say, "I am going on the same trip, and I am going to take along some *tea*." The purpose of the game is to have each subsequent participant name an object beginning with the letter the previous word ends with.

Modifications of such a game can be made to match the grade level of the children. Sometimes games of this sort, with the social reinforcement they abundantly provide for, facilitate learning better than just reading in a textbook. Modifications can be worked out to fit arithmetic and other subjects. Similar games can be played with geography or history subject matter, using places, times, dates, and people as the connecting links. Once the idea of attending to, focusing on, and analyzing the word or concept begins to become clear to the child, he can then apply them to his own work at his desk and can follow through with few words from the teacher.

It is important to point out the enormous social reinforcement that is provided for in these efforts at concentration and the social reinforcement that is provided for cooperative behavior. One could use countries of the world or agricultural products of other nations as a basis for one of these "trips." Like the blasting of the cannon in the overture, the small cues can sometimes provide for surprising efficiency for concentration and for discriminating reactions to the environment.

Immediate concentration and proper selection of and attention to stimuli do not guarantee achievement. Prompt focussing on the material at hand is certainly good, but it is not all that is necessary for learning. A child may focus well for a few minutes, then lose interest, and wander off to other matters, or he may generate considerable enthusiasm at the beginning but lose it as time goes by. He may not sustain the attention necessary for prolonged work and achievement beyond the quest of the moment; the teacher may need to learn how to produce longer and more durable concentration.

The problem of sustaining attention requires a flexibility of approach and the correlation of material to the child's developmental level. This problem is similar to that of providing a first impression and the immediate focus of attention. To sustain attention one has to keep the child at the task. One often has to bring the child back to the task in the same manner as that which gained the child's attention in the first place. Thus the immediacy of attention getting, tuning in, or discriminating responses needs to be captured and carried out in lengthened sequences of activity to sustain productive learning. Reinforcement has to gain in importance as complex activity increases.

THE PROPER ROLE OF DRILL

Drill is often misused at this point in disciplined learning. The child may be asked to write 50 or 100 times, "I must pay attention in class," or "I must do my entire lesson before I stop." What the teacher is requiring here is not attention to the work at hand, but attention to some evaluation of the work. It would be better if he spent the time and energy on having the child *do* the work rather than writing about doing it. It is extremely doubtful that this type of punishment—and it is more punishment than corrective disciplinary action—increases the child's attention to prolonged work.

Drill should be made as effective and efficient as possible. Drill certainly has a place in education, especially for materials that need to be thoroughly memorized—such as words on a spelling list, foreign language vocabulary, forms of speech, multiplication tables, the position of letters on the typewriter—but the drill should revolve around an opportunity to increase knowledge or to gain facility with knowledge which is already known to some extent. Prescribing old material in novel ways rather than just repeating it is one approach; it establishes more associations with the material to be learned. Drill should not be used to try to obtain concentration and focus attention. The game we suggested above shows that in learning some subjects, drill might depend more fully upon concentration and focussing through some medium or knowledge that is already present. If drill is carried on without sufficient concentration, it becomes a matter of practicing at random or even practicing bad habits or poor concentration. For example, we see the student who reads his lesson three or four times and then "doesn't remember" what he has read. He has been doing something; he has been drilling in a sense, but to no purpose. In fact, he is really practicing the *wrong conditions* for learning.

We hear about the concept of "negative practice." This is the attempt to eliminate a bad habit by practicing it and concentrating on its undesirability. Thus, if you are prone to type "hte" for "the," you would deliberately mistype, quite conscious of the error, and in this way overcome the error because you discriminate out, so to speak, the incorrect response. It is like purposely practicing a motor skill in the wrong way, so the characteristics of the error involved become more discernible and thereby more readily correctable. Then when the correct motor acts are brought into play again, they are more fully and skillfully mastered because the wrong moves are better known, more easily detected and eliminated.

If he uses this approach, the teacher has to be careful to insure that the student distinguishes between negative practice with a purpose and simply poor practice that has only negative or interfering results. The teacher who requires a child to write a hundred times "I must pay attention in class," thinks he is helping the child to concentrate, but really he is probably worsening both the child's general attitude toward the classroom activities and his skill in applying himself. Teachers do not use this type of drill as much as they once did, but some do resort to it when they are perplexed by the child's lack of attention and achievement. They also tend to use it too frequently as a disciplinary measure.

Rote memory can be overstressed in the same way. The wrong emphasis in rote learning exists in not applying the to-be-learned materials better. To commit to rote "I must behave" or "I must be kind to others" is of no particular value, unless these sentences lead to some *decisive action*. Perhaps there is still too much rote learning in the form of dates, facts, words and phrases in education today that is not translated into and validated by deeds.

UNDERSTANDING VERSUS DRILL

The importance of learning through "understanding" has been a big issue in modern education and it has a bearing on our discussion of achievement. Understanding was discussed earlier. The emphasis on understanding stems in part from a rebellion against drill and rote learning, which were still paramount in educational practices at the turn of the century and even later.

There may be a middle ground between the emphasis on drill and rote learning and excessive reliance upon understanding. We have seen and worked with many children who have been expected to learn such materials as the multiplication tables without recourse to drill or practice. We have seen too much reliance placed on learning the various subject matter fields based on a cursory and superficial notion of understanding. When as a result of overemphasis on understanding, to the neglect of concrete learning, the child does not learn the expected skills, it is sometimes explained that the child is not "ready" for the learning or suffers from emotional blocks. We believe, more often, the child does not learn the skills because sustained, disciplined exposure to the material was lacking.

It is true that some bright children do learn very effectively when they are given freedom for individual exploration in the subject matter;

classroom drill may be unnecessary for their learning and understanding. It is as if they bring a background of skill to the new learning situation and can apply it in a way similar to that of a person who is already accomplished in playing a musical instrument and who takes easily to a new one. These children with a gifted learning capacity often understand what is being presented the first time. However, when one pursues the reasons for lack of ordinary achievement in average children, one finds that their exposure to the subject matter is often too cursory. Reading lessons are given perhaps only once a week; no effort is sustained to get students to correct inferior work; too little emphasis is placed on completing work assignments; and so on through a long series of ineffective ways of handling assigned work. The teacher who then "explains" the child's lack of achievement as "failure to understand," may well be asked how the child could possibly understand when his exposure and attention to the subject matter had been so perfunctory. The teacher should find a middle ground between drill and understanding. In doing so, he should be fully aware of the strengths and limitations of each technique, as well as the status of the learner at the particular time.

THE IMPORTANCE OF VIGILANCE

The modern school curriculum is rich in its offerings. It is wonderful that students have such full and varied choices before them. But the variety of choices can be a liability as well as an asset. With indiscriminate exposure and opportunity to "sample" in a cursory manner the various fields of learning, the student may end up with no substantial gain. We may rely upon a "smorgasbord" of offerings, and then find ourselves saying to the student and his parents, "What is wrong with this child that he cannot learn in this rich and stimulating setting?"

As educators, we often offer explanations based on the child's readiness to learn or his emotional state, but do we always first examine the *learning situation per se* for clues as to why the child is not learning as he should?

Too often teachers and parents begin to realize at the end of the first semester that the child has done virtually no studying or learning. What has happened in such a case? The teacher may have assumed that because the learning tasks and materials had been presented, they have been learned. Perhaps because of oversized classes and pressing schedules, no one has stopped to determine day by day and hour by hour just what studying and learning are occurring. Neither parents nor teacher may have stayed close enough to the child's learning situation to determine precisely how much progress there was. Children observe this looseness but lack ability to judge the ineffectiveness and so may feel they are "putting something over" on the teacher. The looseness may eventuate, then, not only in poor achievement but also in poor attitudes—attitudes which may gradually deteriorate in ways we will discuss later into active emotional and social problems.

One problem that affects achievement adversely is an absence of sufficient home-school contact. The vigilance under discussion requires the joint involvement of home and school. Children are very often skillful in their ability to dodge responsibility. They frequently look upon such maneuvering as fun. They may act as if they are studying or pretend to do a great deal of work. They may come to school without handing in their homework from the previous evening. They may forget to take homework from school. They get assignments confused and do the wrong ones or do them in the wrong way. At each point, then, the *structure of requirements* is broken; the child proceeds to circumvent his obligations, and his achievement suffers.

There are innumerable ways in which a hypothetically clear and efficient model of classroom learning and achievement may be damaged. There is need for always keeping the program of learning and achievement alive and well directed.

WHY BLAME THE PAST?

There is a tendency to blame current failures on earlier teachers or levels of learning. A high school teacher of freshmen English remarks, "Well you can hardly expect me to teach them much composition if they don't know how to read, write, and spell—they should have learned all this in elementary school." The teacher is correct. The student should have acquired more basic skills than evidently he did. But if we could slip back to the fifth or sixth grade teachers and talk to them about the same children, we no doubt would get a similar remark about even earlier grades. Perhaps the children did not get enough grounding in the first three grades. The primary teachers might admit this but ascribe the child's limitations to some still earlier state of affairs, such as inadequate ability, doubtful readiness to enter school, or excessive emotional dependence on the parents.

Where then can we begin? How do we solve the problems? We are talking here primarily about average children scoring in the average range in intelligence tests and making average progress.

Each teacher whom we consult on this matter looks backward in time for an explanation for the achievement deficiencies of his students. Too seldom does a teacher say, "Here and now we have these achievement problems and all that goes with them: poor spelling, poor reading, lack of concentration, inadequate study habits. It is here and now that we have to overcome them." This is the role of remedial and makeup courses. But every child cannot be put in such courses. Much of the corrective work has to go on at the same time that new learning is in progress. If we leave the problem unsolved or only partly resolved, the high school senior teacher will have the same complaints and more. The college freshmen English teacher, the business college English teacher, and the boss who hires the high school graduate and finds that he cannot do elementary writing, all will have the same complaints. Too few of us are ready to sit down with the problem and plan what to do *now* regardless of how it came to pass.

What is now defective with achievement in these instances is also wrong down the whole educational pathway, perhaps from the first grade or even earlier. Whatever has to be corrected now could have been corrected countless times before and probably more easily. Whatever remedies we might apply now could have been applied earlier, but at least they should be applied now rather than later.

Our job is clear. Now it is our turn. It does no good to blame all current educational faults on previous teachers or previous conditions. Otherwise, the child will never gain tomorrow what he lacks today. Passing the buck backwards has to stop. One assumption underlying this tendency is that the readiness problem can always be postponed. In most instances, this is probably educational folly. Data from early childhood and preschool age children indicate that they can learn readily and well. While it is possible to try to crowd in too much at an early age, recent research and educational-clinical observations suggest that we have probably stimulated the child too little.

There are many reports of children learning to read, to some extent, at tender ages (3 and 4). Others report that concepts, arithmetic relations, and the more formal structure of knowledge need not be avoided with even the young child if we approach the matter correctly. This means finding their entering level of competence, proceeding in small steps, keeping the materials interesting and subject to reinforcement for the child, and applying other good learning and teaching practices.

We know from research, too, that nursery and kindergarten experience help to boost the child into academic work at the first grade level. These preschoolers are stimulated by and learn from not only the specifics of reading but they learn better how to concentrate, how to get down to work, how to follow routine (when needed), how to share and otherwise cooperate with others. The become acquainted with, and learn how to use the whole educational milieu. Thus, the tendencies of the teacher at any level to postpone educational remedies, simply contributes to the educational logjams that so often develop at the higher levels of education.

THE PROPER USE OF HOMEWORK

One remedy for achievement deficiencies is to set down a policy of homework and to persist with it. There are limitations to homework as an effective educational device, but there is much to commend it. If it is properly handled, it can be a good way of promoting achievement. Homework should be done on a *daily* basis, not used just occasionally. If it is not a daily task, students do not develop the very important set to do the work, and they do not set aside time or establish attitudes supporting homework. When homework is given on a hit-or-miss basis, parents do not know whether there is homework; therefore, they cannot help regulate the child's activities at home so as to support the work. The lack of structure inherent in an intermittent policy is almost as ineffectual as no policy at all.

The amount and difficulty of the homework assigned should naturally vary with different individuals and with the purposes of the course and the teacher. For the gifted child, it may involve a review of an article in an encyclopaedia in relation to a classroom discussion; for the slow learning child, it may simply provide a new way of enhancing or extending previously learned materials.

Homework can teach the child to implement and rely upon an explicit home-school relationship involving him. It can teach him to work on his own, to accept and complete assignments, and to adapt to varying amounts of work on his own. Homework can teach responsibilities in ways which are important in our effort to aid achievement.

"Busy work" is not a desirable type of homework. Homework should not be a filler, something the teacher assigns because he does not know what else to do, or as a way simply of keeping gifted children out of trouble. It is proposed as a strong, positive aid to achievement.

Along with daily homework the teacher can send home an accumulation of papers which the student has produced for arithmetic, spelling, or writing. This enables the parent to learn, on a periodic basis (perhaps every week or two), the trend in the child's work. The folder of completed work may be sent home at the end of any designated period of time compatible with the objectives of the course; it probably should be sent home at least once or twice a month.

Along with parent-teacher conferences and report cards, the folder of completed work is a way of demonstrating the child's progress or lack of it. It also provides a day-to-day cumulative account of what the child has produced. Ups and downs can be related to other events in the child's life, and the feedback to the parent is relatively clear and immediate. It can mean much more than the generalized and often superficial remarks on report cards, and it can make much more meaningful the conferences between teacher and parents. The child's progress can be studied in terms of his own ability, in this he compares himself with his previous performance rather than with other people.

Without homework and periodic school-to-home reports other than report cards to review, parents are often in a quandry. They frequently complain that they do not know just what Johnny or Mary is actually doing at school. They do not know to what degree the child is progressing in qualitative ways; how well he pays attention; whether he makes up his work; how he does on written examinations as compared with classroom recitations. These matters differ with children, with grade levels, and with teachers, but through them runs the common thread of training the child to accept responsibility and of firming up structure in the interest of better achievement.

Parents share equally in this responsibility with students and teachers. Many times teachers are conscientious in following the above suggestions but find that some parents will not accept a part in the program. Sometimes, too, these uncooperative parents are the ones who make the greatest fuss when their children fail at school. However, what is important here is what the teacher can and should do, rather than what the parents do not do.

The teacher's evaluation of the child is best tested when supported by the child's homework efforts and the parent's encouragement of them. If the teacher has given him proper homework, if he has really stimulated and challenged the child's ability and interest and followed up appropriately, the teacher has done his best. The parent, then, should be better prepared to accept whatever remaining limitations there are on the child's achievement as perhaps characteristic of his basic ability and habits. Parents cannot properly blame the child's lack of achievement on the teacher.

The emphasis on understanding, in some aspects of modern education, has a bearing on attitudes concerning homework. "The child does the work in the classroom, and we know what he can do," the teacher may say in response to the homework emphasis. The teacher may add, "In this way we know what he can do, what he understands, and not what he turns up with when he has taken the work home and gotten perhaps too much help—or confusing help—from well-meaning parents."

While this discerning teacher has raised a legitimate issue, it probably does not come to grips with the most useful parental role. We discussed drill and understanding earlier in this chapter. Many kinds of learning require much exercise of what the child knows, not only an understanding of the problem at hand. Too frequently, children who knew their multiplication tables last year do not remember them this year or cannot employ them in word problems or in sequences of exercises. The child needs the repeated exercise of his knowledge and skill, and this kind of homework, with drill, can be aided by the parent if the teacher tailors the work properly.

Too little attention, then, has been given the matter of homework and programming it well, we believe. Homework can be put to the service of increased achievement without affecting adversely other important concerns in the educative process. Homework need not be a substitute for classroom work or a way to pass the teacher's responsibilities on to the home.

USING GRADES MORE EFFECTIVELY

Passing and failing are problems integral to achievement. Promotion should be, of course, a sign of adequate achievement; conversely, failing should be a sign of insufficient achievement. Issues arise, not so much with promoting children—although promotion may occur for reasons other than genuine achievement—as with failing them. But failing should be used only if it has value in the learning process, if it corrects achievement problems.

Some elementary schoolteachers have commented to us about failing in these ways: "Well, if he doesn't get down to work pretty soon, he will have to repeat his grade." Or "I have tried to get him to work—he will just have to fail and maybe that will teach him a lesson." Or "When the end of the year comes, he will know that I meant business when I told him I would fail him." Obviously all the children in question were having achievement problems. Is failure the best way to handle these?

These achievement problems were basically matters of *daily self-discipline in studying.* Our concern is with teaching the child good study habits, good attitudes, and good mental hygiene. Failing him at the end of the year—unless all other methods have been tried during the interim—is probably not a good device. Why not? The answer follows the same reasoning that constitutes the theme of this book. A well-disciplined, well-regulated program day by day, hour by hour is needed. If the child still does not succeed after such deliberate efforts have been diligently made, then failing him or, still better, trying to cope with his lack of achievement in some more constructive way is indicated. But simply to level a remote threat of failure—an "F" on the report card or a statement that Johnny will have to remain another year in the eighth grade—is not sufficient. Our efforts to get him to learn have to consist of more immediate and meaningful stuff than is connoted by the threat of eventual failure.

The trouble, as many teachers admit, is that the failing student often does not do better the next year when he repeats the grade. He will probably be bored, and his already inadequate study habits and self-disciplining habits will deteriorate further through lack of stimulation and challenge.

Attitudes of blaming others, resignation, or indifference may predominate.

We should examine what the word "failure" means here. What it really means is that we have the child in the wrong channel or we are teaching him the wrong subjects at the wrong time on the wrong level. There should be no failure in a general sense but only specific failures— failures to perform in particular ways which then require the responsible educators and parents to find methods by which the student will be successful. These might include putting the child in a different kind of school, in classes for special education, in courses that are much more concrete and detailed than usual, or in accelerated classes.

It is important, however, that the student earn his promotion just as he earn a passing grade for each day's assignment. This is no "soft" attitude on promotion and failure. It is to say that the results of the student's work should be felt by him in the manner that will motivate and direct him most effectively. Most instances of failing a student at the end of the year, especially at the elementary level, accomplish nothing positive.

Perhaps at the high school level, a failure in a course can have a more constructive effect. It can mean, for example, that the student should not take algebra at this time but perhaps should take a course in general mathematics. It may mean that he is not ready for a foreign language at this time but needs more instruction in grammar in English. Because of the student's age, the obligation he has may be clear to him, but he may choose to "test out" the teachers to see whether they actually will fail him. Perhaps on such occasions a failure can be constructively absorbed by the student if he is re-directed into new channels.

It should not be assumed, however, that all high school students are sufficiently mature to absorb failure constructively, and the importance of the daily discipline and achievement for those of this age as well as for younger children should not be overlooked. Failing a student is no simple or inconsequential matter. It should always be assessed, with very deliberate and careful thought, how good the effects will probably be for educational purposes. Teachers need to guard against a tendency to use failure as a retaliative effort or as an implicit statement of the inability of the teacher to cope with the child.

SUMMARY AND CONCLUSIONS

Aiding achievement is at times a complex matter.

At all turns in the process of daily learning and achievement there are pitfalls. Most, if not all of these, revolve around some lack of discipline or structure in the set of requirements the child faces. A number of these conditions, but certainly not all of them, have been discussed in this chapter.

We believe that most problems of learning and achievement can be remedied. The remedies will *not* be some new and startling discovery about teaching or motivation, nor some mechanical device that will end all problems or greatly simplify them, nor some magical button-pressing that moves the lagging child to industriousness. They will involve painstaking and persistent effort to keep the student to his tasks in firm, fair, intelligent and rewarding ways.

In this chapter we have covered some of the ways in which this program can be brought to bear on the achievement problems of the child in the classroom.

SELECTED READINGS

BLAIR, GLEN M., and R. STEWART JONES, "Readiness," in C. W. Harris, ed. *Encyclopedia of Educational Research*, 3rd ed. New York: Macmillan 1960.

CRUICKSHANK, W. M., and G. O. JOHNSON, *Education of Exceptional Children and Youth*, 2nd ed. Englewood Cliffs, N.J.: Prentice-Hall, 1967.

GELFAND, D. M., and D. P. HARTMAN, "Behavior therapy with children: A review and evaluation of research methodology." *Psychol. Bulletin*, 1968, *69*, 204–15.

GOLDIAMOND, I., "Self-control procedures in personal behavior problems." *Psychol. Reports*, 1965, *17*, 851–68.

GOODLAND, JOHN I., and ROBERT H. ANDERSON, *The Nongraded Elementary School*. New York: Harcourt, Brace and Jovanovich, 1959.

HILDRETH, GERTRUDE H., *Readiness for School Beginners*. New York: World Publishing, 1950.

LUMSDAINE, A. A., "Educational technology, programmed learning and instructional science," 63rd Yearbook, of the National Society for the Study of Education, Part I, 1964.

MCGUIRE, C., and G. D. WHITE, "Social-class influences on discipline at school." *Educ. Leadership*, 1957, *14*, 229–31, 234–36.

MALPASS, L. F., "Some relationships between students' perceptions of school and their achievement." *J. Educ. Psychol.*, 1953, *44*, 475–82.

PHILLIPS, E. LAKIN, DANIEL N. WIENER, and NORRIS G. HARING, *Discipline, Achievement, and Mental Health*. Englewood Cliffs, N.J.: Prentice-Hall, 1960.

SCHRAMM, W., J. LYLE, and E. B. PARKER, *Television in the Lives of Our Children*. Stanford, Calif.: Stanford University Press, 1961.

SOLOMON, J. C., "Neuroses of school teachers." *Ment. Hyg.*, 1960, *44*, 79–90.

TYLER, LEONA, *The Psychology of Human Differences*. New York: Appleton-Century-Crofts, 1947.

WHITLEY, H. E., "Mental health problems in the classroom." *Understanding the Child*, 1954, *23*, 98–103.

6

VIEWING
ACHIEVEMENT
IN TERMS OF
LEARNING PRINCIPLES

Teachers who have had courses in child development, educational psychology, and personality theory will remember sections of these courses based on learning theory. Learning theory is probably the core of psychology, whether we think in terms of child behavior, teaching, abnormal psychology, or any other specific subdivision of psychology.

Learning theory, or the study of learning, is so important because it attempts to account for human modifiability. The plasticity of the human organism is so vital a fact in human behavior that any book on education, child development, or personality which overlooks it is certain to lack concreteness and usefulness.

In this chapter we will relate our previous discussion to learning principles.

REINFORCEMENT PRINCIPLES

The central concept in most learning theories is that of reinforcement. *Reinforcement* is generally defined as some event in the environment which, when it occurs in a consistent manner and when it follows closely upon the performance of certain behavior, will greatly increase the likelihood of that behavior occurring on subsequent similar occasions. Sometimes the word "reinforcement" is used loosely to mean "reward." However, in scientific analyses of behavior, the term "reward" can become very misleading, while the term "reinforcement" can be more precisely denoted.

If a child looks in a drawer and finds a piece of candy, the chances are great that the child will rummage through the drawer again when the opportunity arises. We might say, "The child is looking for another piece of candy." To be more exact, however, we should observe simply that the business of rummaging through the drawer is increased in likelihood in relation to the fact that the child found a piece of candy there. The candy was the reinforcing event.

If a person interested in certain intellectual activities goes to the dictionary or reference book in order to find the meaning of some term or to get relevant information on some topic, we can say that his behavior has been reinforced and that in the future, the dictionary or the reference book will serve to reinforce his quest for certain kinds of knowledge.

Many thousands of things can serve as reinforcers, as stimuli of conditions which can reinforce certain tendencies in human behavior. In fact, it is almost impossible to imagine that human behavior would have any relevance, modifiability, or integrity if it did not relate to the environment in ways that would encourage the behavior to serve a useful purpose for the individual organism.

We could say that behavior has *consequences*, that there are some effects or outcomes in the environment which behavior brings about. A child plays in the sand and makes a castle; he fashions a boat out of a piece of wood; he learns how to make drawings with chalk on a chalkboard; he learns to read through the gradual interpretation of funny little marks on a page of paper. All of these behaviors have been *reinforced* in a variety of ways on many occasions. The child learns such activities, and he learns to fashion or influence his environment in these ways. The child's behavior has some effect on the environment.

The terms "effect" or "consequence" have also been referred to by some students of learning as "operants." B. F. Skinner and his followers have emphasized the fact that behavior operates on, or in, the environment. This is another way of saying that it has consequences (or effects) on, or in, the environment. Behavior which is an operant—in contrast to behavior which is merely of a reflexive or respondent type—can be modified. Reflexive or respondent behavior is largely determined by neurological conditions and is set off by special stimulus changes in the environment. Sneezing, the pupil of the eye dilating or contracting, sweating palms, are examples of reflexive or respondent behaviors. Ordinarily we cannot modify reflexive or respondent behavior: it is extremely difficult to modify one's tendency to sneeze when the nasal membranes are tickled or to keep the pupils of one's eyes from dilating or contracting when presented with light changes.

MAKING REINFORCING CONDITIONS
WORK FOR LEARNING

It is important to understand how reinforcement can enhance behavior. In previous chapters most of the learning terms such as "reinforcement," "effects," and "consequences" have been used. In this chapter the term "operant" is introduced as crucial. The concepts represented by these terms all closely relate to each other. Reinforcement is applied for the development of behavior which is held to be of value by the student, his parents, his school, his environment or his culture. Other behavior which is not held in high repute needs to be discouraged or extinguished. Generally the term "extinction" refers to the "absence of reinforcement," meaning that when behavior occurs and is not reinforced or does not have any particular consequence in the environment, its presence or reoccurrence is discouraged, and in time, it becomes weaker or extinguished. We will want then to encourage or reinforce desired behavior. At the same time, we will want to discourage or extinguish unwanted behavior.

The teacher needs to ask himself the following questions: "What behavior do I want to *encourage* in my students for particular purposes?" "What behaviors do I want to *discourage* or eliminate in particular instances among the children I work with?" These are the two sides of the vital coin of education. The teacher must think carefully and plan fully about what behavior he wishes to reinforce and what behavior he wants to extinguish.

STEPWISE PROGRESSION
IS IMPORTANT IN REINFORCEMENT

Previously discussed was the concept that it is often very beneficial to feed new material to a child in a sequential or stepwise fashion. A common error that causes a great deal of frustration in learning is the presentation of material at too fast a rate or in too large amounts for the child to be able to digest. To get a certain result, the teacher may crowd the child too much or perhaps give superficial verbal explanations or assignments of what is wanted, and then feel that the child is "slow" or "not able to concentrate," when he is confused or overtaxed.

Another advantage of feeding learning tasks in small increments is that this enables us to see the consequences of the learner's behavior in the environment. If, for example, the student checks with the teacher after the first twenty-five assigned arithmetic problems, then both the child and the teacher know the child has done the problems correctly (or can quickly arrive at a correct solution if his initial attempt was in error). One need not have the child check after each of the twenty-five problems on all occasions, but one should certainly check after the first few individual problems until the student is on his way to a more facile and skillful performance. Otherwise, a large proportion of the problems may be done incorrectly before the child is be put on the right track.

In teaching a child short division and borrowing also, it is important to correct errors very early and to get the child's performance smoothly integrated with the demands so that he does not practice his errors or reach a state of frustration which discourages his performance. While doing twenty-five problems, the child can come under the teacher's tutelage and receive some kind of appropriate reinforcement for his effort ("That's good, John." or "You've earned a play break, Mary."), perhaps a dozen or more times. The learning should proceed more effectively and more smoothly than if these reinforcement opportunities were not utilized.

By the same token, if the child's behavior is in error in his attempt to do short division, it can be corrected or eliminated by having the child redo his work in the correct manner. The word "extinction" might be misleading here; what is wanted is to reduce the student's tendency to make certain kinds of errors and, alternately, to behave in certain select ways. More correctly than referring to extinction methods, we try to superimpose correct or carefully discriminate responses or actions on top of the older, more erroneous, less effective ones. We do withhold reinforcement when the child errs, but more important, when these errors are corrected in a desirable manner, we employ positive reinforcement.

USEFULNESS OF A STRUCTURED
OR PLANNED SCHEDULE

As he grows up, the child passes the point where each separate response or each problem-solving effort can receive a particular reinforcement. He would become too dependent upon our reinforcement if he were asked to check after each arithmetic problem. How peculiar a piece of music would sound if after the child strikes each note, some kind of teacher-controlled reinforcement occurred. We refer here to that behavior goal by which we chain or piece together long sequences of behavior that are integrated and patterned, with the reinforcement coming at the end of the series. For example, in learning to memorize a poem of, say, four stanzas, the child begins by learning the first stanza and getting that set in his behavior in a fairly stable way. His real objective is to be able to recite from memory accurately or to write correctly, with proper punctuation, the first stanza of the four stanza poem. He does not expect to be checked after each word, or perhaps even after each line. His first goal is, rather, the entire first stanza. His larger goal is the recitation or writing of the entire poem.

It is evident here that we are putting together in a large orbit of behavior a lot of small, integrated pieces of behavior, which hang together like the notes in a melody.

Supplementing the notion of reinforcement, then, is some idea of the structure of the entire task to be done. The pattern of the tasks or the manner in which the various components are linked effectively together constitutes the larger learning task and the basis for reinforcement.

EFFECTIVENESS OF PERIODIC REINFORCEMENT

We do not try to reinforce every iota of performance. Occasional reinforcement can carry its effects broadly. If the child is given reinforcement for having learned the four stanza poem, then he feels generally encouraged and perhaps pursues his other schoolwork with more vigor—whether it is memorizing another poem, doing arithmetic problems, or writing a composition. Reinforcement can be considered, then, for application on an occasional basis with a periodicity sufficient for maintaining interest but not so frequently as to make the child entirely dependent upon continuous encouragement.

THE PLACE OF ABILITY

The teacher will wonder whether the strictures cited above in regard to reinforcement do not depend upon the child's ability to perform certain tasks. There is undoubtedly a difference between the amount and characteristics of reinforcement needed for the faster learners compared to the slower. For example, it is often noted that perhaps almost any person can learn many things which he does not ordinarily learn, if the learning tasks and situations are properly programmed or are given in small incremental steps. It takes much longer to teach a slow-learning child algebra than a quick learner, but in principle, the slow-learning child can still be taught algebra, at least to some appreciable extent.

One could look at the problem in the reverse manner and say that while ability affects the amount and quality of reinforcement and perhaps its periodicity, reinforcement also affects ability. There are many people who presumably have the ability to become much more capable than they are, but they have never been encouraged through proper programming and reinforcement to acquire these skills. The student of learning might then ask what value the concept of ability has if environmental events cannot be arranged in a way to facilitate learning. For example, very few masterful scientists or writers have come out of the entire continent of Africa during the last several hundred years. This does not mean that no gifted people have been produced in the cultures of that continent, but in comparison to the European and Western cultures, even in comparison to Oriental cultures, relatively few crowning achievements among the inhabitants of Africa have gained worldwide acceptance. Now surely among all the millions of people there must be talented individuals in the fields of science, writing, abstract thinking, and so on, comparable in numbers to those in Europe, America, and the Orient; missing, however, are the proper environmental events—meaning specific schooling and reinforcing opportunities—calculated to bring about a high level of performance.[1]

PROGRAMMED INSTRUCTION: A WAY OF CONTROLLING REINFORCEMENT

In the last decade there has been a growing interest in what is called programmed instruction. Programmed instruction consists of presenting small bits of information, or frames, in a very tight, logical, and sequential fashion. A response is required at the end of each frame; it is subject to confirmation (reinforcement) or correction (extinction or lack of reinforcement). For example, if a child is studying geography by way of programmed instruction, instead of being presented with a textbook that describes the various continents and water masses of the world, he is presented with a series of small frames, each requiring a response from him which is immediately judged correct or incorrect (reinforced or not reinforced).

The following frames are examples of the way in which programmed instruction in geography might proceed:

1. All maps are described by four major directions: north is most often at the top, east at the right, west at the left, and south at the bottom.
   Question: If a person moved his finger from the center of the map to the right side, his direction of travel would be _____.

   (east)

   Question: If one moved his finger over a map from the bottom to the top, the direction of travel would be from _____ to _____.

   (south to north)

   Question: If a person drew a line from the right side of a map to the left side of the map, he would be going from the direction of _____ to _____.

   (east to west)

---

[1] Also contributing, of course, is the possibility that those of us in other cultures are not yet capable of appreciating the Africans' achievements. This possibility does not invalidate, however, the likelihood that reinforcement deficiencies contribute substantially to the situation.

2. The United States is bordered on the East Coast by the Atlantic Ocean and on the West Coast by the Pacific Ocean.
Question: If we sailed eastward from the East Coast of the United States, we would sail on the _____ Ocean.

(Atlantic)

Question: The _____ Ocean borders the West Coast of the United States.

(Pacific)

Question: California is on the West Coast of the United States. What ocean does it border on? _____

(Pacific)

Question: From Maine to Florida is considered the East Coast of the United States. The ocean bordering this land is the _____ Ocean.

(Atlantic)

Question: If one drives east from the center of the United States, in time he would come to the _____ Ocean.

(Atlantic)

Some of the merits of programmed instruction, which derive from the previously discussed learning principles, are as follows:

1. Presents material in small, manageable amounts (called frames).
2. Requires a particular response, something definitive, so that the student knows what is expected of him.
3. The child compares his response with the correct one, thereby he immediately knows whether he is correct (he is reinforced).
4. Permits the child to proceed at a rate commensurate with his own intelligence and ability. If the material is difficult for him and he needs to go more slowly, then he is paced by his own requirements rather than by the classroom teacher, who ordinarily must get all the children through a particular unit in a particular period of time.
5. Enables a group of children to go at their various rates and to be ready for examination, recitation, or use of the information in particular ways at varying periods of time.

It is possible to arrange the curriculum of a child's entire school day in terms of programmed material. It may not be desirable to do this, in all respects, but it certainly would be possible. If we add to printed programmed material, such as is found in spelling, arithmetic, and geography, the possibility of controlling the informational input and response output by use of a computer, it is not difficult to imagine how an entire class could be taught by programmed or program-like methods, all based on the individual needs of each child.

Presenting materials in programmed fashion provides for the periodic reinforcement that is so important. It also has a reinforcement benefit for the teacher in that his time is freed to do trouble shooting and to give special encouragement or special direction to children in matters not handled by the programmed series.

A whole class could use programmed material in geography, arithmetic, and other fields where the information is fairly precise and easily identifiable. Then the teacher could direct more creative activities, allowing time for initiative and self-direction to develop among the children. The programmed series permits the children to take on as their own responsibility the acquisition of information that is ordinarily the responsibility of the teacher in the more conventional modes of teaching.

Also, it is difficult to imagine the teacher as an effective "reinforcing agent" for twenty or thirty children in the classroom at the same time. Ordinarily, the teacher can act as a careful reinforcing agent only sparingly or in certain highly specific ways. But immediate self-knowledge for the child of the results of his actions on a programmed series or in a test based on a programmed series can act as more or less automatic reinforcement for him, thereby encouraging considerably more achievement and along with this, of course, better self-discipline.

USING REINFORCEMENT PRINCIPLES
IN THE CLASSROOM

Classroom situations are ideally suited to the use of systematic reinforcement. Let us see how this might operate in a concrete situation.

> Miss Jones, the teacher, has a petulant and crying eight-year-old girl in the third grade classroom. The teacher has "tried everything" to understand Peggy and had several conferences with Peggy's mother. Peggy behaves similarly at home and "loses her temper," her mother reports, "at the slightest inconvenience or disappointment."

> Miss Jones has scolded, threatened, punished, and felt sorry for Peggy at various times. She has tried to pair Peggy off in studies and committee work with a jolly, outgoing girl, Sue, but this has not worked very well.

> Peggy's record shows that she has normal intelligence, is achieving on grade level, seems to be liked by others except when whining and crying, but has begun to fall out of favor with her peers, since she has become so hard to please.

> On the basis of several of the school's contacts with the home, and of knowledge about two older siblings in the same school, Peggy's home life is seen as fairly normal and her relationships with siblings, peers, and her parents appear to be at least average in stability and consistency. She has had no special health problems and no recent setbacks in school or in her personal life.

The school psychologist was called in to observe Peggy in her class, and how the teacher handled Peggy's problems, as a preliminary to working out a possible solution for her difficulties. The psychologist observed for two fifteen-minute periods each day, morning and afternoon, for two weeks, before presenting some data and trying to move toward at least an amelioration of Peggy's problems in the classroom.

The following graph summarizes, in brief, ways the data were collected by the psychologist. Notes were taken on when Peggy cried, the surrounding circumstances and what the teacher did on these occasions.

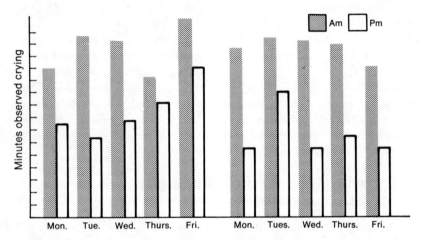

FIGURE 1   Peggy's crying behavior (minutes observed crying), three fifteen-minute samples each day, A.M. and P.M., for two weeks.

This graph shows that, according to the psychologist's sampled observations, Peggy cried almost continually in the morning but not as often during the afternoon. This appeared to be related to unfinished arithmetic work that the teacher reported Peggy said she did not like. She was slow in getting at her work and often left it unfinished to go on to other studies if the teacher allowed this.

The afternoon appeared to be more serene because Peggy had a history class just before recess, which she looked forward to. If Peggy was in a "good mood," the teacher averred, when she went out to recess the others were more likely to include her in their team games, more likely to throw the ball to her and to choose her for competitive activities. Apparently, the reinforcing effects of peer approval of happier and better social behavior had begun to make a difference in Peggy's afternoon behavior compared to her morning behavior—that, together with the dislike Peggy expressed for arithmetic.

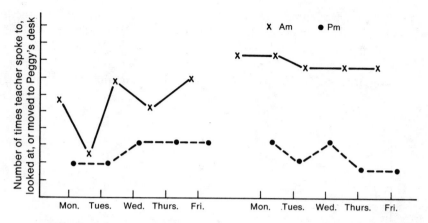

FIGURE 2 Number of times teacher paid attention to Peggy for two weeks, A.M. and P.M., during her crying periods.

A second graph shows what the teacher did when Peggy cried. The data suggest that, possibly out of sympathy, she spoke to, looked at, or moved toward Peggy more often when Peggy was crying. Therefore she tended to maintain Peggy's petulant and crying behavior. At least, Peggy's emotional displays were attended to by her teacher, and there was a strong differential between the morning and afternoon behavior of the teacher vis-à-vis Peggy. (For purposes of changing the behavior, it does not matter whether Peggy's or the teacher's behavior was the more basic cause.) In the afternoon the teacher was busy with a special reading group of which Peggy was not a member; hence she was probably unable to give as much attention to Peggy as in the morning. Miss Jones, the teacher, told the school psychologist before the data collecting began that she thought Peggy felt "unwanted" and "unloved," and she was trying to make up to Peggy what she felt she did not receive at home.

After these data were collected and presented to the teacher and the principal in a conference with the school psychologist, the latter suggested that the teacher make a point of ignoring Peggy's crying in the mornings, on the likelihood that the very act of attending to Peggy's crying made it worse (socially reinforcing her behavior by such attention as eye contact, walking close by, and talking to her). Furthermore, paying attention to Peggy when she was *not* crying would reduce crying and build other behaviors. Opportunities for doing this occurred when Peggy came into the classroom in the morning, when she did a good job on her spelling, when she volunteered to speak in class or to offer an opinion. The teacher was not scolded nor considered responsible for Peggy's moods but was viewed in the same way as a well-intending person who tries to move an accident victim without appreciating the fact that such movement might add to the victim's pain and danger. The teacher accepted this viewpoint objectively and agreed to systematically withhold reinforcement (attention) when Peggy was crying or was about to cry and to increase her attention (and approval) only when Peggy did well in academic work or participated socially in some obvious way.

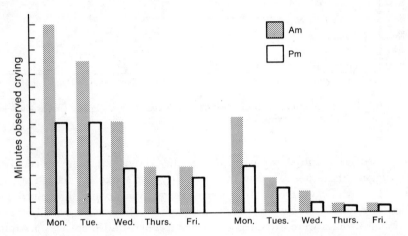

FIGURE 3 Peggy's crying behavior (minutes observed crying), three fifteen-minute samples, A.M. and P.M., for two weeks' time, covering the extinction period (when the teacher paid no attention to crying).

Figure 3 shows how Peggy's crying declined when the teacher made a systematic effort to change the social consequences of the crying. There was a decided drop-off in crying during the first week of extinction effort (nonreinforcement by socially ignoring Peggy at this time), and a dropping to near-zero (after Monday's brief flare-up of crying) during the second week, the remainder of the period over which observations were made. Miss Jones was "delighted to see Peggy happier and more alert in class" and felt that she had begun to overcome a real problem Peggy had displayed in class.

In a later conference the school psychologist pointed out to Miss Jones that when a child is behaving by crying and withdrawing from others, attention given her at such times by the teacher is reinforcing to the child and tends to substitute for more normal peer contacts. In a very real sense, Peggy's teacher was influencing (shaping) Peggy toward dependency, petulance, and crying when Peggy encountered hardships or frustrations.

The situation with Peggy illustrates the power of reinforcement. The first graph shows that the attention of the teacher helped maintain the puzzling behavior, although the teacher did not want Peggy to act as she did. Neither did the parent desire this behavior. Peggy herself wanted to be happier and to get along better in daily school life, but under the circumstances, she was powerless to do much about it. When the teacher's attention was planfully withheld, Peggy was no longer reinforced in her crying behavior; she was left more on her own to cope with the consequences of her actions. Peggy gained strength when she could no longer depend upon the teacher's attention (during the extinction period) and she developed other behavior as she cried less and less. In about two weeks' time, she was hardly crying at all. More positive behavior also began to assert itself as Peggy spent more time playing with others and taking a larger role in school activities. She was seen walking to and from the classroom with other children, between classes and before and after school, rather than sniffling in a lonely and forlorn way.

This teacher was so pleased by the results of her brief therapeutic work that she set about describing *target behavior* in other children which she and their parents agreed was detrimental. And with the help of the school psychologist, she began to work with several children in a similar manner throughout the school year.

The teacher (with the parents and principal concurring) has to set up the target behaviors which are considered as objects for change. Such behavior might consist, for example, of desirable but weak skills in reading comprehension, language (oral skills), and social confidence, which under suitable reinforcing conditions can be upgraded. On the other hand, like Peggy's crying the target behavior may be some activity that all concerned want to weaken or eliminate. In this kind of therapy one must first think about his objectives involving the welfare of the child and then set about to gather data (make systematic observations) on the target behavior. This assures that the target behavior will be more clearly seen over time. Later, the teacher must apply reinforcement principles, using a systematic approach.

Usually, persistent and annoying problems can be overcome in this general manner in a relatively short time. Under the direction of a school psychologist, the classroom teacher can be helped to take many practical steps which result in much more integrative and productive behavior on the part of the child (thus, enhancing his achievement and mental health).

USING REINFORCEMENT PRINCIPLES
WITH SEVERELY DISTURBED CHILDREN

The previous section suggests ways in which fairly normal children with problems can be helped in the classroom through reinforcement principles. Can such procedures be applied with more severely disturbed children or in special education classes?

The following example of intensive behavior therapy with a severely disturbed girl illustrates how these principles have widespread applicability. The more disturbed the child, however, the more carefully the reinforcement work has to be done and the more persevering have to be the teacher and the psychologist.

> T—— was a thirteen-year-old girl of average ability intellectually and of normal size for her age; she showed no signs of organic impairment. She was referred to a school specializing in the treatment and education of emotionally disturbed children[2] because of her repeated failures in social adjustment and academic work. She frequently fantasized "out loud," talking and laughing to herself; she had a very short attention span; she was fidgety and appeared unable to cope with even moderate amounts of social stress (usually began crying and restlessly moving about).

> While T—— had responded somewhat to the use of social and other reinforcements in the classroom in group situations, there was need for more individualized sessions so as to move her along faster and to build generally more resourceful behavior. We began these individual sessions by pointing up undesirable behavior, which was to be overcome, and appropriate behavior, which was to be upgraded or increased.

Statement of Specific Behavior

The following inappropriate behavior was chosen by the teacher to decrease and/or eliminate:

1. Inappropriate verbal behavior such as
   a. talking to herself
   b. humming
   c. squealing and laughing out of context
2. Inappropriate motor behavior such as
   a. rocking
   b. body stroking (auto stimulation)
   c. jumping out of seat
3. Inappropriate staring behavior

These activities interfered with T——'s academic behavior, since they were incompatible with such behavior as sitting still and comprehension.

The teacher chose to increase in frequency the following observable behaviors:

1. Comprehension, defined as percent of correct responses (answers) to questions on reading material

---

[2] The School for Contemporary Education, McLean, Virginia. This portion of the chapter was written by Mrs. Carolyn Adler, teacher, and Dr. Dave Williams, research psychologist, at the school.

2. Ability to sit still

3. Amount of material read

Methods

Fifty-one sessions, each lasting 30 minutes, were carried out over a period of four months (although all data are not reported here). The sessions were always in the morning, during the 30-minute time segment before the lunch hour. The sessions always took place in a research room (with a two-way mirror) except for two sessions held in another room. T—— would sit across the table facing the teacher.

To each session T—— would bring her selected reading material. The Yearling Book Series and The Reading Experience and Development series were used.[3]

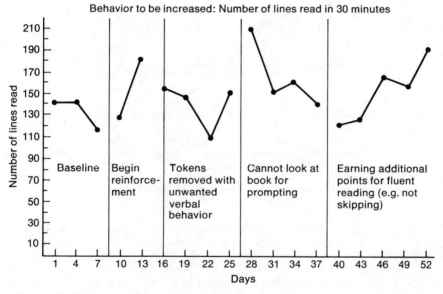

Behavior to be increased: Number of lines read in 30 minutes

FIGURE 4 T——'s performance in reading. A baseline shows where she started: with the beginning of reinforcement, she performed better; when tokens were removed because of her unwanted behaviors (see text), her performance declined. Making the demands on her performance more severe (not looking at the book for prompting), with reinforcement continuing, she showed variability in the number of lines read but fairly good performance. With the addition of more reinforcement—additional points which she could "trade in" (last column above)—she continued to perform on a high level. It was then the task of the teacher to generalize this improvement to performance in all her reading, not just when she was working with the teacher.

[3] In the READ series (New York: American Book), T—— read stories from books numbered 4 and 5. In the Yearling Book Series (New York: Dell), she completed the following books: *Florence Nightingale, Abraham Lincoln, Amelia Earhart,* and *Thomas Edison.*

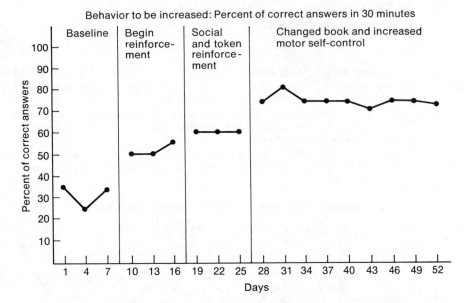

FIGURE 5   Improvement in T——'s quality of performance in reading (namely in the percentage of correct answers during each of her thirty-minute reading periods). The baseline shows where she began. The value of reinforcement is displayed in the next two columns. Finally with the establishment of earning points as reinforcers and her changing to a book providing fluency in reading, she continued to perform on a high level for a number of days. This high-level performance was then more easily generalized to other reading matter.

To begin with, baseline data were collected for eight sessions on the behavior to be *increased* (Number of lines read and percent of correct answers). T——would read a paragraph; then the teacher would ask her two questions about the content. If T—— answered the question correctly within a ten-second interval,[4] it was recorded as a correct response; if the question was answered correctly *after* the ten-second interval, it was recorded as an incorrect response. T——was allowed to look at the book for answers. The number of lines she read, as well as the total number of questions asked and the percent of questions answered correctly, were recorded by the teacher on a piece of paper.

Recording Inappropriate Behaviors

Starting with the ninth session and lasting for seven sessions, baseline data were collected for those behaviors to be decreased (inappropriate verbal behaviors, inappropriate motor behaviors). Baseline data were still continuing on that behavior to be increased. Every time T—— squealed, talked to herself, hummed, or laughed out of context (behavior to be

---

[4] This was a contingency: a response was correct *if* or *when* it occurred within a time limit and *if* it were correct.

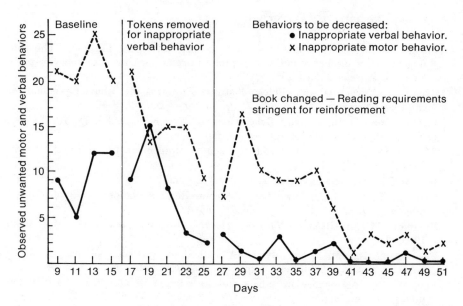

FIGURE 6 Behaviors to be decreased: verbal and motor behaviors were both markedly decreased, beginning with Session 9, concurrent with the reinforcement program shown in Figures 4 and 5. In the final days of this study, we can safely say that T——'s unwanted motor and verbal behaviors were reduced to almost zero for the thirty-minute reading periods during which these data were collected.

decreased), each was recorded by the teacher as one inappropriate *verbal* behavior for its total duration. Every time T—— started rocking in her seat, stroking her body, or jumping out of her seat, it was recorded by the teacher as one inappropriate *motor* behavior for the duration of the behavior. (The behavior was only counted as occurring one time until it stopped, whether the behavior lasted ten seconds or two minutes.) During these seven sessions, the contingency still existed that she give an answer correctly within a ten-second interval for it to be recorded as correct. She observed this throughout the sessions. (Figures 4 and 5).

These data show how one can work with even a severely disturbed youngster, using reinforcement principles. Sometimes people think that reinforcement practices are mainly for children who already have appropriate behavior, but, as this illustration shows, it can be useful even in very disturbed cases. It was necessary to continue the reinforcement practices long beyond the amount of time shown here, and to try to generalize the results to T——'s everyday school environment. In time, T—— was able to enter into fairly normal social behavior with other children, and she required less individual attention in order to read well, answer questions, and control her inappropriate behavior.

SELECTED READINGS

BECKER, W. C., C. H. MADSEN, C. R. ARNOLD, and D. R. THOMAS, "The contingent use of teacher attention and praise in reducing classroom behavior problems." *J. Special Educ.*, 1967, *1*, 287–307.

BEILIN, H., "Teachers' and clinicians' attitudes towards the behavior problems of children: A reappraisal." *Child Development*, 1959, *30*, 9–12.

BIJOU, S., and D. BAER, *Child Development: A Systematic and Empirical Theory.* New York: Appleton-Century-Crofts, 1961.

BIRNBRAUER, J., and J. DAWLER, "Token reinforcement for learning." *Ment. Retardation*, 1964, *2*, 275–79.

BOWER, E., "A process for identifying disturbed children." *Child*, 1957, *4*, 143–47.

CLIFFORD, E., "Discipline in the home: A controlled observational study of parental practices." *J. Genet. Psychol.*, 1959, *95*, 45–82.

EYSENCK, H., ed., *Behavior Therapy and the Neuroses.* New York: Macmillan, 1960.

FERSTER, C. B., and M. DE MYER, "A method for experimental analysis of the behavior of autistic children." *Amer. J. Orthopsychiat.*, 1962, *32*, 89–98.

FEY, W. F., "Acceptance by others and its relation to acceptance of self and others: A reevaluation." *J. Abnorm. Soc. Psychol.* 1955, *50*, 274–76.

GINOTT, H., *Between Parent and Child.* New York: Macmillan, 1965.

HARING, NORRIS G., and E. LAKIN PHILLIPS, *Educating Emotionally Disturbed Children.* New York: McGraw-Hill, 1962.

HEWETT, FRANK M., *The Emotionally Disturbed Child in the Classroom.* Boston: Allyn & Bacon, 1968.

HEWETT, FRANK M., "A hierarchy of educational tasks for children with learning disorders." *Exceptional Children*, 1964, *31*, 207–14.

HOLLAND, J., "Teaching machines: An application of principles from the laboratory." *J. Exper. Analysis of Behavior*, 1960, *3*, 275–87.

KELLER, F., *Learning: Reinforcement Theory.* New York: Random House, 1954.

KRUMBOLTZ, J. D., "Behavioral counseling: Rationale and research." *Personnel and Guidance J.*, 1965, *44*, 383–87.

SKINNER, B. F., "Why teachers fail." *Saturday Review*, 1965, *48*, 80–102.

SOLOMON, J. C., "Neuroses of school teachers." *Ment. Hyg.*, 1960, *44*, 79–90.

WAHLER, R. G., "Child-child interactions in free field settings: Some experimental analyses." *J. Exceptional Child Psychol.*, 1967, *5*, 278–93.

WATSON, G., "Some personality differences in children related to strict or permissive parental discipline." *J. Psychol.*, 1957, *44*, 227–49.

7

AIDING
SOCIAL GROWTH

Social growth and emotional growth, are often considered as aspects of mental health. It is difficult to consider them separately. For purposes of our discussion, *social growth* refers to the emotional maturity with which a child carries on his relationships with his peers as well as with those older or younger than himself.

Social growth pertains to the child's relationships with others as these relationships may be distinguished from the child's feelings and actions in regard to himself, and in distinction to his achievement in school. A child may mature socially, or seem socially acceptable, and yet be deficient in other respects. Usually, however, the various aspects of his life are correlated with each other; they tend to vary upward or downward together. In this chapter, however, we will emphasize those aspects of the child's life in school that have to do with his relationships with others.

PROBLEMS WITH PEERS

First, let us discuss the child's relationships with his peers. These social relationships take up what is perhaps the largest share of his school day and, after his relationships at home, probably assume the largest role in his life. Yet adults often overlook peer relations and, thereby, fail to take advantage of opportunities to know, understand, and guide the child correctly.

Adults are often surprised to learn how much pressure for good or evil children can exert on one another. One rather "nervous" elementary school youngster, for instance, was deeply disturbed by a completely fictitious statement from a peer that the nervous youngster's father had held up a bank the night before. The same child could easily be whipped into a frenzy when his classmates teased him, saying that he was going to fail in his schoolwork; that the teacher was going to give a test in arithmetic that day, which he would fail; or that some people were coming to the school to burn it down.

Another child was admonished to call home by some of his peers who said that his house was on fire and that the police were coming to take his parents away because they had done something to cause the fire. Before the adults realized it, this child had made several frantic calls home, trying to find out what had happened.

You may ask, "What child beyond the third grade would believe such preposterous stories?" Perhaps not many, but some children do. Those who do so are often disturbed, overly sensitive children who need help. The children in these illustrations were affected to a very great extent by their peers. These are extreme examples, but to a lesser degree, they occur with most children.

Children often jeer at or harass each other. By adult standards, they can indeed be cruel to one another, and they sometimes enjoy seeing their victims squirm. In some cases children are so harassed by their peers that they refuse to go to school. School hallways, locker quarters, and the paths to and from rooms in the school are sometimes places where only the sharpest adult eyes and ears are likely to see or hear the little intrigues and the large defeats and victories of child against child. The victimized child may think that the adult does not care what happens to him, and he may regard the adult as very gullible not to suspect a lot of dirty work going on.

Not only are classrooms and hallways the scenes of such intrigues, so sometimes are the laboratories, shops, dressing rooms, and the gymnasium. It is in these larger settings, where discipline is generally looser and the structure very open, that children sometimes become very rough with one another. In some of the distressing situations that develop, it is possible that a child will be injured physically—breaking a bone or perhaps being seriously bruised. We know of an instance where in shop class a ninth grader was attacked by an eleventh grader, resulting in a broken wrist for the younger child. This situation appeared to take place completely outside adult supervision and control, yet upon closer examination, it appeared that a number of small fights had been going on.

This type of situation causes great distress for parents and between parents and the school. Imagine the anguish of the parents of the victimized ninth grader and the equally frustrating and perplexing plight of the school and of the parents of the older child. Sometimes the school is unduly blamed in these circumstances, and the normal role of the school as a judicator or a compromiser is lost because it is already itself under attack. It is very hard for the school to referee a situation objectively because frequently it is placed in a position of blame as well as in one of trying to mollify the offended persons.

Problems with peers can range all the way from minor teasing (practically all children engage in this at one time or another) to physical attacks in which bones may be broken or children knocked unconscious. Generally the more severe circumstances develop when there is a lack of disciplinary control (as with recent gang attacks on schools) or when there is some momentary disorganization caused by factors beyond the control of the adults.

KNOWING THE SITUATION WELL

What is the lesson for teachers in these instances? To try to do therapy with children at odd times in the classroom? Probably not. To know the children better? Yes, but particularly in terms related to the setting, and to how they feel about each other and how they get along with each other, rather than just as they show themselves alone when overwhelmed or in a context with adults. The teacher can listen in on public but informal talk among children. A teacher can ride the school bus occasionally. A teacher can appear in a gym or at a school social function and observe many revealing attitudes and activities. A written theme on an appropriate subject can contribute to the teacher's understanding of deleterious social relationships among children. Teachers cannot, of course, take at face value all the stories children tell on each other, but persistently disturbed viewpoints need to be investigated. This may sometimes lead to a knowledge of cancerous social relationships among peers that can be corrected before matters get out of hand.

The more sensitive and less resourceful child is perhaps most often the victim of unfair play. Such children often are also the most immature and are in greatest need of adult help. It is not the teacher's role to break in and "save" the sensitive child, but rather, at least at first, to apply his skills to modify the aggressor's attitudes, his opportunities for harm, and his insults and to help the victim leave or handle a damaging situation. While the teacher is holding on to the aggressor, so to speak, the victimized child will be given a respite and can be guided toward gaining the self-protective skills and behavior he so desperately needs.

One ten-year-old boy, brought to our attention after a series of episodes involving peers and children slightly older than himself, was in fact a marauder one could only imagine might exist. In appearance the youngster was mild, cooperative, and pleasant toward adults, seemingly contrite about his previous wrongdoings. A juvenile court officer who interviewed the lad at school after he had "caused a girl his age to fall in a race and break an arm," said of the boy:

> He had me completely fooled. He was sweet, somewhat guilty about his conduct, and he readily promised to be more careful next time. I talked with him near the end of the school day after several neighbors had reported to the school and the court that he was beating up other children on the way home from school. We had what seemed to be a good understanding and after 30 or 40 minutes I said "goodby." He started home and I picked up my belongings, went to my car, and started back to the courthouse. On the way to the courthouse I observed a lad about the size of the one I had just talked with, beating up another boy. As I approached the area of the fight in my car unrecognized and probably unseen by the aggressor, I clearly identified my "friend" of a few minutes before—the lad who had been so contrite and so ready to reform after a few minutes' talk.

Children are often smarter than we think. They know how to pretend to subscribe to adult values and how to act beguiling toward adults and teachers, particularly those in authority. A further example of this contrite attitude, in all its superficialty, was the case of a twelve-year-old boy who had been smoking.

> This twelve-year-old youth had been caught smoking in the basement of his home on several occasions by his parents. Each time he promised them he would stop. Usually two or three weeks passed between the episodes, and the parents had been at first beguiled into thinking that the boy's words were to be taken at face value. A complication arose when the mother discovered that the child had stashed away many packs of cigarettes and also loose cigarettes in the basement, where he and his friends could have ready access to them. At the same time at school the lad in question and some of his smoking cronies were discovered smoking in the boys' toilet when their careless behavior set a janitor's closet on fire and caused the fire department to be called.

The ingratiating attitude of this youngster simply led his parents and other adults astray for a time. Their misinformation was finally corrected when a potentially dangerous situation occurred, which the boy had helped to bring about.

Children who are either manhandled by an aggressive child, or who are led by other children into harmful behavior also need protection. The aggressive child needs treatment, to be sure, but unless he is first brought under control or removed from the social scene of the school or until he matures, weak and sensitive children are likely to continue to be victimized by him. The child who leads other children into wrongful behavior also must be identified and, perhaps, even isolated for a while so that he does not become able to spoil the whole environment.

HANDLING BULLIES

The problem of children who bully younger boys and girls needs no more than passing mention. Usually the situation is so obvious that teachers, friends, and neighbors see the mistreated children's circumstance and readily come to their assistance. A bully is more easily detected and restrained than the peer-level aggressor. Most children readily label the bully, and sooner or later, his peers usually retaliate and "put him in his place." The bully is often a child who doubts his own strength more than that of anyone else but who, rather than face his problems with those his own size and age, tests himself on less able youngsters.

HANDLING THE SELF-CENTERED CHILD

A more persistent and common problem is that of the child who constantly makes demands and who lacks consideration for his peers, his elders, and those in authority. This is the child who rushes to be first at every turn; who waves his hand frantically to recite in class, lest the teacher fail to see that he knows everything; who tries to get what he wants ahead of everybody else (such as a drink of water from the fountain).

The administration of simple disciplinary restraint is strongly indicated in such cases. A useful remedy is to require the overly self-centered child either to wait his turn or go to the back of the line. If he gets to the toy box first (preparatory to engaging in outdoor games or athletics), he may be designated to pass out the items needed for the game to the others. Or if he pushes ahead of others, he may be told to return to the classroom and forfeit his play period. This again is the levying of the consequences, discussed earlier, which should be described to the child before they must be assessed. Once the disturbing behavior has been reduced, the child can then be rewarded (reinforced) for good self-control.

The tendency of the child in this illustration toward overly aggressive and monopolizing displays can better be handled by a *choice situation*—"*either* wait your turn *or* go to the end of the line"—than by verbal remonstrations. Usually the remonstrations do not stem the tide of his self-aggrandizing behavior. There is scarcely a time when talk by the teacher is less effective than in coping with the child who is continually challenging the rules of the game and always wanting to put himself first.

When a group of teachers were discussing this problem, one remarked, "But I hate to be so drastic as to make him go to the end of the lunch line when he is obviously so hungry." As the discussion progressed, this teacher came to appreciate the fact that if he did not draw the disciplinary line earlier and more firmly, rather than resorting to simple objections or to threats that could not be carried out, he would probably have increasing trouble with the boy. Ultimately the teacher would have to control the behavior in the cafeteria. The sooner this was done, he decided, the better. It was also unfair to let the other children become victims of the disrespectful boy's relentless behavior. Many times teachers and others in the child's life have a great deal of compassion for the offending one but fail to show similar compassion toward the quieter people who are being victimized. If the compassion leads to rehabilitation, fine, if it merely leads to indulgence, however, everyone involved suffers in the end.

A motto for the teacher in such situations could be: *"Do early what you ultimately must do anyhow."* If discipline will have to be administered eventually, why not do it early and settle the issue, thereby preventing complications and further misunderstanding? The wear and tear on everyone is far less, and the general amenability of the child to learning control in other situations is enhanced by early, concrete action. The teacher is then known to be firm, and a general respect for discipline is more likely to be held by all the children. A precedent is set for order, fairness, courtesy, and consistency in handling difficulties, which then serve as a basis for reinforcing the self-control of the heretofore recalcitrant child.

USING ISOLATION EFFECTIVELY

Perhaps every room should have an isolation area for children who disrupt ordinary routine. Some schools, particularly those dealing with brain damaged and emotionally disturbed children, have installed small booths along the sides of one or more walls so that the teacher can isolate the offending child from the others. In this way, distracting and interfering behavior can at least temporarily be controlled. The purpose of this partial isolation is twofold: first, to halt the disruptive behavior which the child is engaging in and, second, to show the child that you, as a teacher, have recourse and can move effectively in a manner related to the child's social obligations to others. More complete isolation is found in the use of a "time out" booth, which is an office well away from others, where the child goes when he is unusually disruptive.

Here again, simply criticizing or warning the child repeatedly is often useless. A teacher's mere words do not in refractory instances succeed in stopping socially disruptive behavior. The behavior continues; the child accumulates victory after victory (he gets reinforced by this behavior); the disruptive habit becomes stronger; and the teacher's effectiveness is thereby lessened. Also, the other children may lose respect for the teacher, while the troublesome child gains in status.

Offices and libraries are not good places in which to banish the refractory child. There are too many distractions in these quarters, too many interesting activities and objects. Effective isolation requires a separate, relatively barren room or, if all that is possible is separate quarters within the room, the area must be as separate and barren as can be devised. The "banished" child should be held to his academic responsibilities, not left idle or given busy work. The isolation provides not only a respite for the other children and the teacher but also a consequence for the offending child (as all correction should), which says to him, "You are losing your place and your privileges because of your misbehavior; you may return to your group later and try different behavior."

If the child wants to be isolated—very few do—then banishment to the isolation room is not likely to be effective. It is recommended in most cases, however, because isolation is one of the easiest types of consequence to use and usually one of the most potent, from the standpoint of the psychology of the child.

When the child is put in an isolation room booth, he should usually be kept there for a specified period of time. For example, he may be sent there for the rest of the class period or for an hour, or he can be told that he may return to his regular seat and activities when he feels he can do so without disturbing other people. The latter procedure is preferable because it puts the child on his own and gives him the responsibility of ordering and controlling his behavior. The results also tell the teacher if the student is capable of self-discipline. It gives the child an opportunity to try himself out in circumstances in which, previously, he was too immature and in this way, to vindicate himself.

When the child is isolated, it is usually sufficient to set him to finishing his incomplete work. It is not necessary to talk to him further, lecture him on good conduct, or have him write five hundred times, "I must behave in class." The isolation itself, if properly handled, is a remarkably constructive step for most children in most circumstances. To heap on coals by further admonishment or through punishment that has no inherent *corrective effect* not only undercuts the teacher's other constructive efforts but may stimulate unnecessary resentment in the child. If unnecessary resentment is added to the child's thinking, the original issue and the constructive use of consequences could easily be lost.

SENDING THE CHILD HOME
UNDER PROPER CONDITIONS

It is occasionally necessary to send children home from school if they are too disruptive. This too can be a remarkably good device for bringing the average obstreperous child to terms with himself and with the social proprieties at school. Most young children think it is the last thing in the world a teacher would do; sending them home from school for conduct reasons seems to them to be practically impossible. This is not true with older children who have witnessed the expulsion of students from high school.

The step of sending a child home from school for the remainder of the day (this is better than sending him home for the morning only and allowing him to return at noon) requires some forethought and planning. Often it cannot be done effectively on the spur of the moment. It should not be a retaliative measure by the teacher. Also it can easily backfire if it is not handled properly.

The teacher, principal, and parents must agree that this procedure is useful and germane. The teacher may give the child one warning about his conduct, telling him that he will be sent home if he continues to disobey. If the child persists, the teacher can take or send him to the office, where the parent can then be called. The parent can decide whether to come to get the child, have him sent home in a taxi, or let him walk home on his own if the home is not too distant. These should be explicitly agreed upon arrangements, however.

School rules or state or local laws pertaining to school attendance may have to be considered in such cases. However, if all parties agree to such a procedure, then its administration should not be much of a technical or legal problem. The important issue here lies with its proper execution— with careful planning of the conditions under which it will be carried out. For example, a parent might be required to accompany the child on his return to school so that there is full understanding of the conditions for his readmission.

Why is it useful either to isolate children who are social conduct problems or to send them home from school? The reasoning is the same in both instances. It is simply intended to bring a halt to the child's disturbing behavior (and the social reinforcements it often gets from the class members), to demonstrate a consequence of a social behavior, and to indicate what the loss of normal social contact means. It places the responsibility squarely on the child's shoulders for self-control, *but assists him in bringing about this control, through showing him how acceptable and unacceptable behavior earn different consequences.*

WHY CHILDREN MISBEHAVE

The teacher may ask, "But don't we have to know *why* the particular child misbehaves?" We reply, "Regardless of whether the child misbehaves for some apparently mysterious or individual reason, sooner or later most children, to a greater or lesser extent, try out misbehavior. It can and must be handled, in the main, in group settings. Some children will need individual treatment, but this can never be an adequate approach for the many behavior problems teachers face every day."

The reason more children do not misbehave is precisely because they have learned better. This means that they have been taught that different consequences stem from acceptable and unacceptable behavior. Learning better behavior usually entails suffering some unpalatable consequences from the misbehavior. It also involves receiving reinforcement from the desirable behavior, which teaches the children to plan better, to control themselves better, and to respect others. When a child is handled in the manner we have just described—barring very complicated and difficult home situations or especially troubled children—he does learn better to control himself. We have seen this occur dozens of times and so have most teachers or school principals who have tried this approach.

If he feels or knows that he can get away with it, the child often continues to misbehave. This "getting away" is a very important part of the child's misbehavior. The impulsive ends he pursues may not be entirely to his liking in the long run, but in the short run they usually are. This is a case of some rewards or reinforcements occurring before the long-range, undesired consequences befall the child. The child lacks maturity and judgment in perspective. He cannot place his conduct in any long-term social context. Adults must guide children and teach them these long-term considerations. For us to assume that the child should "know better" and then to ignore practical steps to insure that he not only knows better but acts better is folly. Many a child's conduct goes uncorrected, undermining his life as an adult, apparently because the proper people did not take the right stand and set up the necessary conditions to correct mistakes as they occurred. Here again, small corrections consistently applied are very essential.

"But can you impose *your standards* so unilaterally on the child?" a teacher asks. "You are not really changing the child's behavior or his *attitudes* in this way." "You are neglecting the *basic* issue of why he needs to misbehave," said another teacher. "What if you do correct the problem, but another one pops out elsewhere that is just as bad or worse?" a third teacher remarks.

Our suggestions are direct and practical. A child learns what he lives, and he continues to live what he has learned. This is our guiding view. The child's behavior and his reasons for behaving as he does are largely due to the fact that the behavior is permitted or encouraged, however unwittingly (or, in the case of more acceptable behavior, it is purposefully taught), and it obtains some social reinforcement at least on a momentary or temporary basis. We point the way to more acceptable behavior through setting up standards and consequences to reinforce the standards. The positive and negative consequences that we suggest be levied, are but ways of helping the child discern the difference between acceptable and unacceptable conduct in simple, straightforward ways.

Even when such recommendations are controverted, the *ends* seldom are. We all want children to develop as mature and socially desirable behavior as possible in order that they might profit from the freedom and opportunities available to them. The *means* which have been proposed have often permitted these important objectives to be achieved.

MUST "FIRST" CAUSES BE FOUND?

Human behavior is complicated, and even the simplest form of behavior may have many "causes." Oversimplification is a common error of even the most ardently scientific students of behavior. Our appeal here is primarily for applications rather than theory, for economy as well as effectiveness in problem solving.

We need not search for "first" causes in the biographical histories of the children in order to find proximate conditions that make them disturbed or not disturbed. Trying to find first causes, we can easily be seduced into a relatively passive and pessimistic attitude toward what we can accomplish through classroom and other social activities. We may also become so involved in teasing out the "meaning" of a child's behavior or its presumed origins that we neglect taking practical steps when we have an opportunity to solve the problem.

Appendicitis may result from a variety of far-reaching background causes. A headache may have tremendously complex precipitants. But even the most penetrating and searching therapist or scientist seldom knows with certainty what "really" caused a condition he is trying to remedy. All he usually knows with assurance is that he did thus and so and this had a good or bad effect. For determining the most basic causes of the human condition, our knowledge is pitifully inadequate. We must be practical about finding solutions, now. We must act to solve problems, but we must act intelligently.

Many children go untreated while their behavior worsens. Adults often act paralyzed, helpless while they wait for someone to find the reason why a child behaved as he did. In *Two For The Road*, an obstreperous little girl is allowed to indulge herself, uncorrected by her parents, while adults nearby grow disgusted with the child's behavior and the parental attitudes. In the movie the situation was treated humorously, but in real life the humor is quickly lost, and eventually, the child usually suffers penalties and pains.

This is not to say that understanding the child, his problems, and his development is irrelevant to effective action. Understanding can be applied in an effectively active way, or it can simply be words that are revered. Our suggestions are predicated upon the fullest knowledge we could obtain about the behavior of children, teachers, and parents. The great desirability of obtaining this knowledge in all specific instances should be emphasized so that actions can be taken which are commensurate and applicable to the child's condition and behavior, as in the example charted in the previous chapter.

Here we only eschew that analysis of children's problems which continues a process of attempted understanding vaguely and indefinitely at the expense of setting goals, structuring situations, and taking other actions that would help children reach these goals.

Eventually something must be done to solve a problem. Unless one believes that understanding by itself solves all problems, as the parents in *Two For The Road* apparently did, one must sooner or later attempt to influence the child's environment and to affect his behavior directly or else forfeit many excellent opportunities for accomplishing some good ends.

THE ADVANTAGES OF TAKING ACTION

If the teacher acts in the ways we recommend to correct undesirable and self-defeating behavior in the child, he usually will get some reactions indicating the effectiveness of the measures. Although a small number of very seriously disturbed children may need further help and more intensive care, most behavior needing correction can be dealt with directly, by intelligent planning and proper follow-through. The average teacher is capable of rendering sound judgments, most of the time, of the behavior in his classroom. He can act with reasonable methods and hope in most instances. Generally, the teacher is going to have to do something; he cannot allow the child to continue to be disruptive or negative indefinitely. Even if there is no outside intervention, the teacher's job itself might be eventually placed in jeopardy if he did not take effective action.

The teacher can put some simple, direct, proven corrective measures to work. But we are suggesting that the teacher put them to the test in calculated ways, with some kind of planning, in ways based upon what we know about learning, education, misbehavior, punishment, and the related phenomena of social behavior.

USING CLASSROOM SOCIAL PRESSURES CONSTRUCTIVELY

During World War II Dr. Kurt Lewin showed how group decisions and group pressures can get individuals to do many things they would not otherwise do (for example, change food habits and buying habits). Since then there has been continuous application of group-decision research to psychological and social problems. It would appear that, as Glasser suggests,[1] these measures could work well in the classroom.

Group discussions or classroom meetings can be used to foster academic or achievement goals. For example, the class can be asked to discuss and decide upon objectives to be obtained in a given unit of work; to judge each other's work (written or oral); to give opinions on the selection of educational content in a course; to submit examination questions derived from their own understanding of the materials studied; to write critical (but positive) reports on the work of subgroups, committees, and individuals in a given classroom or course.

Less structured or more open group discussions may pivot on current political, economic, or social topics of the day, resulting in a group decision to write a congressman, interview the mayor of the town, or petition the school administration regarding matters that have achieved a group consensus on in the classroom. The pros and cons of the matter under discussion may be aired extensively before the group is ready to support a group decision. Unanimity may not be the desired objective here but at least majority opinions, minority reports, and the like can be fostered as goals for the group process to achieve.

In a similar vein, classroom or school-related conduct problems may be discussed openly, with a view toward producing *decisions* and *actions*. One class in citizenship considered the problem of litter around the schoolyard and decided to set up several procedures to rectify the situation: increasing the number of receptacles available for trash, a daily "round-up" of trash, and a reward system for the class bringing in the most litter and trash from the schoolyard each week. This procedure worked so well in organizing group decisions and actions regarding social problems that a class set about discussing conduct problems in general in the school. Group discussion resulted in a more objective and more easily enforced set of conduct rules and ways for students to state grievances to the school administration. Had the school year not ended, this particular class would have

[1] William Glasser, *Schools Without Failure* (New York: Harper and Row, 1969).

gone on to tackle many other problems that a school referendum indicated needed solutions. A system of effective student participation was in the making.

If they know how to tap the latent resources in groups, especially in classrooms, teachers can use group psychological and social characteristics to solve many social problems. Group discussions are relevant to the objectives of the class academically. The group either articulates its standards or develops standards where none existed before or overcomes its objections to the extant standards of the school milieu.

HOW SOCIAL GROWTH OCCURS

How do these recommendations facilitate social growth?

Social growth—growth toward maturity in relation to other people— implies some kinds of standards for behavior with others. These standards may be related to the child's age at any time, or they may be standards toward which we want to move the child, over the coming years. They are general standards of conduct toward which the growing child moves as he gains experience and new social discriminations. This chapter will not, however, be concerned primarily with specific standards and how they are arrived at but rather with the *means*, with the daily routine methods, of aiding social growth.

The child will change in his social behavior as he matures neurophysiologically. Some kind of change is inevitable. Left entirely untutored, the child would change anyway. He would move toward some kind of maturity though not necessarily the one desired by those responsible for him —or even satisfying to himself. Educators, parents, and psychologists enter the child's world to offer *direction* to the course of his development. If they cannot offer direction, then they are failing in their assignment with him. Offering direction means *interceding* in the child's behavior, *altering* his course, and *guiding* him, according to specified standards.

Most of the job of social education—of teaching socialization—is a matter of *steering*. Many more children might become delinquent if it were not for the steering agencies operating for the benefit of society: parents, school, church, and other conventional institutions. No adequate substitute is yet available for them in our society. There is no clear way to appeal to the individual unless we set and teach some standards for him to use. The child cannot be depended upon to do his own job in this respect except at a heavy cost in unnecessary inefficiency and defeat.

Ordinarily the home has the largest influence in promoting social growth, but the school can, and does, do much of this job. There are situations where the school can do a better job than the home, and these instances are where our present interest lies.

CONSTRUCTIVE STEPS FOR TEACHERS

Children often love and respect their teachers, at least during the early elementary years. As a result, the teacher can often sway the child when the parents cannot. Many a parent has recognized his dethronement when the child comes home and announces that teacher said thus and so —a new and different view—indicating the child's respect for this newly found source of authority. Sometimes the child contests the parent's point of view by quoting the teacher or perhaps the scoutmaster or some other authority. At certain periods of the child's life this new authority can be more influential and more objective than that of the parents. The teacher can exercise great influence in the child's life at times and should be sensitive to the child's attitudes toward him.

Many cases of emotional disturbance resulting from conflict at home, immature social behavior in peer groups, or extreme shyness can be handled better by teachers than by parents. A teacher has a fresh, unprejudiced start. The child usually is not able to intimidate or dominate the teacher, as he often can a parent. In a sense, the child begins school or a new term with little prejudice toward his specific teachers. If the teacher can fully realize this, he can start off a new term on a firm footing. The teacher can know in advance the child's proclivities for misbehavior and be ready for him with clear direction.

Miss C. was a teacher who realized the opportunity for dealing with children with social difficulties. She asked that they be put into her class instead of going into the other three available fourth grades in the school and usually received three or four of the most challenging children. She studied the cumulative records of each child before the beginning of the fall term and "met them at the door coming in," as she expressed it.

Miss C. discussed how she proceeded to get to know one of the social problem children better and how she managed each child in terms of corrective and maturing experiences.

> I knew that Jimmy was a showoff, according to his behavior record in school for three years. I decided early in the year to let him begin the "Show and Tell" period with his own story. If he acted too pert at this time or he in any way disrupted the stories of others, I used his favored starting position as a lever point, and I suspended it for a day or two. I only had to do this twice before I had Jimmy controlling himself well. The music, art, and the cafeteria teachers all commented after the third week of school on how much Jimmy had improved.

Jimmy's parents were equally grateful. They had not been able to control the boy's disrespectful and disruptive behavior, and they had been scolded by more than one teacher for allowing him to act this way. They had done the best they knew under the circumstances. It took another person with a fresh outlook, who felt it important enough to create a new set of environmental conditions in order to bring Jimmy to terms with himself.

Miss C. was able to find solutions to other social problems in her class the same year that she helped Jimmy. She proceeded in the same manner we have suggested: Knowing the child well; knowing what he is able to do; knowing what he is most likely to do, in the way of misbehavior; setting up situations requiring choice; applying pressures toward social behavior in persistent, fair, and firm ways; reinforcing progress once it began to appear.

Teachers are not miracle workers; not all of them can be expected to make socially mature all the children who have had severe problems throughout their school careers. On the basis of much work with many teachers, however, we believe that the average teacher can contribute a great deal to the child's social maturation, often to the teacher's own surprise. The teacher has to learn to view the child's socially disturbing behavior as *his way of coping with the problem situation as he sees it*. He has to regard it as capable of being changed through environmental or interpersonal manipulation. The teacher can then enter into the social field and into the environment of the child and rearrange factors to direct a corrective effort and to help the child toward more adequate and socially mature behavior.

GROUP CONFORMITY FOR THE DELINQUENT

The conflict between group conformity and individual freedom is acute today. These two objectives need not be considered mutually exclusive, but often they are so viewed. Many critics of contemporary society say they discern a distressing trend toward conformity for the sake of conformity. They also see a neglect in the classroom of individual freedom and the individual's right to be different. And there is the related problem of outright rebelliousness and antisocial behavior. At its extreme, it may pull society apart; as the pressure for conformity, in its extreme, can seal society against change.

The nonconformist who beats his chest and proclaims his difference as his major purpose in life is not the same as the creative or inventive person who may be different from others but does not make an issue of the matter. Both types of persons may suffer from the same indiscriminate restraints imposed by a neutral, or indifferent, society; but one is unwilling to accept the consequences of his difference and wastes his energy futilely trying to change them, while the other, not without special strain and occasional outbursts, puts his creativity first and moves ahead with it. The proclaimer is—like the moralist or the righteous man of any ilk—the preacher of his own virtues.

Many delinquents then are not merely "protesting" against unfair social action. Many of them are working out their personal problems in a social context.

This is not a case on behalf of conformity per se. It is not proposed that all teachers should think or act alike or that they should try to fit their students to the same pattern. It is to propose *that degree of conformity that maximizes individual freedom and personal expression for the greatest number of people.*[2]

Among the least free people are those who cannot accept the consequences of nonconformity. If one cannot conform sufficiently to meet some social demands, then he is bound to battle continually with society's rules and regulations. He may well spend so much time battling that he cannot find time to create or to use freedom. As a result, freedom, especially to the child or youth, becomes a mirage.

The outright delinquent will tell you about his conduct, his problems, his troubles with the law—and that he wants "to be left alone." He feels constraint everywhere and that the consequences of his misdeeds are unfair. He blames others for his plight and takes little responsibility himself. He is not able to direct his activity—even his propagandizing efforts—in a way to satisfy himself. These feelings are so common with delinquents, those who have been serious social offenders, that one can almost write the script before the youth is interviewed. When the adolescent is interviewed he speaks almost entirely of all the things that others are doing or have done to him. These "evils," as they are felt and reacted to by the adolescent delinquent, are only hindrances. He is trying to "break out," to have his own way. Many delinquents, then, are not merely "protesting" against unfair social action. Many of them are working out their personal problems in a social context.

Is the delinquent's type of freedom necessary? Is lack of freedom really the core of the delinquent's problem? We think not.

Could the delinquent ever find the total freedom he wants? He wants *no* limits, and he gives only minimal consideration to others or to changing himself. He is likely never to be satisfied until he learns how to control and direct himself in social living.

The answer to the delinquent's problems lies, we believe, in more conformity and constraint, not in looser bonds. The issues that confront him have to do with restraint, with socially propitious behavior, with modifying the impulsive behavior that grates against the social ends that have to be commonly agreed upon if men are to live peaceably together and yet be creative as individuals.

---

[2] We simply do not encompass here the argument of the revolutionary who speaks for temporary restrictions to accomplish, presumably, a longer-term goal of more freedom for all.

Actually the issue here with the delinquent or the social offender resides in the fact that individual freedom is pushed to the limit—without positive gains or purposes or acceptance of consequences. It is pushed to the point where the freedoms of others are impaired or precluded.

FREEDOM IS RELATIVE

Freedom is relative to the total of affairs among people in a social context. If you are the only swimmer in the pool, you may dive, jump, swim under water, and cavort as you please, but the instant another person enters the pool, you must share your freedom with him. The person who has to share in such a case may look upon his plight as being discouragingly constricting, but if he does not limit his own freedom, he damages the other person's freedom. Likewise on the highway. If you were the only driver, the road would be yours; there would be no question of constraint nor of conformity to rules. But the moment another driver enters the same context, the problem of constraint, freedom, individual rights, and group rights emerges.

Conformity, from our point of view, becomes a matter of specifying those minimum conditions necessary to maintain an optimum condition of freedom for all who are part of the group or who wish to participate in the process.

Conformity should not be merely a matter of whim or of vested interest. It should always stem from some calculations of cooperative and optimal freedom for members of the group.

Most of the problems of conformity in the classroom stem not from an initial constraint upon the rebellious person but from what the group does to protect its collective freedoms. Ideally, these are the only constraints. But they are difficult to interpret and apply (our Supreme Court is constantly called upon to adjudicate such issues). Our interest in helping children to mature socially is not in trying to fit them into a predetermined pattern but to enhance their opportunities for individual expression. We believe, however, that this cannot take place except relative to set group standards. Improper group standards are wrong and can be labeled sooner and more clearly in terms of the shrinking of individual creativity than by labeling all constraints bad. Group pressures and standards should always be open to question; there should be criteria to determine their effects.

The free individual then, we believe, is one who is able to determine his course of development and to pursue his creativeness without continuously fighting battles over prerogatives and standards of conduct in the group that, in the long run, do not harm him. Perhaps no creative person is completely easy in this respect because the group is not static nor all wise, but the youth who can direct and control himself to create without placing himself and his group in jeopardy is vastly different from the student who challenges standards only for the sake of his own momentary impulses.

The psychology of the creative person we think is an open, forward-moving, constructive one. That of the primarily rebellious person, while it may be socially useful, more often represents a penchant for conflict with the group, often to foster his transitory impulses and at the expense of his creativity. The teacher can spot the latter "type" in the classroom. He can move toward bringing the rebellious child into sufficient conformity so that whatever justification he has for his complaints which will free him to learn and create better will be given a chance to flourish in an atmosphere of acceptance by the group. The teacher can help him to stop fighting those battles with himself and others which are unnecessary, and get on with the business of learning and achieving and creating in ways that will satisfy him.

SELECTED READINGS

Bandura, A., and R. H. Walters, *Social Learning and Personality Development.* New York: Holt, Rinehart and Winston, 1963.

Benedict, R., "Child rearing in certain European countries." *Amer. J. Orthopsychiat.,* 1949, *19,* 342–50.

Bijou, S. W., and D. M. Baer, *Child Development.* New York: Appleton-Century-Crofts, 1961.

Bush, R. N., *The Teacher-Pupil Relationship.* New York: Macmillan, 1954.

Gelfand, D. M., and D. P. Hartman, "Behavior therapy with children: A review and evaluation of research methodology." *Psychol. Bulletin,* 1968, *69,* 204–15.

Gewirtz, J. L., "A factor analysis of some attention-seeking behaviors of young children." *Child Development,* 1956, *27,* 17–36.

Giles, H. H., *The Integrated Classroom.* New York: Basic Books, 1959.

Glasser, W., *Schools Without Failure.* New York: Harper and Row, 1969.

Greenberg, H., and D. Fare, "An investigation of several variables as determinants of authoritarianism." *J. Soc. Psychol.,* 1959, *49,* 105–11.

Hartup, W. W., "Social behavior of children." *Review of Educ. Research,* 1965, *35,* 122–29.

Jourard, S. M., and R. M. Remy, "Perceived parental attitude, the self, and security." *J. Consult. Psychol.,* 1955, *19,* 364–66.

O'Leary, K. D., S. O'Leary, and W. C. Becker, "Modification of a deviant sibling interaction pattern in the home." *Behavior Research and Therapy,* 1967, *5,* 113–20.

Thorpe, L. P., et al. *Studying Social Relationships in the Classroom.* Evanston, Ill.: Science Research Associates, 1959.

8

AIDING
EMOTIONAL GROWTH

In the last chapter social development and emotional growth were viewed as aspects of the same behavior, the difference lying only in the particular context of consideration. What we call emotional growth is also strongly related to a person's self-discipline, his social skills, and his general problems of mental health.

Unfortunately the term "emotional growth" is often used loosely and vaguely. Here it refers to the development of how the child feels about himself, in terms of his own behavior and performance, particularly relative to his own standards, although the standards of other people enter in. The emphasis is on the child's *behavior* and his evaluation of it.

Emotion is often put in terms of some sort of disturbance. However, all of us are in a sense emoting all the time. We strongly feel a preference for sugar in our coffee or for cream, we have an emotional reaction to certain colors and foods, clothes and friends. In effect, these are all emotional reactions. They may be of relatively low intensity, but they are nonetheless acted upon and persistent.

Children who have not grown-up emotionally comprise from one-half of 1 percent up to, perhaps, 10 percent of the school population, depending upon how severely or loosely one wishes to draw the line. That is, something has gone wrong in the normal emotional development of the child, owing usually to many different circumstances. These children may feel bad about themselves, harbor resentments and ill feelings toward others, cannot manage to do things that are developmentally normal for their age group, and are unable to control, express, or manage feelings. We do not intend in this chapter to delineate all the emotional problems of children, rather we will place our emphasis on helping the child achieve positive goals, which we call emotional maturity. And we will consider this objective in the light of the whole book's emphasis on mental health.

Further to relate this chapter to the previous one on social growth, we can consider that the child who has immature or unsatisfying social characteristics may not recognize this; he may not have insight into himself or see that his relationships with other people affect his own feelings about himself. Thus, he would lack objectivity both about himself and other people. A person who does not clearly recognize what his effect is on other people may have an adverse social effect on them and fail to take any responsibility for changing his behavior or his attitudes. He may fail to see the relationship between his behavior and the reaction of others and not feel impelled to improve.

Another possible relationship between social development and emotional growth is seen when the child is relatively introspective, tends to be hypersensitive or hyperreactive to the opinions of others, and tries too hard to please, such a child can be said to be excessively (emotionally) concerned about his social behavior. He is paying the price emotionally for what he considers to be his social inadequacies. He may be excessively concerned, may feel upset and uncomfortable at the slightest cues from others, and may continually evaluate himself unfavorably. He tends to feel inferior, even though he may be adequate in objective social terms. He may try to reflect on his problems, but he goes around in circles without ever breaking through to effective solutions from new approaches.

HANDLING FEELINGS OF INADEQUACY

The observer is often surprised when he discovers that a person who, by all appearances, functions adequately is one who considers himself inadequate.

Miss B., a sixth grade teacher, asked the children to write about how they had spent the previous summer vacation. One of her children, Doris, wrote a beautiful, descriptive account of her reactions to summer camp, to a trip the family had taken, and to miscellaneous activities in her neighborhood. What amazed the teacher was the fact that Doris indicated through her theme that she had done poorly in her summer activities, had wasted her time, and been unpopular and disliked at camp. She had these feelings despite the *objective* evidence that she had adjusted to the routine at camp and had been a popular and fully accepted child there. The teacher examined Doris's previous school record and found that she had always been a popular child and had always seemed happy and well adjusted at school—as others saw her.

Doris' own story was one of misery. How did she happen to write such a seemingly self-pitying account of herself? Our belief is that she might well have had expectations for herself which she could not fulfill. She apparently had ambitions that went far beyond her present adequate behavior, and as a result, she distorted her view of her current social status.

How many of us know adults who appear to be successful financially, professionally, occupationally, yet who may be chronic complainers, may end up in mental hospitals, or in extreme cases, may even commit suicide. The relative value of one's own achievement and accomplishments viewed subjectively versus the standards applied by society, may be grossly discrepant and may account for a miserable emotional life despite objective achievement.

It usually does little good to try verbally to convince children like Doris that they are adequate. A more constructive approach seems to be to let them tell you how they feel about themselves, through themes or other forms of expression, and then to sit down with them in private and discuss the matter more fully. This is not to suggest that the teacher should try to be a full-fledged therapist but that the teacher should take advantage of his relationship with the child to try to solve emotional problems.

> One afternoon after school Miss B. sat down with Doris and said to her, "Doris, your theme was well written and you have used your knowledge of English to good advantage, but what I wanted to talk with you about was your feelings about yourself, your summer, and the other activities you wrote about in this theme."
>
> Doris then began to say in a number of ways that she was unhappy with herself because she felt she did not live up to her own standards. These standards were, of course, learned primarily in her home and in her school environment. We might say that they were even learned too well, because Doris had taken a basically good idea—that of achievement and doing well in one's undertakings—and had pushed it so far as to damage her own opinions of herself. She tried hard and failed miserably in her own estimation, but she had always done well in the eyes of others, in the light of objective observations, test results, and teachers' opinions.

After this talk, Doris's teacher understood some of the pressures the child felt. She encouraged Doris to think about her own values and question whether she (Doris) was not being too hard on herself, to look a little harder at reality and, hopefully, come to some better appraisal of her work and results. Several such sessions between Doris and Miss B. helped, over the period of a school year, Doris to develop a more realistic set of self-appraisals and to feel relieved and happier as a result. Doris's better morale was reflected spontaneously in her behavior, her comments, and her writing at school. She received "feedback" rewards in the form of compliments, good grades, and better relationships with her classmates, which now meant more to her. The teacher discussed Doris and her problems with the school psychologist from time to time. It had been decided that it was much better to try to work, at least initially, within the classroom than to send Doris off to therapy, which would be largely out of the context of her school living and also expensive and, perhaps, unnecessary. Actually, therapy in the formal sense of the term was not called for. Focusing on the child's behavior and on the discrepancy between her behavior and her own self-estimates was sufficient treatment.

HANDLING OBJECTORS: SETTING LIMITS

A more common type of problem than Doris presented arises with children who openly and temperamentally object to school and classroom requirements. These children express their displeasure by fussing, whining, or complaining in disruptive ways. Usually they do not act very drastically to implement their feelings, and they are not usually outright social problems—unless the teacher responds irrationally. But in many annoying ways they protest or criticize, and sometimes they stimulate others to do the same. So the teacher who is not fully aware of their emotional attitudes and prepared to deal with them may get into undue troubles.

The teacher can often handle these children in matter-of-fact ways, allowing them to voice their objections but not giving in to them when they have no merit, and not permitting the children to think that they can avoid their obligations through complaining. A fourth grade teacher had boys in his class who often voiced objections to arithmetic. The teacher reported this condition to us, saying that he had handled their comments in this way:

> Soon after school started, Mr. G. called each boy in to talk with him at separate times. They were not doing adequate work in arithmetic and were "ganging up" on the teacher, perhaps by prearrangement. Each boy would at various times make complaints to the teacher or, through side comments to other children, censure the teacher's behavior. Each boy was told that the teacher understood his objections to the arithmetic, that he didn't think that was so bad, and that when it was possible, he would be making some changes. However, this did not mean that they would be permitted to escape the arithmetic, Mr. G. told them. Not liking the work was one thing, but not doing it was quite another. The boys could remain after school, as often as they liked, to tell the teacher how they felt about the arithmetic; to let him know fully their problems with it; and, perhaps, to receive some help; but in class they were to settle down to the arithmetic assignments without comment except when they needed help.

On two occasions after these talks between the teacher and the three boys, one boy persisted in offering critical comments. This lad was reminded that he could stay after school that day and the teacher would be willing to go over the whole matter again with him. One such episode handled firmly sufficed, and thereafter the more recalcitrant boy settled down and did acceptable work in arithmetic. It should be pointed out that all three of these boys could do their work acceptably or even in superior ways. There was no issue of basic intelligence or of understanding the problems; rather it was an issue of their "emoting" about the work and harrassing the teacher, evidently, to try to escape the work if they could. Also, they had formed a "gang" and were socially reinforcing each other's emotionalized attitudes, trying to gain some momentary advantage over the teacher.

What did this teacher do that was constructive? First he did *not* condemn, threaten, cajole, or try to talk the boys out of their attitudes. The work was to be done, and that was that! The teacher made this clear at the outset. The teacher did accept the boys' feelings as familiar and understandable. He did not tell them they could not feel that way. It is not generally a good psychological tactic to tell somebody he should not feel a particular way, but it is a good psychological tactic to take the feelings as given and then see what circumstances can be altered that, hopefully, will result in a change in the feeling.

The teacher simply made the issues as plain as possible; in arithmetic class we do arithmetic; if you do not like arithmetic that is one thing, and you are free to feel this way—you may even try to change the curricula and the teaching methods—but the fact still remains that the arithmetic is to be done in arithmetic class.

This approach may seem simpleminded. However, why complicate the situation unnecessarily by trying to "work through" emotional meanings which are distant from the task at hand, especially with children who are not greatly disturbed psychologically. In these cases the boys' protests could be viewed and handled simply as protest. Initially, at least, they were apparently not the facades of serious emotional problems. They were "reluctances," a balkiness which all of us feel some of the time about a myriad of matters, though as mature adults, we know that we cannot always have our way that we have to buckle down to a realistic attitude or forfeit some of our advantages in life. A child often does not understand this. He cannot always act realistically and discriminately. We, as adults and teachers, have to help him make the realistic judgments and take the proper actions to gain his goals and rewards. Our behavior can serve as a model for him. If we expect a certain course of events, and if we hold firm to such a course, the child will in time fit in and feel natural about it and do the necessary things more or less routinely. This assumes, of course, that our judgment is realistic and the child's condition is such that he can in time learn or adjust to the requirements.

In these rather straightforward instances of emotional display accompanying reluctances to do schoolwork, the teacher can greatly simplify his problems by assuming from the first that there will be such displays of protest by some students in the class. The teacher can assume, too, that he may get these reluctances now and then from nearly all of the class members. The teacher can, therefore, prepare himself. He can take the matter in stride and not feel that his educational program is being drastically hamstrung or that the group of children this year is hopelessly recalcitrant. That progress will occur smoothly would be a false and misleading expectation. But disciplined procedure on the teacher's part can greatly modify the extent and persistence of problems of this type among the children.

HANDLING OBJECTORS: GIVING ALTERNATIVES

To return to what the teacher did constructively with the three boys, a second suggestion in procedure was to give the boys a choice. Either they do the work during the time the arithmetic class is in session or they stay after school and settle the matter later. The alternative, it should be clearly realized, is not whether or not they will do the work, it is simply *how* and *when* they will accomplish it. The boys seem to begin with the assumption that they may be able to get out of doing the work if they object sufficiently. The teacher corrects this assumption and puts matters on a more realistic basis by pointing out that the issue at hand is *when* and *where* the work will be done. The teacher leaves off all critical or emotionalized comments; he doesn't even *feel* them after a while. He gains in confidence so that he can handle such cases of academic reluctance and skillfully move ahead without being disrupted. To be sure, there will be cases where matters cannot be handled as easily as this by the classroom teacher. Even in the first grade there will be children who are too immature emotionally to fit into the daily schedule and profit from it (we are not speaking here of brain damaged, retarded, or severely disturbed children; we discuss them elsewhere). But by and large, the average teacher can handle a majority of emotionally immature children in this kind straightforward way. The teacher can expect to have from one to four such children in a class of thirty or so youngsters. Our experience is that the teacher can expect to be reasonably successful with most of them most of the time.

A BASIC QUESTION: WHO'S IN CHARGE?

One issue at stake is whether the child primarily is going to determine his educational course or whether the teacher is. A child will try to have his way, often proportionately to the degree of his disturbance, or to his degree of past success. The emotion that the teacher witnesses is generally not mysterious nor serious but simply one strong method by which the child tries to get what he wants. The emotional disturbance and immaturity in these cases are not usually things apart from the behavior that is observed and dealt with by the teacher; the attitudes and behavior *are* the emotional disturbance.

Although what the teacher observes in the classroom is sometimes described as but the "symptom of a deeper process," we strongly question the general applicability of this concept. If the average teacher can handle most of the emotional immaturities of children in the manner we have suggested—in our experience the teacher can learn to do so—then there seems to be no good reason why the teacher should not act in the direct ways suggested. For those few exceptional cases where the teacher cannot succeed by the methods described, he can be much more certain after trying them that he has done his best as a classroom teacher and can with greater assurance turn to the school psychologist, special educational director, or others for more specialized, detailed, subtle, or prolonged help.

Thus, if the classroom teacher is not scared off too soon by the emotional immaturities of the children, he can help a significant percentage of them in substantial, lasting ways. Just as parents have to reassert their prerogatives and their more mature behavior day by day with their children, so do teachers. Both teachers and parents can give children rewarding experiences with learning and achieving by enlarging the child's emotional life to the point where he does not expect or try to get his way in an immature fashion. The teacher need not separate the emotional elements from the rest of the child's educational and personal life; rather, he should use the emotional elements to reinforce and to extend learning and achieving. There is no better way than handling the emotional whims of a child to show the relationship between discipline and the child's achievement and his general well-being.

THE PROBLEM OF CONCENTRATION

In earlier discussions we have already noted the importance of concentration. The problem of concentration is often confused with or becomes part of various expressions of emotional maturity. Too frequently the teacher and other specialists who work with children use terms like "emotional immaturity" or "emotional block" as if they were explanations for the child's lack of concentration, rather than being simply descriptive. A better way to account for poor concentration, we believe, is to say that the child has learned poor habits of applying himself. The more that concentration is required, the more he reneges, diverts himself, or wool-gathers. This latter hypothesis is a good deal easier to test out by actions, and to control in the classroom.

Undoubtedly, emotional problems will reduce one's power of concentration. Stress and being caught up in conflict, with indecision and inadequate feelings, commonly and forcefully impair the ability to concentrate. However, it does not necessarily follow that because there is evidence of poor concentration, there must be an emotional problem of some hidden significance in the background that has to be analyzed before anything else can be done. If this were actually the case, the human race would have ceased a long time ago to be able to solve its problems. Most of the time most people, including children, solve their small emotional problems by taking the kind of action that seems most sensible to them at the time. If their judgment and action is poor, they then tend to accumulate the distress and, thereby, impair their ability to concentrate. On the other hand, if their behavior solves their problems fairly well, which it does for most people most of the time, then their concentration is not seriously impaired or curtailed.

Sometimes children don't concentrate because they are simply too busy engaging in social and play activities. A very good example of this can be seen in the case of Paula.

> Paula, a healthy, happy eight-year-old girl of above average intelligence, seemed unable to concentrate on her studies. An investigation of her achievement through standardized tests showed that she was nearly up to grade level. However, she must have learned much on her own, since she did not follow class discussions very well, did not keep her place in reading groups, and seemed unable to concentrate on the mechanics of arithmetic. With an IQ of 115 she was not achieving up to her ability, although she was learning enough to get by on tests.

In discussing Paula with her present teacher and the previous one, we learned that both had observed nearly the same characteristics. Paula was a gay, fun-loving, popular child who appealed to adults and appeared socially and emotionally healthy. The trouble was that she would not concentrate on her schoolwork, especially arithmetic. It was observed by her parents and teachers that Paula would, however, concentrate when she wanted to, when there was a clear issue at stake (such as getting her schoolwork done before going to an assembly program or out to play or to watch television). If one considers the connection between learning and reinforcement and desirable behavior, Paula's own behavior gives the teacher a clue to get her to concentrate better, namely, to hold off some cherished activity until she has accomplished the assigned task. Generally this will bring many problems of poor concentration under control.

However, Paula's teacher, despite observing how the girl worked, tended to follow the hypothesis that there was some deep type of emotional block that prevented Paula from concentrating. And the teacher held to this hypothesis despite much evidence to the contrary—all the teachers who knew Paula and her parents felt that she had no deep disturbance. Paula could do the work when she was held to it, and she had learned enough to remain nearly at her grade level, even though she was not achieving up to her capabilities. Unfortunately, because of the teacher's analysis a semester went by before we were able to bring a relatively simple disciplinary regimen to bear on Paula and her concentration problem. How was this done?

HANDLING THE CONCENTRATION PROBLEM CONSTRUCTIVELY

Since the classroom teacher held firmly to her opinions about Paula's emotional disturbance, we had to begin work on the problem indirectly. The situation was discussed with Paula's principal, and the principal's opinion was solicited about using a tutor to help break the jam among the adults concerned. He thought this a good plan and sanctioned it; he discussed the matter with Paula's teacher to seek her permission to use a tutor. Paula's parents had previously decided to engage one. A tutor was obtained and Paula saw her twice a week for about three months, then once a week for the remainder of the school year.

There was no disturbance of Paula's classroom procedure or activity. The teacher and Paula continued together as they had. Since the teacher felt the problem had more to do with Paula's emotional block, which was outside the teacher's scope, than with educational skills and attitudes, she ignored the tutor whose job then became relatively easy. The latter implemented the psychologist's suggestions about how to get Paula to concentrate and how to go about improving the whole situation. The tutor was told that

> Paula is evidently a normal child without any pressing emotional problems. The issue at hand is how to get her to work consistently and to develop the power and habit of concentration needed, which she had somehow been able to neglect. We could do this by setting definite limited requirements at the time of the tutoring session, reinforcing even her feeblest efforts and giving her homework that she was to perform between sessions. Since the classroom teacher had objected to giving Paula any homework, which would put pressure on her, we worked with only the tutor on this.

After about six weeks of tutoring according to this general plan, Paula began to show some improvement. She seemed "more willing to tackle her work without wincing, frowning or changing the subject," according to the classroom teacher. The teacher was glad to see the progress the girl was showing and was flexible enough and willing enough to capitalize on it by giving Paula more work in school and more encouragement in order to exercise her newly found strength and determination. Fortunately then, through this type of arrangement, the teacher was won to the side of the principal, the school psychologist, and the parents who tended to see Paula's difficulties in terms of skills and attitudes and application, rather than in terms of deep emotional blocks.

By the end of the school year—and it often takes one to two semesters to bring children to attitudes and skills whereby they are achieving up to their capabilities—Paula was handling her schoolwork in a fully acceptable manner. Moreover, she had begun to take some pleasure in doing her arithmetic. She brought home her good papers in this subject to show to her tutor and her mother. She was willing to get down to work at proper times without protest and she sloughed off her former techniques for avoiding educational requirements. She was reinforcing herself by recognizing her own progress. ("See, Mother, I got *all* my problems done on time— now may I watch TV?")

We cite this case in order to make two points: first, in the absence of clear evidence to the contrary, a concentration problem need not be thought of as symptomatic of deep emotional disturbance; it can be attacked at its own level—namely, as a problem requiring closer and firmer teaching, supervision, and reinforcement.

In Paula's case, the tutor had to see that the mother got Paula to do her assigned homework by placing the work period *before* some cherished activity or free play period. The cherished activity or free play acted as a reinforcing condition for Paula's having done the work. As she did better work, her own performance acted as a reinforcer also. Gradually, Paula came to see the logic as well as the convenience of work before play. This feature alone helped Paula settle down and concentrate at the time of study. She knew there would be nothing else to do until the homework was done. All kidding, cajoling, and fussing aside—the work had to be done!

The second point to be stressed grows out of observations of the relationship among the adults—the parents, the teacher, the principal, the psychologist—as they tried to work together to overcome Paula's problem. They were not stymied by a difference of opinion; they did not lose sight of the primary issue of how best to help Paula. They arrived at a practical plan (albeit a substitute for direct teacher action), put it into operation, and followed through in good faith and with rewarding results. What they all wanted to do—help Paula—got accomplished, and no professional toes were stepped on, no unfortunate side effects were generated, and no other symptoms of disturbance arose in Paula.

There are however instances where children presenting complaints and symptoms similar to Paula's would show other clearly emotional problems. We do not imply that children with concentration problems have no emotional problems. It is impossible ever to be sure that a child or adult does not have some emotional difficulties, but we don't need a clear bill of emotional health in order to proceed successfully with direct action. Not only is the postulation and solution of an emotional condition not prerequisite to the skill development, but the emotional condition actually changes as a *result* of changed skills and attitudes.

We have to be practical. We need to look about us in the classroom, in the daily routine, for the opportunities to work through homework assignments, through tutors, through some parental supervision, through whatever we can devise that offers hope, to see what we can do to solve problems.

Judgments and courses of action depend upon alternatives. Problems can rarely be solved ideally; they must usually be solved in terms of the available alternatives. We cannot judge the value of our proceedings with Paula or anyone else unless what was done can be compared to alternatives open to us. What were the alternatives in this case?

EMOTIONS AND CONCENTRATION

Judging from the literature on the subject and our experiences, two broad courses of action have usually been followed in handling children with concentration and achievement problems similar to those of Paula. One has been based on the attitude of "let the child alone; she has already been pushed too much." Lack of concentration, in this point of view, would be attributed to tension or repressed feelings, which in turn are considered to stem from some kind of mistreatment or misunderstanding on the part of the parents or teacher. Conditions must exist, it is thought, that produce tension, which is expressed in various ways and which may show itself in schoolwork that is below the ability level, as with Paula.

Following this viewpoint, a frequent prescription is to try to reduce pressures toward achievement in schoolwork and to "free up" the child as much as possible to doing anything he or she wishes. Ordinary expectations of the child to stay in his normal grade placement may be lifted, very permissive handling may be encouraged. The reasoning goes this way: If pressures make him too tense to concentrate, then perhaps reducing the pressures will naturally lead him to move toward better concentration and better schoolwork.

This hypothesis has further extensions—such as reducing school and home pressures as a necessary *beginning point*, but also providing the child with "play therapy" so as to allow him to "work off" his already accumulative tensions. The play therapy routine is often complex; it may take a long time, and bring one or both parents into therapy also. The reasoning behind it is that the child has to be drained, so to speak, of his tensions so he can gain the freedom to do his work unhampered by emotional conditions.

In the case of Paula, we have observed already that, judged on the basis of Paula's behavior with peers within the school setting and at home, there was little or no evidence of emotional problems. The too ready use of a hypothesis of emotional problems stems not from any direct observation of such problems in cases like hers, but entirely from a *theory* that problems of concentration and achievement *must* have emotional origins.

The simpler alternative hypothesis that we favor is that the concentration problem stems from a deficiency of self-discipline, a lack of the habit of staying with tasks and getting them done, and a too neglectful educational environment (which indirectly abets these poor habits and attitudes). This hypothesis is much easier to test.

FINDING THE MOST EFFICIENT APPROACH

Some problems with children's behavior cannot be solved quickly and reliably, at least not as quickly as in Paula's case. It often takes some time to determine whether a given course of action is useful. If we can adopt the habit of trying out the simplest "explanation" first (the "law of parsimony" in science), then we can learn whether the most direct methods will work. With Paula, it was very useful to discover that the simpler hypothesis worked well and produced results which could be critically and objectively evaluated by a number of people. Often with the more complicated and indirect methods of handling this type of child, progress cannot be judged in as clear-cut a way, and whether the child has gained emotionally may remain a matter of subjective opinion.

Sometimes longer-lasting effects are claimed for longer-lasting treatments. Here any conclusion is purely conjectural. No proofs whatsoever are available that longer treatment is better than shorter treatment, no matter what the goals are. The literature in psychotherapy, in behavior change, and in overcoming psycho-educational problems of children all attest to the fact that short-term methods and direct methods of treatment are highly productive. Most of the literature suggests that some of the more parsimonious methods of treatment are not only more economical but also more effective than the long-range, deep probing techniques.

While accepting the importance of emotions, we would like to try to put emotional behavior in a less crucial position than usual—not in the driver's seat of the educational process. Emotions become dominant factors in classroom problems no less often, we believe, as *by-products* or poor problem-solving ability and poor achievement than as precipitants of these factors. Emotional difficulties are often a *result* of poor structure in the psycho-educational environment rather than a cause of the psycho-educational problems. If we believe that emotional confusion is a result of a poorly structured psycho-educational environment, then we proceed to change this environment. This provides a direct and short-term type of treatment.

HANDLING POOR WORK HABITS

That bright children can often get by at school with minimal effort, is discussed in Chapters 5 and 6. They "play it by ear," using their ability to learn just enough to pass or to make an occasional good impression; this ultimately leads to poor work habits and, perhaps, emotional difficulties. Poor work habits and related problems are common among bright children, and much research indicates that a significant percentage of college students who fail do so because of poor work habits rather than a lack of capability. Typical of others, one city superintendent of schools told us that it was difficult to get superior students to take accelerated courses in high school because they were concerned about facing a more demanding program with their poor work habits and other cumulative results of the years of neglect of work habits.

The point is perhaps already obvious, namely, that poor work habits themselves can lead to emotional problems. Gradually, as he moves up the educational ladder, the typical youngster is brought into more and more demanding programs. After a while he finds that he cannot keep up, usually not because of a lack of ability—or primary emotional problems—but because he lacks habits of perseverance and efficient work. *Then* he begins to feel inferior and to develop a failure pattern instead of a success pattern. *Then* he creates his own problem, or he works in subtle ways in a kind of "self-fulfilling prophecy," which says that he cannot do it. *Then* he blindly interprets these failures as caused by emotional problems rather than realizing that the emotional condition results from the poor working habits.

If this kind of youngster—that is, the brighter, superior student—is told that the remedy for his problems is to let up on work, that he has been pushed too hard, and that too much has been expected of him, we see no immediate hope for him. A hypothesis that may apply to others is being

indiscriminately applied to relatively normal boys and girls. The consequences seem evident. The bright child continues with his failures and negative attitudes; he looks for others to blame for making him this way. He is
reinforced in *not* taking responsibility for himself in his educational and
emotional plight. He continues with as easy a program as possible and
ultimately may accept low goals that do not challenge his true capabilities.
If he does not come to grips with his external problems and try to overcome them, he gets on kind of a downward spiral or a tendency to adjust
downward. Because the failure pattern that is associated with going on in
an unguided fashion tends to overcome him, he tries to downgrade his
hopes. If he does not take himself out of the curriculum, he is put out by
others because of his continuing failures.

THE FOURTH GRADE—A TURNING POINT?

By the time the child reaches the fourth grade—sometimes sooner—
clear evidence of his poor study habits and meager accomplishments begins
to emerge. At the fourth grade level the child is expected to work more
independently, to apply his basic educational skills to such new areas of
learning as science, geography, and library work. If he cannot branch out
at this time and if he cannot read and keep up with the assignments or do
work outside of class, he becomes increasingly hamstrung in his efforts. As
a result, he may develop a failure pattern and a sense of inadequacy.

This is common soil from which spring many emotional problems
relating to schoolwork. Sometimes, in such circumstances, children will
develop a strong "don't care" attitude and may spend considerable amounts
of time daydreaming in class. They may increasingly incur resentment from
their parents because of poor marks. The parents often do not know how
to cope with the problem except to try to pressure the child with words,
to make him work.

This is precisely the point at which the school can make or break a
child's educational progress. Enlightened teachers have saved many children
from educational and intellectual failures, but more often than we care to
admit, the child in this situation is not saved but is dragged along and
eventually lost to formal education. The accumulation of years of inefficient application and unrewarded effort—there is often little to reward—is
enough to lead many able children to drop out of school as soon as they
legally can, usually between the eighth and twelfth grades. During the
interim, the child who is failing tends to develop noticeable problems of
attitude and emotion.

A suitable curriculum and a program of disciplined daily study will
not eliminate all emotional problems that occur in the classroom setting, but

they will greatly ameliorate a significant percentage of them. As educators, we must use all our wits and educational skills to assist in the emotional development of children in our classes who display such problems.

SUMMARY AND CONCLUSIONS

It must be evident by now that we do not believe that most classroom problems involving emotional behavior are solved by rolling away a large stone, an "emotional block," thereby clearing the way for easy development.

Growth toward maturity is usually a slow and sometimes painful process. This is especially true when growth depends on learning rather than upon simple biological maturation. Problems have to be solved by and large in a slow, careful manner; they tend to build up slowly and to require solution in the same manner.

One difficulty with the "emotional block" theory is that it seldom provides specific guides to action; rather, it is a hypothesis that often leads us into effectual and untestable procedures, or at least unnecessarily long and painful ones, to reach the specified goal.

We first need to look not for blocks in the road but for wrong turns. The child turns away from the task at hand to think about something he would prefer to do. He concentrates only partly or not at all; hence, he cannot retain what he has presumably learned. He may not have learned the material in the first place because he was only faintly exposed to it. He tries to take our attention away from what we want him to do; he sulks, cries, or acts put upon, and otherwise attempts to divert us from our legitimate task.

On the other hand *skills* in educational pursuit are too often neglected. The skills are the accumulated products of proficient application and reinforcement. If there has been too little application, then the skills cannot help but suffer. If the skills suffer, then the child is at a disadvantage in his environment. The condition of being handicapped results usually, we believe, not because of too much pressure on the child, but rather *too little pressure of the right type* and too little reinforcement of cumulative skills. We consider skills a prime necessity for self-discipline and educational accomplishment and an aspect of behavior that can be handled directly and through an emphasis on direct and short-term methods of treatment and psycho-educational remedial work.

It follows logically that if inadequate skills are so large a factor in emotional problems in the classroom and if acquiring skills can be as important an antidote as we have suggested, then the role of the classroom teacher is enhanced, and at the same time, *simplified*.

The teacher can now consider as part of his domain, the emotional refurbishing of the lagging and the recalcitrant child. The teacher can help the moderately disturbed child, along with the others in class, by setting up the types of achievement requirement that will bring about successful accomplishments by all of the children. The teach can do this through a disciplined educational procedure which carries with it many connotations for emotional development and maturity, without splitting the child into "emotional" and "intellectual" parts, which must be considered differently and treated differently. In this new, more disciplined way the teacher can help to integrate the child's development in a unified manner.

SELECTED READINGS

ATKINSON, JOHN W., ed., *Motives in Fantasy, Action and Society*. New York: Van Nostrand, Reinhold, 1958.

BANK, P., "Behavior therapy with a boy who never learned to walk." *Psychotherapy*, 1968, *5*, 150–53.

COMBS, ARTHUR W., and DONALD SNYGG, *Individual Behavior*. New York: Harper and Row, 1959.

EYSENCK, H. J., "Learning theory and behavior therapy." *J. Mental Science*, 1959, *105*, 61–75.

HARING, NORRIS G., and E. LAKIN PHILLIPS, *Educating Emotionally Disturbed Children*. New York: McGraw-Hill, 1962.

HURLOCK, ELIZABETH B., *Child Development*. New York: McGraw-Hill, 1964.

KRUMBOLTZ, J. D., "Behavioral goals for counseling." *J. Counseling Psychol.*, 1966, *13*, 153–59.

PHILLIPS, E. LAKIN, DANIEL N. WIENER, and NORRIS G. HARING, *Discipline, Achievement and Mental Health*. Englewood Cliffs, N.J.: Prentice-Hall, 1960.

RETHLINGSHAFER, DOROTHY, *Motivation as Related to Personality*. New York: McGraw-Hill, 1963.

SPOCK, B., "What we know about the development of healthy personalities in children." *Understanding the Child*, 1951, *20*, 2–9.

WAHLER, R. G., G. H. WINKEL, R. F. PETERSON, and D. C. MORRISON, "Mothers as behavior therapists for their children." *Behavior Research and Therapy*, 1965, *3*, 113–24.

WHITLEY, H. E., "Mental health problems in the classroom." *Understanding the Child*, 1954, *23*, 98–103.

9

THE TEACHER
AS A PRIMARY
CHANGE AGENT

The teacher is certainly in a tactically and strategically powerful position in helping the child to discipline, achievement, and mental health in that order. The purpose of this chapter is to show how the teacher can operate as a primary change agent in some explicit and intelligent ways, and can thereby move toward the accomplishment of the objectives discussed in this book.

WHAT IS A PRIMARY CHANGE AGENT?

A *primary change agent* is any individual operating in a fundamental and crucial role with the child, where this role can serve as an agent of behavior change.

The purpose of a change agent is to change the child's most important behavior. We are not interested in superficial kinds of change, change just for the moment or just to suit some whim of an adult. We are talking about change that is integrated with the rest of the person's behavior and that serves the most significant socially and individually desired goals.

Besides teachers, parents also are primary change agents. And in contrast to these primary change agents, we may think of secondary change agents who play a less significant role in the child's life; namely, boy or girl scout leaders, tutors, music and art teachers, recreational instructors, camp or athletic instructors, parents of friends, relatives—and indeed anybody who plays a small but effective role in the child's life.

We propose concentrating on the teachers and parents as primary change agents because they have the greatest influence on the child and the greatest responsibility to deal with the child. There is another reason for talking about primary change agents and that is to reflect credit on the business of bringing about change itself. Growth brings about change; in fact, growth and change are pretty nearly synonymous, except for the fact that growth is a directed change in terms of certain biological and maturational goals which are set by the history of the species and by the nature of human development.

In another sense, however, education and child-rearing practices leading to the acquisition of self-discipline are also change producers and act almost as inevitably as the biological factors—though in much less predictable or understood ways.

The emphasis on the primary change agent also recognizes, as previously discussed, that direct and short-term types of change or treatment methods can be highly useful and are often highly efficient. Rather than ask the teacher or the parent to hold back efforts in regard to the child's development, they who know the child best and who bear the greatest responsibility can be helped to direct the effort effectively.

The role of teachers as primary change agents should become clearer as we discuss the terms "change objects" and "change plans."

THE CHILD—THE CHANGE OBJECT

The child can be regarded as the *change object*. The child is the one, who in the educational process, is to be changed in some specified direction. We want to help change behavior and attitudes, to aid his movement toward becoming a self-disciplined, efficiently self-fulfilling human being.

When talking about the child as a patient, in a mental hygiene sense, we still call the child the change object, as we do in this book, where discipline and achievement are primary, and mental health is viewed as a useful outcome from them.

The child is not to be regarded as a pawn to be moved about on a chessboard; rather, he is simply the focus of operation in the change effort to achieve his own (though *at first* his parents') goals and those society sets generally.

THE CHANGE PLAN

Having a change object—the child—and the presence of a primary change agent—the teacher—it is necessary to integrate them in the form of a *change plan*. The use of the term "change plan" implies several things. First, it implies that there is something to be changed or developed, there is some circumstance or condition that should be changed. Secondly, this change should bring about an improvement in the child's life in some specifiable ways. It might be that educational progress and mental health considerations are intertwined, which is usually the case. It might be that there are very specific problems—such as those dealing with concentration, or the child is acting as a bully, or the child is bright but unaccomplished— which would be specific goals of change.

The change plan can be thought of as operating in terms of a series of steps. The first step would be to delineate the problem or problems as carefully as possible. To delineate does not mean merely to name but to state some of the observations that support the naming of the problem and its concrete nature. For example, if the problem has to do with concentration, then the change plan would be composed in part of instances where the teacher or the parent has observed deficiencies in concentration on the child's part and also the nature of these deficiencies. This would be a kind of "chapter and verse" documentation in order to generate specific change efforts.

The change plan will also take account of efforts that have been made heretofore to overcome the problems indicated. The teacher may have resorted to threats or punishment, or the teacher may simply have given up after fruitless attempts to change the child. It should be known whether people who are responsible change agents have, in their previous efforts, tried many approaches too briefly, applied inconsistent measures, or been hopelessly discouraged and halfhearted in their attempts.

A third part of the change plan consists of setting down what it is possible to do at the present time in the present context of the child's school and home life. For example, any one of the measures that has been discussed so far in this book may be an item in a change plan. It might be useful on some occasion to remove the child from the classroom or even perhaps to put him in a special class. It might be useful to have parent consultations in regard to particular problems that affect both home and school. It might be useful to change the child's position in the class or his role on the playground in athletics or sports events. Many small measures might be considered for the change plan.

The fourth aspect of the change plan would be to decide on some kind of priority in executing the items considered in the third stage of the plan. Even though there may be six or seven things possible to do, there may be a very important hierarchy of events. Some matters are more important than others, some are more practical to initiate, some offer more hope for success. In some cases the priority may mean working first with the parents on a particular issue, such as how the child leaves home in the morning preparatory to coming to school (particularly important in so-called school phobia cases), and sheer presence in school should be given first priority.

Other conditions may exist where the home environment would seem to impose a particular condition on the school. In still other instances it may be that some kind of change at school would be the prior one, with the change at home seeming to be secondary. If we consider the change plan as some rational method of working out the interrelationship among the various alternatives, we realize how frequently our efforts in trying to bring about change in children are vague, misdirected, and haphazard.

Traditional methods, which have related the child's educational problems to an "emotional block" and have suggested referring the child and his parents outside the school for therapy, often do not utilize any change plan. Often this kind of referral simply assumes that through therapy the child's educational behavior and attitudes will change automatically. We recommend instead the development of *articulate change plans* which can be rationally arranged, tested, and adjusted.

Change plans may also utilize secondary change agents such as the teachers who appear infrequently in the classroom (art, music, recreation teachers) and other individuals with whom the child may have occasional dealings. Secondary change agents may be used to support change efforts involving primary change agents. For example, the classroom teacher, who is the primary change agent, is dealing with a problem child in a particular manner or is trying to overcome educational problems with special procedures; he may enlist the cooperation of other teachers who have some effect on the child, to coordinate their efforts. If a classroom teacher who has difficulty handling the disciplinary problems of some children finds that these children are left to do as they please in gym class or in shop class and turmoil builds up which acts adversely on the change efforts of the classroom teacher, then the matter should be discussed among all the teachers involved, to try to integrate their efforts.

INTEGRATING CHANGE EFFORTS

Perhaps the best way in which to integrate a change effort could come through conferences among the teacher, school psychologist, school principal, and others as needed. In such a conference the teacher, along with the psychologist, would be able to present facts and observations which underlie the change plan; that is, the teacher would be able to give specific descriptions of the child's problems and also tell what he has done about these problems. In such a conference the school psychologist could apply his observations to the child and the results of any tests and previous data. These data placed alongside those of the teacher could then be used, with the principal's concurrence and participation, to generate concrete attempts at remedy.

A conference with the parents could come into the picture at this point, when the school has formulated its own change plans. This is not to exclude the parents from participating in the plans but to let them know that the school has done some groundwork of its own and has certain objectives in mind, which can be shared with the parents. The parents, of course, might object and propose changes in the plan, or they might enlarge the picture, or they might act in a way to implement significantly what the school proposes.

Many conferences of this sort, however, can be carried on efficiently through the efforts of school personnel alone. Most classroom problems need not be referred to parents nor involve any out-of-school personnel. In fact, most of the problems would seem to yield to simple classroom management. But when secondary change agents and others are involved, the school should stand ready to provide crucial leadership for its proposed change plans and to act intelligently with respect to them.

MAKING THE MOST OF CHANGE PLANS

Even with minor problems, conferences are frequently held. And large amounts of time are spent collecting data and discussing them, often without developing a specific plan, or without realizing what the school can do or what it expects of parents or other concerned parties.

Formulation of a change plan may seem a bit formalized at first, but in the long run it can have several good effects. It will make the effort the school is already engaging in a much more efficient one. It will present a cohesive viewpoint to the parents or to other individuals who may be concerned (sometimes the court may be involved in an exceptional case, for example, or a social agency). It will give school personnel roles to play and help to prevent contradictory or conflicting courses of action and wasteful overlap in their various functions. And there is a side benefit in that once school people get the knack of formulating change plans, thinking of the child as a change object, and utilizing the teacher as a primary change agent (with the principal and others as secondary change agents), then their facility can help them view new problems and engage in new sets of plans for succeeding children who present difficulties. They gain a certain momentum and a certain skill in handling problems, and this means more efficient operation than when there are no plans.

FURTHER INTEGRATION OF CHANGE EFFORTS:
THE TEACHER AND THE SOCIAL GROUP

As we have indicated elsewhere in this book (see Chapter 7 especially), the social group can often instigate and direct change. The social group (the classroom, committees, other subdivisions of the school population) may serve as a primary change agent in some cases (when integrated with the teacher's primary change agent role) or as a secondary change agent. A child who has latent musical talent may be placed in a band, orchestra, or chorus and given the opportunity to flower; we could call this action part of a change plan, and the musical group would serve at least as a secondary change agent. The same may be said for dramatics instruction, the development of skills in selected class placement (art, handicrafts, shop, science lab, for example), and the like. All of these may be thought of as opportunities to "bring out" the child who has need for directed stimulation or to channel energies that otherwise would go to destructive or fruitless purposes.

Moving a step further in this rationale of group pressures, the teacher can set up discussion groups, committees, open classroom procedures, and the like to involve a given child—or perhaps several children—who appear to be in need of some enrichment, direction, or structuring likely to be gainful. Often when youngsters can be given some responsibility, a useful place in the classroom, even in small ways, this action channels their energies, directs their attitudes toward socially useful purposes, and may overcome behavior problems or academic underachievement or foster social growth.

The main point here is that the teacher, acting as a primary change agent, has within her purview, the opportunity to restructure elements of the average classroom in ways to benefit one or more children who otherwise present problems. The action of the teacher need not be limited to placing the child here or there in already existing classes or programs such as special education classes or a changed curriculum—important as these may be in many instances—but can also take the opportunity to restructure the social group to meet new goals or to set up new procedures in her already existing classroom structure. This, in a way, is making optimal use of the "social psychology of the classroom" to solve important problems.

It is important that the teacher (and educators, in general) *not* think of the individual and the group as mutually exclusive or oppositional. Actually, most of us as individuals come to life in groups, working exceptionally well in some settings, not so well in others. We want to use the group to optimize individual integrity and growth—and to change unwanted behavior—in a way that enhances the group also. The individual is not, in such instances, taking something away from the group; rather, the group is made richer and more versatile by gaining the new behaviors which the individual is capable of implementing when he or she is given the opportunity.

Other plans for change may be arrived at from the use of tests and observations, or from some experimental procedure that might be set up, such as counting the number of times that children act in a particular way in the classroom. These research data can be very valuable in the long run

(See Chapter 6). Basically, there may be very few different *types* of behavior problems that children display in the classroom. Perhaps the apparently wide assortment of problems or emotional difficulties can be distilled down to a few types of problems in terms of remedies. Research should be done to test the observation and provide a basis for more solid decision making and planning in the future. If, on the other hand, the plans that have been developed have been shown through research not to be effective, than a firm basis is laid for correcting them.

It would be very useful for a school system to keep track of the number and variety of problems that it deals with in the classroom, during an entire school year, and the solutions attempted. Generally, such a record or research investigation is not complex and may prove very illuminating for school personnel. The use of a change plan, thinking of the teacher as the primary change agent, and viewing the child as the change object, may well enhance the capacity to do research on this kind of problem and may distill data to some fairly fundamental description where it is more easily interpreted and acted upon (see Chapter 6 for further illustrations along these lines).

SELECTED READINGS

ALLPORT, GORDON W., "Values and our youth." *Teachers College Record*, 1961, *63*, 211–19.

BERNARD, H. W., *Mental Hygiene for Classroom Teachers*. New York: McGraw-Hill, 1961.

CROW, L. D., *Mental Hygiene for Teachers: A Book of Readings*. New York: Macmillan, 1963.

GINOTT, H., *Between Parent and Child*. New York: Macmillan, 1965.

HOVLAND, C. I., and I. L. JANIS eds., *Personality and Persuasibility*. New Haven, Conn.: Yale University Press, 1953.

KRUMBOLTZ, J. D., "Behavioral counseling: Rationale and research." *Personnel and Guidance J.*, 1965, *44*, 383–87.

SKINNER, B. F., *Science and Human Behavior*. New York: Macmillan, 1953.

STEVENSON, GEORGE S., and HARRY MILT, "Ten tips to reduce teacher tension," in J. M. Deidman, ed., *Readings in Educational Psychology*, 2nd ed. Boston: Houghton Mifflin, 1965.

WATSON, G., "Some personality differences in children related to strict or permissive parental discipline." *J. Psychol.*, 1957, *44*, 227–49.

WHITLEY, H. E., "Mental health problems in the classroom." *Understanding the Child*, 1954, *23*, 98–103.

10

SPECIAL
EDUCATIONAL
AND
CLINICAL PROBLEMS

Interest and progress in the field of special education has grown rapidly since the first edition of this book was published. Any book dealing with the general problems of discipline, achievement, and mental health must give some attention to special education problems, or to the general "clinical" problems which concern not only the special education teacher but require the attention of the regular classroom instructor also.

Every teacher recognizes that some classroom problems confront him. However, unless such a teacher has had direct contact with or at least has observed special education classes, he will seldom realize how much more difficult disciplinary and achievement problems are with such groups—and easily he may overlook the lessons such classrooms hold for him. In the ordinary classroom there are the usual tugs of war between child and child and between teacher and child; in special education classes, where the students have more severe personality problems and occasional problems with organic brain damage and retardation, what would be ordinary problems are magnified considerably.

The trend toward separating the most educationally and clinically disturbed children and putting them into special classes and, in some cases, in special schools is growing. Compared with regular schools, such special classes handle the children in smaller groups, prepare them for particular educational methods, and give teachers more help in dealing with the children. Very often these classes do not exceed ten or fifteen children and, perhaps, should not exceed eight to ten. In addition, helping teachers and other kinds of supportive personnel are on hand for part of if not for the entire, day, and other aids are available.

One perplexing aspect of many of the special education problems is that these educational and clinical groupings do not easily subdivide themselves into entities. Even in a class of retarded children, there will be special cases of brain damage, of cerebral palsy, of physical handicap, of sensory-motor disturbances, and of emotional disturbances. There is no "pure" diagnostic classification.

In this chapter, however, we arbitrarily have divided these various clinical and special education problems into groups for purposes of *descriptive account only*. We do not imply that brain-damaged children are qualitatively different from retarded or emotionally disturbed children. The groupings will overlap, and the individual differences among children in any group, for example, among the cerebral palsied are likely to be great.

BRAIN-DAMAGED CHILDREN

These children range from slightly brain damaged to severely damaged; they show gross speech, motor, and general intellectual defects. Some have such slight handicaps as not to need any special class placement or special educational techniques. Some have only slight perceptual-motor problems.

As many psychologists and physicians are coming to realize, all of us are probably to some extent brain damaged. Perhaps there is no such thing as a perfect brain, but the amount of defect can have very wide and encompassing implications in the education of children. Some are so severely handicapped as to require not only special teachers and classes, but special equipment and even schools built to accommodate their limitations. There is, for example, a tendency toward erecting school buildings restricted to one story so as to facilitate passage in wheelchairs and other devices from one room to another, from classroom to bathroom, from school to bus. Add to these gross matters of floor plan, building size, and room arrangement, a host of new kinds of teaching machines, electronic equipment and other aids, and the novice usually is amazed at the array of special accommodations and devices useful and in some cases, necessary, in the education of brain-damaged children.

Research suggests that an important aspect of the education of the brain damaged consists in simplifying their physical environment as much as possible so that they are not distracted by sundry stimuli. Too often in our attempt to help the handicapped learner, we overwhelm him with too much stimuli and too much complexity. We should go in the opposite direction—namely, simplifying and paring down environmental stimuli.

Classroom and teaching materials for children with various learning difficulties have undergone much change in the last decade. The materials to be learned are placed in bolder relief, so to speak, and the nonessentials of the environment reduced in importance. As a result of this stimulus simplification, the children can focus better on their educational tasks. They can absorb the materials they need to learn and thereby achieve more. To use the language we used earlier, they learn to discriminate between important and unimportant stimuli, to produce the correct response, and to receive the reinforcement associated with it. The problems and solutions are similar to those discussed in the chapter "Facilitating Achievement," in that the "mind" is conceived of, in part, as a kind of radar system which takes in, digests, and imparts information. If too much information is fed into the system, it "jams" or becomes confused like a person trying to take orders simultaneously from others as he drives through unfamiliar territory. If on the other hand, the information to be learned is regulated, simplified and focused, and put in the proper serial order, then the receiving organism —in this instance, the brain-damaged child—can receive better and can thereby process and learn more effectively. This concept is especially important with these children.

In addition to improving learning, this environmental simplification also helps to control the behavior of the brain-damaged child. Some of these children are extraordinarily active. They literally try to climb the walls, race all about, often interact at random in destructive ways with one another, and can quickly become unmanageable. Also, once they have been given too much freedom, they tend to increase their hyperactivity rather than to spend it. Therefore, any quieting of their behavior makes them more tractable as far as educational stimuli are concerned, more agreeable socially, and more amenable to learning.

In many classrooms cubby holes or wall booths have been a considerable help in teaching the brain damaged. These consist simply of wooden screens, thick enough to prevent any direct contact between the youngsters as they sit parallel to and facing a wall. The booths are about ten to fifteen feet square. Ordinarily five or six of them can be placed against a smooth wall that is unbroken by windows or doors. The children are taught to work alone in them for brief periods of time. They may return to the teacher's desk for help when needed, or they may sit in the ordinary classroom chairs and at desks part of the time. However, ordinarily they should not sit where they can openly stimulate each other for very long periods of time. The isolation booth provides a much needed respite for the child and the teacher and offers an opportunity for the child to develop some semblance of self-discipline.

Many observers are surprised to see a classroom of children facing the wall separate from each other, rather than interacting. Educators have placed so much emphasis on social adjustment and social exchange that it was long overlooked that the handicapped learner often cannot accept this complexity of interaction without untoward effects. So the observer in the classroom of brain-damaged children and, perhaps, in other classrooms offering special educational techniques has to reorient himself to these different objectives.

DISCIPLINE WITH BRAIN-DAMAGED CHILDREN

Regardless of their presumed causal conditions, the problems of brain-damaged children are effectively handled by techniques of discipline similar to those used for normal children, with some adaptations. Some kinds of control or structure must be imposed on their behavior so that they do not run rampant. In this regard the handling of the brain-damaged child is similar in nature to the handling of any normal child in the classroom, who may on occasion stir up disciplinary problems. As we shall discuss later, the classroom management of other types of exceptional children or atypical children requires a similar viewpoint, though with modification for particular cases.

In exercising classroom control, there are two special major limitations for brain-damaged children. As we have already seen, one has to do with the *amount* of control that must be exerted over their behavior and their learning efforts, that is, the number and complexity of stimuli which they can handle. The whole physical environment of the brain-damaged child must be better controlled than that of other children. The classroom teacher of brain-damaged children, therefore, has a much harder job in regard to setting up and maintaining control. The second major difference in the disciplinary regimen is that the classes for the brain damaged have to be smaller. A class of 30 to 35 normal children is too large for the most effective learning, but trying to educate brain-damaged children in classes this large would be preposterous, if not impossible. No educational objective would be realized; only a modicum of control of overt behavior could possibly be accomplished in a class of that size. Class size must be held to a minimum. Even the use of teacher aides and other incidental personnel can easily become profitless if too many brain-damaged children are kept together in the same classroom. There seems to be no substitute for a small class for these children, although this is by no means all that is needed.

Other considerations include the following: If they are to profit from educational stimuli, the children should be helped to achieve somewhat sustained attention to their work and to learn to appropriately estimate themselves against environmental demands. Also the brain-damaged child tends to be exceptionally liable emotionally. He often has acute sensitivity to failure, an unusual reluctance to try new things, a guarded and almost animal-like alertness to what he perceives as "danger" or "uncertainty" in his environment. These vulnerabilities have to be fully appreciated by the teacher or by anyone planning a program for the brain-damaged child. It is impossible to deal with him as if he were a normal child with just a little more than the usual fear of the new. The various approaches to discipline discussed earlier apply to the brain-damaged child, but they must be executed with considerably more finesse than with other children and must be bolstered with a greater amount of consistency and perseverance on the teacher's part. The tasks and requirements must be put to the brain-damaged child in smaller amounts, with greater care, with more supervisory follow-through, with much greater patience and with immediate, well-tailored reinforcement.

It may take weeks to get a brain-damaged child to perform a task the teacher knows he can do but about which he feels very insecure or confused. In addition, the solidifying of any gains may take many weeks. Meanwhile, the ups and downs in behavior and performance level of the child may be so great as to discourage even the most patient teacher. Besides flighty distractability, the brain damaged also shows much variation in his efforts and his performance from day to day and week to week, as well as from minute to minute and hour to hour. It is often necessary to consider any results in the perspective of months or even years compared to days, weeks, and months with more nearly normal children.

This high degree of lability is one reason why many educators and psychologists have turned their attention to machine-assisted learning. The machine can present problems or learning material item by item without tiring or becoming emotionally upset with the child. While more normal children could become bored with the monotony, the brain-damaged child needs this kind of consecutive presentation. Machine-assisted learning is relentless, whereas the human teacher frequently is distracted or emotionally incapacitated after a period of time.

Altogether the problems of educating the brain-damaged child are considerable, and the disciplinary regimens are sometimes almost unbelievably complex. Such a child is in dire need of structure, and this structure has to be a flexible one that keeps long-term aims and goals in mind but can, at the same time, accommodate to the great momentary turbulence the brain-damaged child may show at times.

In a sense the disciplined routine is needed more than with the normal child, but the amounts of discipline and control must also be more carefully regulated. To take off controls and let the child act impulsively in order to "work off steam" or to express himself is to miss the point of the brain-damaged child's hyperactivity. To assume that he mainly needs love and will calm down when loved enough also seems to miss the mark. To overcontrol and overdiscipline as if he "knew better" and were simply being mischievous is also fruitless. If nothing else, this is likely to exhaust the adult involved within a short time, as he tries to keep up with the hyperactive child. The teacher must rely as much as possible on a firm regimen that has built in flexibility and not try to react primarily on an emotional level.

In essence, these children are often highly intractable and need very carefully planned daily routines. Ordinary measures will not suffice either to control them or to educate them. They are truly a difficult but fascinating and challenging group of children who need specially designed and specially executed teaching, supported by the proper educational-assisted teaching aids, and careful reinforcement of their small efforts and gains.

RETARDED OR SLOW-LEARNING CHILDREN

Retarded, or slow-learning, children constitute probably the largest category of exceptional children. One may call slow-learning those with IQ's between 50 and 75. Children below 50 IQ are considered mentally deficient (although educable) and require even more specialized environmental regimens. Some would skip the handicapped category and call all children with IQ's below 75 either feebleminded or retarded.

The exact delineation of the IQ range is not the important matter, however. What is important is to realize that, in general, the lower the intelligence, the slower the learning and the more exposure the child needs to acquire a given amount of knowledge or skill. In fact intelligence is defined in part on the basis of time needed to learn something. Also the slower the learning, the lower tends to be the ultimate intellectual ceiling. Recognizing these limitations of the slow-learning or retarded, the teacher then has to set about exposing these children patiently and consistently to their learning tasks. The need for a disciplined routine is still present, but the teacher has to recognize that his results will be less, even though efforts are greater than with other children. The slow-learning child cannot be expected to make the advances that the more normal child makes and not primarily because of emotional problems nor the lack of proper teaching techniques. There is simply a limit to the child's ability to learn (on the basis of rate of learning), which is lower than that of other children.

To stress the importance of the low limit on the learning of the retarded child may seem unnecessary. However, one must recognize that parents and well-meaning friends often do not understand what is meant by low intelligence. Parents may feel that it is just the child's speech which is not up to par and that if he could be taught to speak better, the other intellectual problems would be solved. Or one may think that such a child is just slow but can eventually learn as much as the average child or that what the slow-learning child eventually learns is better retained. Another misapprehension, and one frequently encountered, is that the slow-learning child is limited only in a specific area of learning. Generally this latter assumption is not borne out, although there are specific instances in which it is true. A final misapprehension one frequently encounters is that the slow-learning child will catch up one day and overcome his educational deficit.

The emphasis on "hope and help for the retarded" has its useful and constructive aspects, but it is too often interpreted as a road to normalcy. Perhaps someday scientists will learn how to make the retarded child normal, but this simply cannot be done at this time. In order to help the retarded child, it is better to recognize and work within his limitations (as it is, indeed, to accept those each of us has in some regards) than it is to hope that if just the "right thing" is done, he will be normal again. The latter road seems to lead only to disappointment and resentment. An example of this sometimes pathetic state of affairs follows:

> Betty, a nine-year-old, retarded child, was the oldest of three girls. Her mother, hoping to overcome what she felt to be Betty's "emotional problems which made her retarded," had been to just about every professional person in the area who worked with retarded children. She thought that although Betty was retarded (IQ 75 on several tests by different examiners over a period of time), this state of affairs was due to her emotional problems. She had misunderstood the report of a psychologist who said that Betty did have emotional problems, but that she was also clearly and unmistakably retarded. Betty's mother had gotten the cart before the horse and was searching for someone who would agree with her interpretation of Betty's troubles. In her quest for this confirmation she had solicited numerous professional opinions and had garbled most of them. Finally she found someone who agreed to a program of "play therapy" for her child, hoping that this would allow her to work off her emotional constraints and thereby become normal intellectually. We were able to keep track of Betty's progress over a two-year period; it was only that which could be expected—knowing her intellectual level and rate of intellectual growth—although she did seem to show some improvement in emotional stability in the classroom.

There are many mothers of Bettys, hoping for across-the-board improvement of their retarded children, attributing the problems to the wrong causes, and failing to utilize good existing facilities for the education of their children.

Equal caution is needed in another direction—the tendency to relegate certain children to slow-learning classes when they do not belong there. Children may get placed in such classes because of poor emotional and social development or low scores on group intelligence tests which penalize them for poor reading ability and poor motivation. One such child was:

> Ivor, a twelve-year-old boy, the middle child of three children, who had been in classes for slow-learning children for five of his seven years of school. He was reading and doing arithmetic on the fourth grade level (three years behind his chronological age level) but showed signs of better intellectual ability in other ways. However, as occasionally happens, his teachers had somehow discounted or even overlooked the peaks in his otherwise retarded performance and assumed that he belonged in the class for slow-learning children. Referring to early intelligence and achievement tests which put him in the slow-learning classes, it appeared that his low score (IQ equivalent score of 72) was obtained on a short group test, which probably unduly reflected his poor reading skill and lack of confidence.

On what grounds do we become suspicious of Ivor's diagnosed ability but not that of Betty's? Betty had scored low (around 70 IQ) on a number of tests, individually administered by several competent examiners over several years' time. Ivor, on the other hand, had scored low on only one test—a short group test based on following directions by reading—in a group situation (not on an individually administered test, where motivation, interest and reading are better controlled). Also Ivor had shown spontaneous evidence of better intelligence in his hobbies; some achievement scores, which were not as low as would have been predicted from his group IQ score; and in understanding behavior in the classroom. No one had tried to prove that Ivor was normal intellectually, but test after test had been made to try to prove Betty's normalcy, and it had continually been found lacking.

Further indication of Ivor's near normalcy came during the following two years. It was decided that he had probably been underrated and relegated to an unchallenging (for him) classroom, and he was moved to a class of normal but *underachieving* children. Within a year's time Ivor made up about one and a half years' of his three years' educational deficit—a rate of growth considerably faster than would have been predicted from a valid IQ rating of 72. As Ivor remained in the more stimulating and more nearly normal class for him, he continued to progress, and after two years he was apparently stabilized, with his average achievement scores about one year instead of three years below his chronological age and with a retested IQ of 84 (on an individually administered test) instead of the IQ of 72 originally obtained from the group test.

Thus, we were able to correct in this instance an educational deficit and an educational misplacement of a child. Ivor's progress was attributable in part to the revival of his formerly dormant ability but also to the greater challenge he encountered in the more disciplined and achievement-oriented class. He learned how to study; before he had not been required to do so since it had been felt that he was too retarded to profit from studying. The new class produced better achievement and also better social and emotional adjustment. The teacher commented that "Ivor really came to life." While the nature of the classroom routine has to be modified to fit the needs and limitations of the slow-learning or the retarded child, a challenging and disciplined routine is still needed. If all challenge and all disciplined routine are cast aside, one risks even more than a vegetative educational existence for the slow-learning child. As teachers who have worked with them know, these children are often surprisingly acute and perceptive, even though the sensitivity does not generalize to all their behavior. If one does not realize that much growth can occur in a sufficiently challenging program, one may exaggerate to hopelessness the meaning of their retardation.

CHILDREN WITH ORTHOPEDIC HANDICAPS

There is likely to be an overlapping between physical handicaps and emotional problems and also between brain damage and other physical handicaps. Children with severe physical handicaps often present emotional problems because of their inescapable abnormality. The child who cannot run and play, test and encounter, fuss and fight and go on to make amends lacks the common background of experience from which realistic self-appraisals and appraisals of others arise. Generally speaking, the more severe the physical handicap, the more restriction it places on the child's life, and the more restriction the child experiences, the more likely he is to be emotionally disturbed.

Physical handicaps, of course, are usually obvious. An impaired gait or stance from cerebral palsy, a hunched back or curved spine from some congenital condition, show plainly and call the victim's plight to the observer's attention. Usually people are strongly sympathetic to the child with an obvious physical handicap. The many campaigns to raise money for foundations serving handicapped patients testify to the strong emotional appeal that can be made on behalf of physical handicaps. One sees a picture of a child with braces and on crutches, sympathizes with the victim, and supports one's feeling with money, even if the number of victims who may be involved is relatively small.

There are good reasons why people are sympathetic to the child with obvious physical handicaps. Without such concern, the handicapped person would lack the direct support and care he sorely needs in order to make a place for himself in society. But as is often the case, good practice and good intentions can be overdone, leaving a residue of undesirable *dependency* on the part of the handicapped child.

> Monty was a very charming ten-year-old boy who had suffered from polio at age three. He had to stay in a wheelchair most of the time because of residual leg weakness. Despite his handicap he was a likeable and outgoing child, who made friends quickly, especially with adults. If he had to take responsibility, however, such as with schoolwork, he usually reneged. The world came to him so much that he had not been forced to make an effort on his own part to learn, to take his exercises, to follow routines set down for him at home, at school, and in the hospital. He became a problem to the nurses and to other patients in the hospital. With his cheerful, friendly manner, he encouraged their interest in him, but when it came time for his work, he hated to give up his sociable behavior and get down to business. During his frequent hospitalizations, he stayed up too late at night, talking to interested adults, watching television, and getting about in his chair. Efforts to pin him down to a schedule, to schoolwork, or to exercises met with strong, stubborn resentment on Monty's part. With those who had direct responsibility for him, he was far from popular.

It would be easy to call Monty spoiled. He had been catered to because of realistic needs he presented. Necessarily he had a somewhat artificial life, and people continually tried to make up to him, through their generosity, what he lacked in the way of a normal boyhood. These efforts sprang from good intentions, but they misfired in Monty's case (as they frequently do with handicapped children) because of the self-centered, dependent, playful attitudes they indirectly and unintentionally engendered and reinforced in the boy.

Lessons can be learned from Monty's case. In school settings where handicapped children are taught, teachers must have the courage and persistence to treat the children *as normally as possible.* A general rule to follow is to encourage the handicapped child to do as much for himself as he can. The handicapped child has to learn to struggle with his feelings of reluctance even more than the normal child. He has to explore his range of response as much as the normal child does. Too much sympathy affects his future in a way which pays poor dividends, as is shown by the case of Ann.

> Ann was an attractive and likeable child of seven and a half. She was diagnosed as having cerebral palsy, with mental retardation (IQ in the low 70s on the basis of individual tests). Ann also had to wear braces at night.

Among the many problems that she presented was one of persistent bed wetting. She would often wet the bed two or three times a night, according to her mother's report and the record the mother kept on a calendar at home. Ann's mother would get her up about midnight and again about 4 in the morning. If she got Ann up at 10 or 11, she would have to get the child up again at 2 or 3. Even then Ann was often wet at 6 or 7 in the morning, the normal time for her to awaken. The mother was inadvertently promoting the child's bed wetting by trying to do for her what she should do for herself. Despite the mother's efforts, the child continued to be wet, and only rarely was the mother able to get the child through the night dry.

A change in the regimen that Ann's mother followed—by skipping the 2–4 A.M. arousal and by having Ann awaken around midnight to an electric alarm clock (she had gone to bed between 8:30 and 9:00)— allowed Ann to become sensitive to her own toileting requirements. Within two months, Ann was able to stay dry about 20 out of 30 nights on the average, and with this improved performance, her mother was no longer required to get Ann up during the middle of the night.

In the cases of Monty and Ann the adult environment had supported the children beyond what was required. This extra amount of emotional and social support, this doing things for the child and showing attention to the child when adult interests were not required, led the children to be more dependent on the adults. In these cases it was the adults rather than the children who were trained! Or we could put it this way: It was the adults' misconception of the child's difficulties and the adults' approach to a solution that led to the child's continuous dependence.

HANDICAPPED CHILDREN AND FEAR

The handicapped child generally shows more realistic fear responses than does the normal child. This tendency toward fear springs from consistent causes such as a lack of balance, hence a proneness to fall; a fundamental muscular weakness, hence a lack of strength; misperceptions about gravity and other physical phenomena in relation to his body. Learning to protect himself against damage in vital ways is important if the afflicted child is to avoid developing strong fear. Knowing just when to let the child work out some matters for himself is a delicate and important problem which nurses, teachers of handicapped children, and parents often have to find out for themselves through trial and error. Too frequently, however, the child's limitations are better appreciated (and hence overprotected) than are his strengths.

Routine is often lacking in the home and school life of handicapped children. Here again, giving in to the childrens' whims and placating them out of sympathy and affection is too often the rule. Though a well-intentioned error, this does not soften the effect which, in the long run, shows itself in the form of general emotional immaturity and instability.

The handicapped person has to make his place in life just as anyone else. The more care we exert in teaching him self-discipline, a sense of his own strengths and weaknesses, a feeling of responsibility for himself and his progress, the more able he will be as an adult. In talking with handicapped adults who have risen above their limitations, one is impressed with the objectivity with which they view their handicap and with the matter of fact ways they go about daily living. They do not wait for others to do for them what they can do for themselves. They regard their handicap not as a negative state of affairs (an important difference between the adjusted and the unadjusted person with a handicap), but as a realistic set of limitations within which they have to live and enjoy life. They do not focus on the handicap itself but rather on the limitation. This brings them closer to most people, and most of us do have limitations within which we manage to live —poor eyesight, flat feet, tendencies toward certain types of illnesses, minor but irritating digestive, eliminative, and other disorders. Nobody is built or functions perfectly, and everyone must accept his limitations and live within them. Most people are also less strong and agile than athletes and less creative than artists, but they usually do not compare themselves to others in such negative ways. It actually handicaps people beyond their natural limits, in terms of poor attitudes, if they continually compare themselves with those who are superior in some respects.

However, the obviously physically handicapped person has a somewhat wider gap to bridge than most others. We can help him do this by teaching him to accept his limitations and to live productively within them. There is no better way to go about helping the child live with his limitations than to teach him to rely on a self-disciplined program of schoolwork. In this way he learns to accept small tasks commensurate with his limitations and to accomplish them as well as he can, just as the normal child does. It is the prerogative and the privilege of the school to bring these important discriminations to the orthopedically handicapped child.

CHILDREN WITH SENSORY DEFECTS AND LIMITATIONS

These defects, referring mainly to sight and hearing, are exceptional conditions with which the classroom teacher has to cope, and they provide additional instances of the importance of the child's learning to live within his limitations.

All handicaps carry with them general tendencies toward certain psychological reactions. These tendencies are not inevitable, however, and they are sometimes exaggerated by the individual differences among people with the same handicap. But generally speaking, sight and hearing limitations impose psychological restrictions on the child that other handicaps do not typically impose.

One psychological problem that the hard of hearing or deaf child experiences arises from being unable to follow many communications among people. He does not know what people are saying, and he does not perceive the vocal inflections, the plays on words, and other subtle interactions that spoken language allows. In the language of modern communication theory, he lacks immediate auditory feedback by which to regulate his own behavior. As a result, the child may grow suspicious of others, may fail to differentiate between others laughing with him and at him, and can readily become self-pitying, and discouraged.

A certain amount of protection is required in such cases, just as the poorly sighted or blind person needs protection from the traffic and other dangers about him. The tricky problem educationally—and also from the standpoint of social and emotional maturity—is to determine how much protection is necessary and the limits beyond which it will unduly impede the development of independence and responsibility in the individual.

It has been a common practice, whenever possible, to put children with sight or hearing problems in special classes. In being with others who have the same types or degrees of handicap, the child with sight or hearing deficiencies learns that others share common problems with him. He gets to see himself as a normal person in many lights. This leads him to feel less alone, less different, less exposed to a confusing and complex world. Also, the child with deficient sight or hearing learns how better to cope with communication problems by sharing solutions with others similar to himself, and this experience indirectly aids his self-confidence. He becomes more willing to take on new learning and responsibility as he matures. Complete isolation or protection for the exceptional child, however, is not desirable. There should be some interaction with normal children.

For some reason educators and others dealing with children with hearing and sight defects have tended to protect them less than children with obvious physical handicaps. This may be due to a difference in the appearance of the handicaps, to some stereotyped evaluation of what the handicap calls for, or to the observer's own anxiety as he views a handicap and thinks what it would mean if he had a similar one himself. Or perhaps the children begin school with already differently shaped reactions which affect education. In any case, the greater willingness to give the child with sensory defects more independence and to expect more maturity from him results, we think, in his having fewer emotional problems than many other types of exceptional or handicapped children. While there is no good research to support this generalization, many clinical observations support it.

Such children do have problems, however, and the teacher needs to be aware of their general limitations. But the teacher can usually find a way of dealing with this type of child more easily than with many other handicapped children. The teacher can rely on careful, individually directed and well-disciplined educational programs similar to those we have outlined earlier. As he proceeds in a manner geared to individual differences in capacities and limitations, he gains encouragement that his children, though handicapped, can achieve well—educationally as well as emotionally and socially. The teacher can see the three broad objectives of discipline, educational achievement, and generally good mental health being secured simultaneously.

OVERLY SHY AND OVERLY AGGRESSIVE CHILDREN

A wide variety of children and problems are subsumed under this general heading; they are too numerous and complicated for one to try to delineate carefully. Also they do not form as clear-cut a grouping as the other handicapping conditions discussed in this chapter.

As with most emotionally disturbed children, our purpose is to draw out some general similarities among them in order to arrive at specific ways of improving their achievement and helping them to mature psychologically. Our emphasis here will be on the extremely shy and the extremely aggressive child, probably the most frequently disturbing elements in the classroom.

If the term "emotionally disturbed" has any precise meaning, it probably refers most specifically to children who feel excessively disturbed about themselves, about their relationships to others, and about their general ability to cope with the world around them. The shortcomings they see in themselves are not primarily due to low intelligence, brain damage, or any known physical or organic condition. In brief, they are due to faulty learning, the accumulation of faulty habits, attitudes and feelings. The emotionally disturbed child may range in attitude from shy reluctance to blustery hyperaggressiveness. People try to solve their emotional problems in different ways. Some retreat, feel inadequate, or are loath to take action in the face of social or environmental demands. Extreme cases include children with prolonged school phobia, or children who have a highly irregular pattern of school attendance caused by emotional disturbances often masked as physical symptoms. These shy children tend to wait for others to set the style of interaction. They hesitate, vacillate, reach decisions slowly or not at all. They are easily made "nervous" or upset; they readily translate their apprehensions and reluctance into outright fears and can be scared off from taking normal or even necessary action. They may become dependent upon others who are more resourceful or more self-confident. They also tend to develop an attitude which can be described as expecting others to help them out. Their shyness is compensated for (rather than overcome) not by their own effort but by the efforts of others who take up the slack for them.

Those who are blustery and overly aggressive, on the other hand, may have problems similar to those of the shy person—lack of self-confidence, for example—but they exhibit their tendencies differently and try different means to cope with their unrest.

The aggressive child does not "look before he leaps." He tries to take over, although he lacks the skills or attitudes called for. He is often selfish, domineering and a show-off. When he is uncertain, he uses bragging and assumed confidence to cope with situations. In the place of true confidence and skill, he pretends to attitudes, experiences, and capacities he does not possess. This is not to say that he might not possess these capacities, but his momentary actions are based on an assumed prerogative or an assumed capacity rather than a demonstrated one.

There are many gradations between the extremes of shyness and over-aggressiveness. There are also children who exhibit in seemingly random ways, now shyness and reluctance, now blusteriness and arrogance. In one situation their lack of sureness may lead them to take one tack, in another situation a different one. We commonly call them unpredictable, or all mixed up. We attribute these descriptive terms to them because we perceive that they lack self-control and self-understanding, and also it is very hard for us as teachers and observers to understand and follow their inconsistencies.

In coping with such children, the classroom teacher tries to bolster the shy child and slow down the overconfident one. The problem is to help them reach a better balance, a steadier and more stable equilibrium. This is not to say that all children should adapt in the same way, but some— the overconfident child, for example—have to be taught to be more affected by other means than to try to force themselves on people when unsure of themselves. They have to be taught to evaluate situations better, and only then act. Shy children, on the other hand, have to learn to make an effort even a provisional one, to snap out of their reluctance sufficiently to test themselves against the demands of the situation. *Each one in his own way needs to be taught to be more realistic and more self-disciplined.* The same general remedy can be applied to the child with the motley assortment of in-between symptoms and to the child who varies between shyness and overaggressiveness. With in-between or variable cases, more of a breakdown of usual situations is ordinarily necessary. For example:

Johnny, a ten-year-old boy, was an overconfident, aggressive lad in some of his schoolwork. He sang too loudly in music class. In arithmetic class he relished a race in addition at the chalkboard, and told the others he could beat them doing arithmetic fundamentals. But when it came to reading or to sharing with others in a cooperative venture, (for example, making articles to celebrate Thanksgiving), he bowed out and acted as if he had no confidence at all. The teacher did not let him withdraw from the latter type of situation and tried to "tone him down" in those situations in which he was too aggressive and overconfident. By discussing with him his effects upon others, by setting clear limits, and by differentiating underconfident and overconfident situations with this child, the teacher and Johnny were able to bring Johnny out of his dilemma.

When Johnny felt confident he "went to town," as he expressed it, and bragged. He wanted to "hog the whole show" when he felt able, and he did not want to participate at all if he could not win or show adequate skill immediately. His shyness and his overaggressiveness were extreme reactions which did not bring him his goals in the long run.

The teacher came to understand these different ways of looking at the daily demands put to Johnny. The teacher now understood his motivation and his varying performance; he did not let the matter rest there, however. Steps were taken to teach Johnny a more realistic attitude in both sets of circumstances so that in time he became less of an extremist and could work and learn more effectively in the classroom in various situations.

Generally speaking, the teacher can set tasks for the shy child in terms of requirements the teacher feels confident the child can meet. The teacher can stay with the child during his reluctant moments, keeping the demands alive, and thus gradually help him to experience, firsthand, the success he needs. The teacher can help him see that often his expectations for himself are too high or unrealistic—like Johnny's always insisting on winning—and that if he modifies these expectations, then he can begin to do a good job and receive reinforcement for his efforts and accomplishments.

An overconfident child openly and deliberately acts on his superior attitudes ("I can do it easily"); he may even demonstrate remarkable skill and achieve his ends in some cases. However, he cannot be sure of doing it all the time and performing up to his expected level. No person's skills are flawless, and no one is likely to perform excellently all the time. The overly confident child generalizes too freely from some instances of skill and achievement to all opportunities, and as a result, does not learn what he should and would from efforts to improve. He, too, has to be taught to be less rigid and insistent upon or confident of success. Athletic teams that are too confident can end up losing a game because of carelessness and failure to profit from errors. They may fail to estimate correctly the size and skill of their opponents and of themselves and go blithely along as if they "had it made," thereby not preparing themselves for the true situation.

THE DISCIPLINED MANAGEMENT OF
SHYNESS AND OVERASSERTIVENESS

In cases of both the very shy and the extremely aggressive child, realistic assessment of expectations and disciplined management are remedial steps the teacher can take to help. He can help such children measure their efforts step by step, and thereby elicit their best achievement. They learn to overcome their unrealistic overconfidence and excessive shyness and come to estimate more accurately what is expected of them by their environment in and out of school. It is the teacher's role to help clarify and simplify the situation to a point where childrens' self-estimates are made more realistic and are pursued with greater confidence.

INTELLECTUALLY GIFTED CHILDREN

It may seem strange to some readers that the problems of intellectually gifted children are discussed in this chapter on special educational problems. The term "exceptional children" is used to connote not only children at the lower ability rung but also those at the upper end of the ladder.

In some ways the most challenging educational problems arise with the superior child. Possessing the greatest potential and often the greatest variability, he directly challenges the teacher with the possibility of a most rewarding victory or a most saddening defeat. We say this not to slight the importance of educating *all* youngsters but out of a growing respect for the importance of truly educating the bright child, and the belated recognition that educators have been neglecting the gifted child and his importance to society.

One answer to the problem of most effectively educating gifted children lies in the direction of more support for their education. In recent years it has been encouraging to see money spent for educating various types of exceptional children such as the physically handicapped, but there has been no corresponding support for the educational needs of the superior child.

One persistent and insidious educational problem of the bright child is that he is able to get by with little work and to make acceptable, even above average grades with minimal effort and application. Such a child may even brag about how little work he does. Escaping real effort may be momentarily satisfying to him, but in the long run, it develops poor habits and attitudes, for which there will likely be a day of reckoning.

A large percentage of college failures (perhaps as high as one-third or even one-half) stems from lack of adequate work habits, not from insufficient ability. Many bright students graduate from high school never having learned to study. As a result they may never get to college, or if they get there, they do not apply themselves well. Their bad habits reduce opportunities for advanced or specialized work, for vocational opportunities, and for the general pleasure of living more fully each day.

Many large and some small school systems have programs for advancing bright students through accelerating their academic schedule. Such programs allow first-rate students to take more courses, to progress at faster than the average pace, or to take enriched programs. But often bright students are reluctant to take accelerated programs in the freshmen or sophomore year of high school. It is as if they have existed on a bare subsistence level educationally for so long that they do not fully recognize it and take the advantage of a better "diet." Also they are loath to take on more work if they do not need to do so in order to graduate. In such cases not only has the actual educational achievement of the bright child lagged but his morale, self-respect, and self-discipline have also been harmed. For example:

> James, age fifteen, was a very capable high school sophomore. He had a tested IQ of 140 but had made "C" and "D" grades during his freshman year and the first half of his sophomore year. As his story goes, he would attempt to study, but he would get "nervous" and have to give up after 15 or 20 minutes. As he sat down to the task, he easily became discouraged when he could not master the material in one reading or with a cursory effort. He did not take college preparatory or accelerated courses because of his poor ability to concentrate. As a result, his estimate of himself continued to decline, and he dropped more difficult courses to take easier ones. He would report headaches or stomachaches prior to examinations at school, with a regularity that finally suggested his educational trouble.

Fortunately, a program was worked out for James. It combined a brief period of psychotherapy, directed primarily at the youngster's immediate problems, with the teaching of good study habits and methods of application. Through it, James was able, within a year's time, to increase his academic average from "D" to "B." And this average was based on some college preparatory and even more advanced courses. James learned to study, to apply himself, to sustain effort, and to produce good results from his effort. Consequently, he felt more adequate and happy, participated in more school functions, and improved his social behavior by becoming less critical of himself and others.

James's case fits well our previous outline of ways in which to get a student down to the business of achievement. He was a prime example of how one should not study, now he is a good example of how one can and should study. Many bright children have not had the good fortune to work with a competent school psychologist, who is able to fuse the achievement and mental hygiene aspects of their school life.

Often intellectually superior children demonstrate their abilities early in their formal education. All teachers know many instances of superior intellectual achievement in young children, such as reading before entering the first grade, handling arithmetic concepts two or more years in advance of those of the same chronological age, possessing a large fund of information about science or the social-political world. Sometimes, however, the bright child is not suspected to be as capable as, in fact, he is.

> Linda, a nine-year-old earned a Stanford Binet IQ of 188, a most remarkable score. This level is often called genius. Looking into her school record, we found no evidence that she was regarded as more than just a capable student. Although she was taking some French lessons during a free period at school, she was making only moderately good grades ("B") in her regular work. She was interested in art, read widely, and conversed unusually well with adults, but her general school status was mediocre compared with her test scores and her potential. On the Stanford Achievement Test she scored from three to six grades in advance of her actual grade placement. Actually, Linda was bored with normal schoolwork. She was suspected by her teacher of having some problems in adjusting to children, but this was not related to her evident boredom at having to share educational material on a mediocre (for her) level.

Such an unusually bright child does not belong in the usual class of her chronological age. She cannot, however, be promoted on the basis of intellectual ability alone since this would place her with children three to six years older than she—children who are much larger and much more mature socially. Nor will a one-year acceleration contain much intellectual stimulation for more than a month or two. Linda belongs either in a very much enriched, largely individualized program with her age group or with a group of children of comparable abilities. In most large cities (say, above 250,000 population) there will be enough superior children to form such classes.

If most educators could free themselves from biases concerning bright children, they would recognize such children more readily and work to provide additional educational stimulation for them. The biases seem to fall into several categories: The children are bright and capable of getting along well on their own; consequently, nothing extra need be provided. They should go right along with average children, lest they get the impression that their intellectual superiority is something that should provide privileges or nondemocratic types of special social experiences. A third bias is probably more rooted in fact: Frequently, teachers do not know *how* to enrich their educational program; may be somewhat afraid of them and their perceptiveness; may hate to expose them to teaching methods designed for average students.

The latter attitude is particularly relevant in the case of intellectually superior children above ten or eleven years of age. They are by this time able to challenge adult knowledge in a number of ways; therefore, adult leaders and teachers have to know their fields well and know how to continue to stimulate and guide these children. Entertainers sometimes like to show off the extremely bright child via quiz shows and other public appearances, but such procedures are a long, long way from recognizing and guiding their intellectual superiority properly. At best they are extremely poor encouragement of what the children *are* rather than how well they have developed themselves. And the intellectually gifted suffer in the long run from not cultivating and advancing their unusual talents, rather than simply exploiting them.

THE SOCIALLY DISADVANTAGED CHILD

The socially disadvantaged child presents many of the problems cited above among the more clinical of the special education cases, but for different reasons. Such a child generally has a slow start, poor cultural background for school as it is, and is not given much encouragement to achieve. Much of his life is spent keeping the various problems of mere survival (economic and social, mainly) under control. He is, moreover, not part of the mainstream—middle-class mainstream—of American life that dominates the schools. He senses this, is resentful of it, and often tries to "break out" rather than "develop out" of his circumstances.

There has been much written in recent years about the ill effects of socially disadvantaged living, its influence on child growth and development, especially on education, vocational preparation, and eventual mature citizenship. We are not able in a book of this length, with its broad coverage of educational and achievement topics, to treat the problems of the disadvantaged child in detail. It will be necessary, therefore, to present only a few highlights of the difficulties that may especially affect the principles of this book, and around which the reader can assemble his thoughts.

1. Socially disadvantaged populations contain as many, if not more, children in the categories cited above, such as brain damaged, orthopedically handicapped, and emotionally disturbed. They simply tend not to be detected as early in the lower economic levels, and they do not get professional attention as readily as other children.
2. In conventional schools, class and social prejudices prevail against the socially disadvantaged child. These prejudices are, of course, present at all social levels, but there is more pressure exerted on those in the lower levels than is true for middle-or upper-class people.
3. Schools, libraries, parks, community recreational and other facilities are often lacking or poorly kept up in the geographic areas where the socially

disadvantaged child is found. This is part of the definition of *socially disadvantaged,* namely, the absence of the opportunities provided by such facilities. The socially disadvantaged "system," as some would put it, keeps the child down or at least limits his opportunities.

4. Socially disadvantaged parents are generally less well educated and they are less interested in education and social-economic betterment. The "system," here again, perpetuates itself: The child learns the values of the parent and lives them out in his own (disadvantaged) life.

5. The number of school dropouts and cast outs is much above average in disadvantaged populations. Schools are mostly middle-class institutions, and the lower-class or disadvantaged child (these descriptions are often synonymous) is not motivated by the school's offerings; consequently, he drops out or gets "invited out."

6. Unemployment and other economic pressures tend, also, to keep the disadvantaged child "down." He drops out of school, lacks skills, has poor incentive, cannot get or keep jobs, and cannot compete in the marketplace for the better jobs or for those circumstances that would allow him to lift himself out of his disadvantaged status.

Many other points could be added, but the many permutations and combinations of the conditions already cited would cover most issues. The impact of the socially disadvantaged child on the existing school system is only beginning to be clearly perceived and worked on. Perhaps in the future there will be no socially disadvantaged persons but only those with idiosyncrasies and personal handicaps; but until time arrives, we shall be increasingly concerned with the socially disadvantaged and the myriad of subconditions they are subjected to which are inimical to education, growth, self-discipline, and mental health.

SYMPTOMS AND SOLUTIONS OF
SPECIAL EDUCATIONAL PROBLEMS

The range of symptoms of emotional disturbance in handicapped learners among children with superior backgrounds, as well as among the socially disadvantaged, is so great that neither the psychologist nor the teacher can cope with them all. It is often possible, however, to make sense of symptom complexes. The teacher can try to see beyond the particular symptoms and catch a glimpse of what the child is trying to do, what he is saying about himself through his behavior or his attitudes.

Symptoms are only a guide to the presence of problems. For educational purposes, symptoms are not a good basis of classification.

If the teacher is able to see beyond some of the presenting complaints or symptoms and gain a more relevant *understanding* of the child, he can devise new educational practices freely or learn of his own limitations in this respect.

Teachers are too frequently interested in merely finding explanations for the disturbances among exceptional children. The teacher often wants a simple concrete answer like "brain damage," "low intelligence," or "rejection and lack of love from parents." But such answers, even when they are found, usually have little practical classroom usefulness. In this book we ask the teacher not to think in terms of the verbal explanations but in terms of what to do about problems: "All right, if this is the problem, how then do we go about remedying it?" or "Given this explanation, what can the classroom teacher then do to contribute to better classroom living with this child and to better overall achievement?" These questions apply to all clinical and social problems.

It soon becomes obvious to the teacher that many explanations based on symptom complexes lead nowhere. They lead nowhere for classroom purposes, and they lead nowhere in the long-range education of the child. They do not relate very well to observable events nor to actions which the teacher can take to remedy the problems at hand. The teacher should ask himself, the psychologist, or other special education personnel for a plan of action that is feasible and that is calculated to remedy the problem in manageable ways.

The teacher needs feasible suggestions and useful procedures, not merely diagnostic categories or statements about constellations of symptoms.

A common complaint of teachers about school psychologists, psychiatrists, and social workers is that they come, see, interview, and test, but very little happens. Much time and energy are spent in conferences and in collecting information, usually about symptoms and their history, but too little effort is put into practical recommendations for useful teacher action. The teacher is entitled to and should ask for useful information from the school psychologist (or whatever mental hygienist is concerned) so that the teacher can see the relationship between the problem he observes (the symptoms) in the classroom and what specifically can be done to remedy the situation.

SELECTED READINGS

BANK, P., "Behavior therapy with a boy who had never learned to walk." *Psychotherapy*, 1968, *5*, 150–53.

BECKER, W. C., C. H. MADSEN, C. R. ARNOLD, and D. R. THOMAS, "The contingent use of teacher attention and praise in reducing classroom behavior problems." *J. Special Educ.*, 1967, *1*, 287–307.

BICE, H. V., "Some factors that contribute to the concept of self in the child with cerebral palsy." *Ment. Hyg.*, 1954, *38*, 120–31.

BLOOM, BENJAMIN S., ALLISON DAVIS, and ROBERT HELL, *Compensatory Education for Cultural Deprivation*. New York: Holt, Rinehart and Winston, 1965.

CARLIN, S., and E. ARMSTRONG, "Rewarding social responsibility in disturbed children: A group play technique." *Psychotherapy*, 1968, *5*, 169 74.

CONANT, JAMES B., *Slums and Suburbs*. New York: McGraw-Hill, 1961.

CRUICKSHANK, W. M., and G. O. JOHNSON, *Education of Exceptional Children and Youth*, and ed. Englewood Cliffs, N.J.: Prentice-Hall, 1958.

GELFAND, D. M., and D. P. HARTMAN, "Behavior therapy with children: A review and evaluation of research methodology." *Psychol. Bulletin*, 1968, *69*, 204–15.

GOLDIAMOND, I., "Self-control procedures in personal behavior problems." *Psychol. Reports*, 1965, *17*, 851–68.

HARING, NORRIS G., and E. LAKIN PHILLIPS, *Educating Emotionally Disturbed Children*. New York: McGraw-Hill, 1962.

KRUMBOLTZ, J. D., "Behavioral counseling: Rationale and research." *Personnel and Guidance J.*, 1965, *44*, 383–87.

KVARACEUS, WILLIAM C., JOHN S. GIBSON, and THOMAS J. CURTIN, eds., *Poverty, Education, and Race Relations*. Boston: Allyn and Bacon, 1967.

MALPASS, L. F., "Some relationships between students' perceptions of school and their achievement." *J. Educ. Psychol.*, 1953, *44*, 475–82.

MILLER, HARRY L., ed., *Education for the Disadvantaged*. New York: The Free Press, 1967.

PHILLIPS, E. LAKIN, DANIEL N. WIENER, and NORRIS G. HARING, *Discipline, Achievement and Mental Health*. Englewood Cliffs, N.J.: Prentice-Hall, 1960.

RIESSMAN, FRANK, *The Culturally Deprived Child*. New York: Harper and Row, 1962.

ROBERTS, JEAN I., *School Children in the Urban Slum*. New York: The Free Press, 1967.

SOLOMON, J. C., "Neuroses of school teachers." *Ment. Hyg.*, 1960, *44*, 79–90.

11

IMPROVING
HOME-SCHOOL
RELATIONSHIPS

A discussion of the lives of children in school is never complete without reference to the home and its relationship to the goals of classroom discipline, achievement, and mental health. Many facets of home and school relations could be discussed. We propose to deal only with the same problems as in our prior chapters, those relating to discipline, to achievement, and to the general well-being of the child, and we shall suggest ways of coordinating and utilizing effectively the interaction of the home and school in these areas. To benefit the child is our purpose always, rather than to benefit the school or the parents. Eliminated from this discussion are serious problems of physical or psychological well-being—the kinds of problems that would put children in hospitals or treatment centers. We shall focus entirely on the great variety of problems inherent in the interaction between the school and the home.

The community is a conglomerate of homes, and home-school relationships become institutionalized or patterned through community action and attitudes; they also reflect these actions and attitudes. School-community relationships and school-home relationships therefore will be discussed in ways indicating how parents and school personnel can improve the training of their children.

THE MAJOR PROBLEMS

Some parents feel that schools try to do too many things and end up doing none of them well. The school spreads itself too thin over a vast terrain, they believe, which results in a diffused purpose and weakened direction. Other parents think that the school does not do enough. They think that the school ought to take over more of the home's responsibilities, since they, as parents, are either unsure of their duties or feel that the school can perform them better.

There is, perhaps, the larger middle ground of parents who more or less go along with present school policies either indifferently, or feeling that the school functions fairly well. From this large majority of parents the school receives very little criticism, not much interest, and very few suggestions for change.

Schools feel conflicting pressures from parents, particularly the more extreme groups, and may spend themselves trying to please too many small groups or to fend off too many foes at the expense of primary objectives. Schools may constrict their outlook; they may reduce their resources severely and thereby fail to offer much needed help to parents of children needing special consideration. It is as if, feeling too much pressure from all sides, school administrators sometimes try to withdraw from leadership. This procedure might momentarily protect the school from criticism, but it is a negative move, which in the long run cannot improve school-home relations or the education of the children any more than a person's withdrawal from society can, in the long run, solve his social problems. On the other hand, the school that throws itself into an extreme expansion of activities can be wasteful in its efforts to handle the most basic and important educational objectives.

Two major problems are most likely to bring parents to school or the school to the parents: One is the misbehavior or other personality problem of a youngster, and this as we know is not an uncommon cause of difficulty; the second is inadequate educational progress by the child. How, then, can home-school relations be improved to help the child the most in these regards?

THE NEED TO WORK WITH PARENTS

The need to work with parents is usually considered fundamental in improving the child's classroom behavior. Parents vary widely in their degree of insight, intelligence, motivation, and cooperativeness, but they have far more immediate, continuous impact on the child's life than anyone else. They cannot be ignored in the effective solution of school problems anymore than in the basic understanding of such problems.

In the long run it is the parent who bears the legal, moral, and social responsibility for the child. In the long run it is the school that has to educate the child. Getting parents and school together is vital to efficient education.

On the whole we have found parents to be reasonable and effective assistants to the teacher in solving classroom problems, just as psychotherapists usually find parents essential participants in the treatment process. Generally, also we have found school personnel interested in the child and attempting to do what they think is conducive to solving his problems within the context of the classroom.

There are exceptions, of course, to both these generalizations. There are situations where parents are themselves so disturbed and disturbing as to require more help than the child, and there are instances where the teacher simply will not or cannot expend the time or energy necessary to enlist effective aid from parents. But these seem to be exceptions to the general rule that parents can readily and effectively be enlisted to complement the efforts of the teacher and vice versa in the ways we will now suggest, if both of them understand their roles, and there is some direction for coordinated effort.

SOME TECHNIQUES OF COOPERATION WITH THE HOME

In the case of a youngster lagging in achievement, when the school is reasonably sure the child has the capacity to achieve better, the teacher can consider some of the following actions:

1. Suggest and provide to the parent a series of homework assignments which a parent can supervise. The parent should see that the child does the assigned work and returns it to school according to a previously agreed-upon schedule.
2. Help the parent set aside a time and place for *daily* study, protecting the child in question from siblings and peers inside and outside the home and from other distractions, such as television and conversation.
3. Set up a program of reporting to the parent every week or two about the child's classroom progress. This report informs the parents how the child is progressing in school; through (1), above, they can already see how he is doing with his homework.
4. Bearing in mind the objectives discussed earlier (Chapters 3 and 4), set up working conditions and general educational expectations as specifically and realistically as possible for the child to follow at school and home.
5. Obtain as much agreement as possible from the parent on how to handle specific situations so that the child encounters the same general approach at school and at home. For example, both teacher and parent might refrain from coaxing or threatening the dawdling child. They might, as discussed previously, simply set the task and keep the child at it for a reasonable period of time. They should then avoid tiring the child by

very long study sessions or getting after him. The child who has not completed his work in the prescribed time can be let off for a while but be sent back after a respite.

6. Avoid criticizing or labeling the child as "hopeless" or a "nuisance" because he should have achieved more or gained better study habits earlier in his school career. If a child is indeed hopeless with respect to a given level of work, then this should be properly recognized and treated, probably by placing him in a lower grade or in a special class, providing tutoring, or giving him a special set of assignments over a substantial period of time. If, on the other hand, the child has simply accumulated bad study habits, which seems to have occurred in a very high percentage of cases, then the above suggestions apply. If the child is simply a nuisance in class, there is no better way to correct this than by structuring active problem-solving procedures such as those already suggested. The negative aspects of the problem can thus be minimized and the issues can be placed on a positive, on-going basis.

To the principal, we suggest administering standardized achievement tests as well as obtaining objective evidence of the child's progress so that any bias on the part of the teacher toward a given child or any refusal of the child to work adequately for a given teacher can be minimized and adjusted.

If a further step needs to be taken beyond enlisting the help of the teacher and the principal, the school psychologist may be called in to make additional observations and recommendations and to help assess the child's progress over a period of time. The emphasis here should be on "over a period of time," in order that momentary expedient decisions do not impair a long-term overall program for the child.

These measures should suffice to start a program of active remedial work, whether such work centers on behavior or on achievement problems in a child. If these particular measures do not suffice, then the school may have to resort to more comprehensive measures. The decision to resort to other methods, however, should not be made lightly, and only after careful consideration has been given to the more direct efforts just discussed.

WHEN AND HOW TO INITIATE CHANGE

Teachers often are too beset by the educational and achievement problems of their students to be able to readily put the above suggestions into effective action for individuals. They may need help. Reducing the size of the class, or engaging part-time assistance can be helpful measures. Even if they get such help, however, the problems of the nonachieving child are not automatically solved; teachers simply have better opportunities to work on the problems more effectively over time.

Overwhelmed with work, teachers sometimes become annoyed with parents who come to school for help with their children. One parent reported to us the following incident.

"When Kenneth, my ninth-grader, got low marks at the end of the first six weeks, I went to school to talk with the counselor," the mother reported. She went on to quote the counselor as saying, "We are a big school, and we cannot take the time to teach your son how to study; he should have learned this before or else he should not have come here to school."

We recognize that the school has an enormous number of students with problems and that to give special consideration to any one of them may be unfair to other individuals or to necessary activities, but is it not the attitude of resignation or blaming, in part, which permitted this ninth-grader to continue to remain on dead center? Is not the counselor in this case—justified though he may be from the standpoint of early causes and his own current workload in the school—passing the buck to other counselors and teachers to come later, the way it has been passed on to him many times before? Where does this round robin stop? *Where can change begin?* Is it already too late *whenever* the problem is observed? Obviously the point of view in this book is that it is not too late, that the time to solve a problem always is *now*, that there are always, continuously throughout life, new opportunities to solve educational and behavior problems.

THE SCHOOL'S ROLE

Even with more efficient teaching methods similar to those suggested, there needs to be a time of reckoning, every second or third year perhaps, in the school life of the average child. A time of reckoning every year would be even more desirable. At such times, a complete evaluation and perhaps overhauling of the child's school program would be considered. This procedure would bring up a consideration of more efficient teaching methods, and it could early intercept those cases of educational deficiency which might otherwise be overlooked until becoming more acute. As pressure intensifies for an improved quality of education, along with massive, worldwide increases in the numbers of students, methods of teaching will have to be made more efficient. This requires not only a positive thrust to be more concerted and effective but the capacity to compensate for any deficits in the child's school career.

Educators say that if parents become more interested in the school, its purposes and possibilities, the school will be forced to carry a greater responsibility. The professional educator will need to develop more resources to deal with common educational problems and will have to train the classroom teacher to use them. And the latter will need to become more of an expert in dealing with the average parent, in providing remedial measures —or better—in preventing the need for so much remedial work. Acting as interpreters or expert go-betweens for classroom teachers and parents, school psychologists and counselors will also have to improve in these necessary skills.

WAYS IN WHICH FRICTION AND COOPERATION MAY DEVELOP

Parents also come to school to discuss childhood behavior or personality problems with the teacher or other school authorities even when no extremely pressing problem exists. Any experienced teacher knows that these discussions can sometimes provide very constructive direction for both the teacher and the parent, but sometimes they may also flare up into emotional scenes where feelings are hurt and no good results for the child.

The parent may feel accused in adverse interactions between parent and school; the teacher may feel unfairly burdened by a difficult child or a difficult parent. If the parents feel blamed, they may lack the courage or the objectivity to rise above the immediate emotions involved and may set forth on a plan to remedy the problems of the child's conduct at home. School personnel may take a similar attitude, leading to resignation on their part.

To the parent, the school may seem to say, "Here is your child, what are *you* going to do about his behavior?" The parent, on the other hand, may think, "He doesn't cause this trouble at home; there must be something wrong with the school or the teacher." How are such dilemmas to be resolved?

In the first place a cool objective review of the problems at hand is sorely needed. Blaming, accusing, withdrawing, and similar defensive reactions, or waiting for the other party to make the first or only move results in more conflict and little or no problem solving. The child is the loser in such an impasse.

A COOPERATIVE SOLUTION

How, then, can cooperative solutions aimed at resolving the kind of impasse cited above be developed?

Charles was an only child, age nine, in the fourth grade. He acted "silly" at school, refused to do his work in class, tried to entertain others by making faces and doing other distracting things. His teacher corrected him time after time, kept him after school, moved his seat about in the classroom, and in desperation, appealed to the principal for help. As part of this appeal the parents were called in. They felt that Charles was being misunderstood at school; he was "no problem" in obeying them or in performing his daily routine at home. The parents felt accused of sending to school a poorly trained child, and they felt that the teacher was prejudiced against their son or simply wanted to get rid of him. The conference between parent and teacher, with the principal sitting in, turned out to be largely unproductive. Parents and teacher went away feeling resentful of the attitude of the other. The child was buffeted about, with no one seeing the problem in a clear way or suggesting any actions toward a solution. The principal acted more as a referee for the parent-teacher conference, also feeling caught between contestants and unable to do more than to try to placate one or the other party to the dispute.

When this case came to our attention, it had been going on in this manner for longer than one school year. It is very difficult to enter into a clash with such a degree of intensity between parents and teacher and obtain the full cooperation of each. But something had to be done; matters were worsening. Possible solutions such as transferring the child to another teacher within the same school or to another school were turned down by the principal. The principal thought that if this child were transferred, it would open the flood gates for requests from other parents and that it would be difficult if not impossible to draw a line between real hardship cases and parental or teacher whims or prejudices. Some solution evidentally had to be arrived at within the confines of the present teacher and classroom arrangement if at all possible.

It was determined in short order that the parents *did* have trouble with Charles at home. They felt free to admit and discuss this with an outsider, whereas they had insisted otherwise with the teacher and principal, whom they viewed as opponents. Once admitting their problem at home, they were free to start to work on it. The interviews revealed that Charles was indeed a "spoiled" youngster. He carried with him to school expectations for individual attention and privileges which could not be granted by any teacher with a classroom full of youngsters. Nonetheless, Charles kept demanding. This constituted part of the problem.

In time through the consultation they agreed to receive, the parents set up more objective ways of dealing with Charles at home. They saw to it that he had daily chores to perform, obligations to meet, times set aside for study, with free play and television as reinforcement for good work. They kept him to these schedules, not letting him determine his own course completely for himself nor dominate them as he had been doing before.

An agreement was reached, with the school psychologist acting as intermediary between home and school, on how to handle Charles's misconduct at school. Charles was to be given one warning by the teacher; if he continued to misbehave, his mother was to be called to school to take him home for the rest of the school day. The parents agreed to this, and the entire program was sanctioned by the principal, with all the details worked out to suit the situation. When, because of his misbehavior, his mother took Charles home, she agreed that he should not be allowed to play outside throughout the rest of the time encompassing the school day, he was to study and to complete the work he would have been doing at school.

As is usually the case, unless the child is extremely disturbed or unless the adults concerned do not fully cooperate, Charles began to straighten out at school after two such episodes of being sent home. As he progressed in doing his assignments at school and behaving better, he also improved the quality of work and gradually became more accepted by his peers and by the teacher. He no longer felt "tightened up" and he got over the need to "act up" to get attention. Students and teachers quit considering him a troublemaker, and he came to appreciate their respect and friendship more than their attention. And with the progress on Charles's part, the teacher lost her concern with him as an errant student.

What happened to the original problem? Who was right, the school or the home? Neither of these questions is useful except to delineate what happened to Charles. His behavior improved because of a better structured set of expectations put to him at school and at home in consistent, firm, and fair ways in which he could tell just where he stood and what the consequences of various actions would be. He learned to distinguish between the rewards he preferred, and how to obtain them, and the momentary satisfaction he got by drawing attention to himself through misbehavior. He was able to choose clearly and to develop habits that brought him to greater maturity.

Most home-school behavior problems can be treated in this manner. Most of the strong emotional charges between home and school can be avoided in relatively simple ways, usually by assuming that a lack of structure gives rise to the problems and that a firmer delineation of alternative behavior and rewards is needed to overcome them. Otherwise, home and school may stand pat on their separate *misconceptions*; each can blame the other and maintain fixed and incompatible positions, which lead to no problem solutions whatsoever.

SCHOOL PROCEDURES
FOR IMPROVING HOME-SCHOOL RELATIONS

What are some general procedures the school can follow in most instances which require home-school cooperation?

1. Call in an outsider, a school psychologist, child psychologist, or visiting teacher, for example, who can see objectively past the immediate concerns of the school and the parents. This should be done with the parents' permission.

2. Try to get from the outside consultant a clear statement of what is wrong in the parent-child relationship and the teacher-child relationship.

3. Gain agreement between home and school for a set of expectations to be put to the child. It is not efficient to correct matters one place and, carelessly, to leave them alone in the other.

4. Work out a program of homework and a method of controlling disciplinary infractions, with both teacher and parent participating. It is likely that the schoolwork will not improve much until the misconduct is corrected. The child often misbehaves in lieu of doing schoolwork. When the behavior is brought under better control, then the way is paved for a gradual improvement in schoolwork.

5. Recognize and let the parents know that measurable improvement for such children often takes from a semester to a full year, as far as the academic work is concerned. One conference or one session with the psychologist is usually only a starter; persistent and diligent supervision is unnecessary.

6. Try to develop objective ways of viewing each child. Try to see the child's shortcomings in clear but conditional and restricted terms and try not to let the picture of his difficulty override consideration of his otherwise good features. Seek out constructive behavior and encourage it.

7. Avoid quibbling sessions or discussing who is to blame, who started what, and other vague and aimless considerations. What can be done now in the classroom to improve the child's situation becomes the important question. And what actions can be suggested to the parents which will complement classroom measures? The parents' attitudes and behavior should be ascertained and handled.

8. Gather as much valid and relevant information about the child as applies to the current situation. Observations on the child's behavior, present and past grades, and test results are necessary to provide the basis for a remedial program.

9. Have some home-school agreement on short-term objectives and when to reinforce these objectives.

WHAT THE SCHOOL ADMINISTRATION CAN DO

From our observations of and dealings with children having behavioral and achievement problems in school, we believe the school should try to become more flexible in arriving at solutions.

Responsibility for practices listed below resides mainly with the policy makers—principal, superintendent, or school board—but all parts of the educational system can contribute to the following improvements in administrative attitudes and practices.

1. Greater willingness to transfer students from one teacher or school to another. Greater flexibility in this matter will not necessarily lead to a flood of requests from parents, at the slightest provocation, if specific principles are established and maintained. To be rigidly against the transfer of students for any reason is to pass over a useful solution to some of the problems of misconduct and poor achievement. The point is that the transfer should come *before* those involved reach a state of exhaustion so that the transfer can be built on positive possibilities rather than on merely getting out of negative situations.

2. Increased appreciation of emotional problems as intimately related to achievement problems and vice versa in order to arrive at the kind of concrete, direct, feasible solutions within the classroom which have been previously discussed. This often provides an alternative to sending the not grossly disturbed child and his parents into various kinds of individual and group therapy in the hope of somehow indirectly providing a solution to problems the teacher faces in the classroom daily. The solution to many of the school's presently unsolved problems need not require the help of outside professionals.

3. Less reluctance on the part of teachers and school authorities to act on problems *as they see them arising.* The quicker the action on the school's part, the more easily school and parents can solve their problems; to let problems drag on month after month with warning after warning too often serves to encrust the problem rather than to develop alternative solutions. This suggestion requires that the school's reactions will be well-timed, reasonable, and objectively implemented.

4. Recognition that a good system of feedback of information to the parents is strongly desirable. Channels of communication must be kept open; otherwise, normally good efforts may be ineffectual because of misunderstanding. It should be constantly remembered that the parents need to know as much as the school about how the new efforts are working.

5. Provision for a system of "make up" work and times for this work so that teachers, children, and parents alike take the daily obligations of the child seriously. Letting this matter slip by can easily produce poor structure in the school-child relationship. It is primarily up to the school to provide these make up times rather than merely to dismiss unfinished or otherwise unsatisfactory work or to "average it in" when the final grade is given or to penalize the child for noncompliance.

6. Greater willingness to employ or to recommend the use of tutors, assistant teachers, and other in-school and out-of-school specialists. A problem with the child's behavior or achievement requiring outside help does not necessarily reflect adversely on the school. Better to admit the problem and shortcomings in dealing with them than to stand on any formality that provides no solutions. This is a complementary view to that of referring too readily to outside help, particularly to outside help for therapy or handling emotional difficulties.

7. Increased effort to continue to work with the parents. Sometimes parents harbor prejudiced attitudes, but it is better not to make such an assumption until there has been a discussion with them. In a difference of opinion

with parents, even if the school or the teacher is correct, if the latter maintains an unyielding attitude, a constructive solution will not be worked out.

METHODS OF EFFECTIVE COMMUNICATION WITH THE HOME

We wish to simplify here the problems of communicating clearly to the parents the child's educational status. Communication with parents is one of the most important problems in the child's school life. Failure to report properly is the source of much misunderstanding and difficulty. It results in an enormous loss of efficiency in education and can indirectly contribute to poor attitudes and poor mental health in the student.

As previously discussed, a few teachers use the report card, given at six- or nine-week intervals as a punitive measure. They place too much corrective burden on the report card and overlook the daily opportunities for better communication directed at helping the child on a more continuous basis. To young children especially, the occasional report card is simply too remote to have specific application or usefulness for the day-to-day events of studying, achieving, and developing good attitudes. Throughout this book, the great importance of *immediate* reinforcement or correction of the child's effort is stressed. The teacher needs to do more than *present* learning materials or report on the child's progress. It is equally if not more important that a *constant feedback system* operate to give guidance to the student and his parents as well as to his teacher on how he is progressing.

Very often school procedures seem to assume that a failure will stir the child to greater effort. However, failing grades at the end of the six weeks, the semester, or the year is more likely to be a source of further confusion than a source of enlightenment and change. Failure at the end of the term or the end of the school year is an even more inefficient form of appraisal and correction than is the six- or nine-week report card. Failing and having to repeat a grade is not only discouraging to the child and his parents but is an expensive and very inefficient way to remedy educational or attitudinal problems. Failing a child one grade, when an alternative approach is possible, costs the child's parents and society in general an additional 8 percent outlay for his entire education, based on his completing twelve grades. This is an enormous expense to have to pay for failure. The money would be much better spent for attaining better study habits, better achievement, and better mental health.

"Social" promotion for the child, based on his age alone, is a waste of a different kind. It is a way of closing one's eyes to the facts of achievement and merely passing the child along without coming to grips with the problems of discipline, achievement, and attitude involved. What is needed instead are more efficient forms of teaching during the many days the teacher and student face together.

The teacher or principal may not have much time to give to the balky student; this must be taken into account. No more time need be spent with the underachiever in the long run, however, than is *already being spent uselessly*. What is suggested are more efficient procedures so that *less time* actually has to be spent overall and so that other wastes of time (failing the child, for example, for a whole year) can be avoided in many cases.

On the positive side, a more intense and more deliberate followthrough and feedback with parents on the small and manageable daily efforts of the balky child is recommended so that he can again resume his ordinary place in the classroom and thereby save everyone's time. To increase the effectiveness of education may require greater immediate effort, but future economies will be more than compensatory.

An individual conference with the parents or even a series of conferences will accomplish little or nothing if no solutions are proposed. Frequently conferences without clear purposes are held, which are not planned for, nor produce corrective action.

Rather than an hour or several hours of conference with parents, under the pressure of acute problems, would not several well-spaced 15- or 20-minute phone conversations or brief afterschool meetings be better as problems were developing? The brief conferences could acquaint parents with the problems and various possible solutions to be tried.

Many home and school problems arise when the school, with the good intention of posing a problem about the child's achievement or conduct, is unable to follow through and suggest workable solutions during the process of the school term. *We recommend, then, that along with any report of failure or troubles that the school makes to parents, it also prepare a workable, corrective plan and be ready to show the parents how to assist the school in putting the plan into operation.*

In summary, let us try to take some of the mystery out of the child's school problems; let us learn to look more directly at the ways in which the child is using and perpetuating misconduct or underachievement; let us try to develop and apply ways to modify these problems, using all available resources in addition to those of the classroom, especially the home. As we educators develop our understanding and skills, we can improve relationships with the home and develop ways of improving its contribution to effective education.

PROBLEMS IN SCHOOL-COMMUNITY RELATIONS

As one of the most important, conspicuous, and locally controlled institutions in our society, the school often receives the brunt of criticism from anyone dissatisfied in any way with life around him. Not only do parents converge on teachers and principals but various members of our society from time to time try to take a hand at rectifying the school's ills by recommending a sweeping return to the "good old days."

Such proposals, often made in good faith, usually reflect a lack of appreciation of modern education and the demands of modern living. The school administration must often say, "Thank you for your interest; we will take your proposal under consideration." However, if the school administration were forced to consider seriously, much less to follow, all the schemes presented by poorly informed persons, it would never get around to doing the job the critics are hoping to improve: educating children.

It is not our purpose to discuss school administration extensively, however. Rather our concern is with how we can contribute to critical thinking and constructive action between school personnel and the community with respect to discipline, achievement, and the fostering of mental health.

Schools often appear, rightly or wrongly, not to teach the three R's as well as they might. Perhaps the most common public criticism is of "frills" and the neglect of "fundamentals" by the school. The critics do not usually know about the results of standardized tests, comparing the general knowledge and achievement of children today with those of 20 or 30 years ago. They do not stop to consider that because of public demand the average school today serves many more children in many more ways than was true a generation ago. Rather than debate such issues, however, we wish to consider ways to direct school-community relationships toward producing better students.

METHODS OF PROMOTING CLOSER SCHOOL-COMMUNITY TIES

Many schools are expanding their educational facilities and increasing their ability to challenge students by adding special classes in such subjects as foreign languages, science, and the creative arts, and by bringing in, as part-time teachers, well-trained and interested local persons who are specialists in their fields. This procedure provides a means simultaneously of enriching the curriculum of the school and of enlisting community support. As the community plays a more active role in the school's offerings, both school and community gain in appreciation of the other.

Students often hold yearly exhibits in public places. These shows, while they may not represent the activities of the average or typical student, do tend to illustrate what the school can and does do to stimulate able students. For example, science fairs, art exhibits, special athletic exhibitions (other than the common competitive sports), and music festivals show the public what the students are learning, capitalizing on a wide range of talents and interests, yet not neglecting fundamental learning.

Some schools are not only emphasizing "letters" for music, art, debating, and handicraft work (similar to the letters given for athletic skills) but are also extending this practice to superior scholarship. The student, simply as the student, is coming more into his own right. As the school enhances its function as an institution of learning, the community is likely to view it more in this way and be willing to support it better for its primary function.

Some schools hold an annual Education-Business Day. When teachers and businessmen visit each other's institutions, better mutual understanding and respect results. This could serve as a prototype for communication links with other important community groups such as labor, veterans, social agencies, and youth organizations. Such activities should not be permitted to detract significantly from teaching time, but neither can the school stand aloof from its basis of community support, except at a high price.

Perhaps schoolteachers and principals could become better persuaders. Perhaps they are too reluctant to enter into the competition of public interest and funds. Perhaps they could utilize more effectively some earnest and forthright presentations of the assets of their schools by using financial or social contributions, for example, to support their case.

People who complete more years of schooling tend on the average to earn more money. This does not say, of course, that they are happier, or more productive, or they can earn more money *because* they are better educated (both may be a function of higher intelligence or better socio-economic opportunities). But chances are that they have a better opportunity to gain greater personal satisfaction and to contribute more to community welfare, in part, at least because of their better education.

Interest in the dropout problem is increasing, and the relationship between earning power of people who have finished the eighth grade, tenth grade, twelfth grade, or have had a college education is often publicized. As one goes up the educational ladder his productivity, earning power, community resourcefulness, and satisfaction in using himself well appear to increase. Perhaps this vital factor is not stressed frequently enough by the school in its efforts to gain public support.

Schools could also keep a roster of their graduates (especially high school graduates) who have gone on to successful university, professional, business, artistic, athletic, skilled trade, service, and other careers. They could anchor their own current school programs to the factors in the programs that their outstanding graduates in all fields report as most valuable.

An offensive, rather than defensive, stance could tremendously improve the school's standing with the community. The importance of this lies in the fact that the status of the school in the community determines the resources made available to it. If these resources are minimal or substandard (as they often are), then the problems of achievement, discipline, and mental health of the school-aged child are sadly neglected. If these problems are neglected, critics can then point to the school's "poor products" as a reason for less, not more, support. The public's attitude sometimes then is, "Why give them more support when they do not produce?" Thus a vicious circle of too little support—poor resources—poor education—meager products—still less support—is set up, and each successive step in the circle is used to justify the previous one and the following one. Rather, there could be a more open, positive, enlarging circle: good resources—good school products—good reports to the community on the school's accomplishments —supporting these results through community action—leading to community support for the school—leading to better school products.

School people could point an accusing finger at the community when the school is criticized and say, "You get just what you pay for," or "You can blame yourselves because you are not giving us the resources to do a good job." While such a reply is frequently true, like many other arguments it has no corrective value and is ineffectual for solving the problem. Such a criticism directed back at society offers no concrete way to change the school's circumstances. The school and the community each would be waiting for the other to make the first move. Like many parent-child, and teacher-home impasses, no one would profit from the wait or from further arguments.

Whether we are speaking of changing small standoffs between students and teachers or larger ones between the school and the community, there is no merit in trying to stand on "righteous" grounds. This is no way to solve an on-going problem. What must be asked, rather, is what can be done? What are constructive, active ways of gaining more public support on the basis of the merit the school now possesses or could possess? One must always *begin* with the resources at hand. One cannot start with speculations and ask for others to react to the school system differently. One needs to determine—and try out—ways to move the public to greater rapport with the schools.

Many specialists in child psychology and education feel that if classroom size alone could be reduced by, say, 50 percent, the number of disciplinary and related problems would diminish proportionately. This may be true, but it is not a basis for general action here and now. It can be a basis for *limited* action here and now. It is a basis for setting up some classes with reduced enrollment and with especially disturbed children or with slow or inefficient learners, which might demonstrate over a period of time that the smaller class could accomplish more for the education of the children concerned. But the financial resources are simply nowhere in sight for even considering this as a general solution to classroom problems—any more than individual therapy is a feasible solution for all children with problems and all parents with problem children.

As educators we need to become better strategists and persuaders in order to convince the public of those contributions in our daily practice of which we are relatively certain, which we often suppose to be more widely understood than, in fact, they are.

One new development contributing to better strategies for parents and community stems from the formation of parent groups of many kinds over the country. We speak here of parent groups formed not to solve some already existing crises but formed to do *preventive* work. An example is parent groups that have set "conduct standards" for junior and senior high school students to deal with difficulties touching all parents (and indirectly all schools) : Number of nights out per week; nature and control of social group functions (dances, parties) held on school premises; conduct and safety matters where youth drive cars to school; patrolling for safety and cleanliness in neighborhoods near schools; the use of teachers and parents as monitors for nighttime group activities at school; handling problems relating to use of cigarettes, alcohol and drugs in school and at school functions; the relationship between school youth and nearby business areas; the problem of leaving school premises during the daytime school hours; holding night classes for dropouts; the use of local business, professional, and skilled tradespeople to train and employ on a part-time basis youth in school (not just handicapped youth) as part of their educational-vocational preparation; and dozens of other similar problems. The most significant goal here is that parents and other adults begin to realize that their roles vis-à-vis the school (whether they have children currently enrolled or not) are not merely as stop-gappers or critics but integral to the *normal* functioning of the school as part of the whole community. This set of constructive attitudes keeps the school from standing apart from the community and builds, alternatively, many ways in which the school and the community stand together.

PROMOTING A VITAL COMMUNITY INTEREST IN EDUCATION

In recent years, one of the reasons for the success of new programs which deal with various types of handicapped adults stems directly from analyzing and publicizing the dollars and cents involved. The slogan "It pays to hire the handicapped" is a very good example. It is really cheaper for society to reeducate, retrain, and reemploy handicapped people than it is to leave them alone to drift. While it may be unfortunate that support for any human welfare project has to be put on a financial basis, once this has been done and the program is demonstrated to be economically worthwhile, many other human welfare goals can be brought in more successfully. But trying to retrain handicapped people just because it is humanitarian seems seldom to get the program off the ground. This is unfortunately the way society has thought and acted for many centuries. And it is only recently through this new approach that the assault against the prejudice and indifference toward handicapped people has succeeded massively.

There are thousands of worthwhile causes needing support; how can one choose among them? What criteria can be developed to distribute financial and professional resources and energies satisfactorily? In our society, a major answer must involve return for money spent. As educators, with an inclination to stress human welfare values, we often overlook the practical side of the matter. We simply have to look at financial costs and do our best to relate them to our human welfare concepts.

American society was badly shaken when the Russian sputnik was sent aloft in October of 1957. This did more to alert the American public in general and educators in particular to the importance of education than anything written by any educator since the beginning of this century. Is this not a lesson in itself? Is not our guide, more often and more clearly than we are willing to admit, the more practical issues of our society? Educators need to hook on to these practical channels; they must foster their aims and the aims of education by such an alliance. Such channels can be ignored only at the cost of neglect to important educational programs.

Necessity may not have to be urgent to mother invention, but it must be felt to some degree. Perhaps man simply does not proceed ordinarily to try to solve his social problems until some stark reality strikes his awareness. The educator should take pause here to realize that his emphasis on "reason" and the cultural value of educating children simply lacks power with adults. Most adults do not do things for reason alone; they do them out of financial pressures, social pressures and what might be called selfish personal considerations. Perhaps one could argue that we have better schools, better curriculum development, and improved equipment, as a result of the consequences of sputnik, and that we shall have to improve further in the areas of environmental pollution control, safety on our roads, and other urgent issues for improved quality in life. As educators, we should ever keep this in mind. A mere bit of dramatic evidence bearing an economic or health security advantage can be worth more to our cause than all of us together writing or speaking. If we can manage to put such timely lessons into operation in the daily work of communicating to the community, we can probably reap a rich harvest in community support for our schools and children.

What are some of the issues that educators might consider worthwhile if they could tap the community's shoulder and get the attention and support they need? Certainly there should be much more money for the average child in the average school, reducing the pupil-teacher load and seeing that auxiliary services are initiated and thereafter supported. Secondly, considerably more services are needed for all types of handicapped children. This would take the form of smaller teacher-pupil ratios and more auxiliary personnel such as speech therapists, psychologists, and physical education instructors. A third great need is for more equipment and for plants and buildings suitable for all kinds of special education needs. A fourth type of activity that could be developed out of better school-community understanding would be research on all kinds of problems relating to education. We tend to fly blindly a great deal of the time in educating handicapped children. We need a kind of cost accounting to provide proof of the effectiveness of selective efforts with these children. One child who is placed in a gainful occupation is worth thousands of dollars to society and to himself, not to mention the fact that if he were not independent financially and vocationally, he would be a continuous drain on society, as well as a dissatisfied, deteriorating human being.

ROLE OF THE SPECIALIST IN THE COMMUNITY

In all urban areas and in an increasing number of consolidated suburban-rural systems, the classroom teacher must work with specialists outside the school. Within most modern schools these outside specialists are an integral part of the effective school administration. There are, for instance, reading experts and speech teachers, whom the classroom teacher can and should call upon freely for help. Special services of the school itself are usually so much in demand that neither the specialist nor the classroom teacher has time to serve adequately all who need help. Almost every teacher will sooner or later have to talk with psychologists, speech consultants, tutors, and others from outside the school system about one or more students.

Not all outside specialists, however, can find the time or will want to consult with the classroom teacher. Many outside specialists (such as the pediatrician, family physician, the local minister, psychiatrist) turn away from education or feel that education is purely a matter for parents and the school and does not involve them. This is not to accuse any professional group of lack of cooperation with parents and school but to indicate that the school and the parents themselves have probably not fostered the kind of relationship with community specialists which they might have cultivated, and the outside professional is simply not inclined to take the initiative.

The modern trend, however, is for the specialist to consult with school personnel, especially with classroom teachers and principals. This trend is very noticeable in urban areas and is beginning in semiurban and rural areas, with weekly or by-monthly visits of various kinds of therapists and mental health experts to rural or consolidated schools. The child's school environment can be more fully understood and brought under effective direction if those dealing with the child knew firsthand about his school life. The movement today is certainly toward having specialists acquaint themselves with the child's problems *in the school setting*.

PSYCHOLOGISTS, PSYCHIATRISTS, AND PEDIATRICIANS

The *psychologist* is a specialist in child development, in tests and measurements, and in learning, personality development, and other behavioral problems related to education. The psychologist who specializes in work with school-age children almost always has education and experience in a broad range of child development and education. He is also likely to be professionally prepared to do individual or group counseling with children and to consult with parents. These services may come within the purview of the psychologist attached to the school system. Usually, however, the school psychologist does not have the time for many individual or specialized functions, and the psychologist in private or group practice outside the school system can be utilized.

Teachers may, therefore, receive calls from or make calls to psychologists in private practice; counselors, classroom teachers, or principals may refer children or parents to such psychologists. Psychologists may come to the school to give lectures, hold conferences on general topics concerning child development, or consult with school personnel on behalf of a given child. In some cases the psychologist in private practice or one available at a public clinic may briefly study children who are problems in school and consult both with parents and school personnel about the child. Through arrangements with PTA or with other groups they may also help plan, organize, or conduct special classes for the mentally retarded, emotionally disturbed, the blind, or the deaf. Or parents may consult them on their own on behalf of a given child. The psychologist may then, as part of his service to the child and the family, get in touch with the school in order to help the child as much as he can. This is a cooperative effort and not a matter of the psychologist telling schools or parents what to do.

Psychologists are generally oriented very strongly toward research. They may do a variety of testing, interviewing, or developmental studies on children, which bring them into contact with the classroom teacher. Sometimes these research studies have implications for the education of special groups; sometimes the findings apply generally to all children (like the development of intelligence tests and personality or achievement tests).

The psychologist with research interests may have only a secondary interest in the individual child and his problems and may not have the skill and training to help with emotional, conduct, or achievement problems. Most psychologists who work with children will, however, have a major interest in the individual child and will have much to offer in the way of specific help.

The psychologist's role has begun to change in recent years. He is less a person who is merely a "tester" and more a professional who can give high level consultation in classroom management to parents, teacher, principals, and other school personnel. It is a more efficient use of the psychologist's time to call him to a particular school or classroom for the purposes of observing a child, doing some testing, or consulting with the teacher or the parents, and perhaps repeating these visits over a period of time, all to improve the child's achievement in school. The psychologist who merely tests and then files a written report, leaving its interpretation and all the other judgments and decisions to chance or, perhaps, biases which he has not been able to influence, has a very weak, inefficient, and wasteful role.

In effect, the psychologist can be the behavioral expert, the kind of person who can help to develop a broad change plan, such as we have discussed in a previous chapter. The school psychologist can help the teacher and the principal to formulate the broad kind of plans that will be very useful, not only to the school at large, but to each individual child as well.

The *psychiatrist* is a specialist in mental health with training in medicine and in the treatment of mental illness. Traditionally the psychiatrist has been concerned mainly with the more serious types of mental disturbance and has not been prepared generally to deal with the everyday problems of the relatively normal child in the classroom. Some individual practitioners, however, are interested in the less serious problems of children in schools.

The psychiatrist has usually kept to his office and has only lately branched out to the social environment of his patients (community mental health). Some school systems now employ psychiatric consultants or offer limited consultation services to teachers or to school officials on the general topics of mental illness. The skills of the psychiatrist, while important and useful, are usually highly specialized and for school purposes are limited to the few problems of mental disturbances. Ordinarily the psychiatrist in private practice will work best through a school staff specialist, such as a psychologist or counselor or perhaps the health officer in the school system, each of whom can act as a go-between for the school and the psychiatrist's work in a specific classroom setting.

The *pediatrician*, a medical specialist in the physical diseases of children, is concerned with organic pathology more than with general development, although the latter is of concern to him and forms a backdrop of understanding necessary to the practice of medicine with children.

Most often the pediatrician does not have the time and inclination to work actively with the classroom teacher in regard to a given child unless that child has to go to school under some severe or chronic handicap. The functions of the pediatrician with children who have nonorganic behavioral, emotional, or achievement problems are minor; this is not their speciality. Their role in the case of blindness or deafness or some chronic disease is most important but still usually involves the classroom teacher or affects the school life of the child in relatively minor and indirect ways.

COOPERATION BETWEEN SCHOOL AND SPECIALISTS

Since, after the home, the school constitutes the main experience and learning medium of the child, any specialist working with children ought to have some knowledge of the child's school setting. When an out-of-school specialist comes into conflict with school authorities as sometimes occurs, it is usually because the specialist has failed to understand the school's problem with the child. The professional often would like to individualize the child's environment without sufficient accommodation to the necessary school structure.

The parents may consult a child specialist of some kind—let us say they seek their medical practitioner's opinion on whether their child is intellectually normal and can be expected to make average progress in school—and give him their side of the story, an important side but not the whole story. The doctor may render a judgment or write a recommendation which reflects that he does not have a complete picture of the problem and which irritates the school.

Similarly the psychiatrist or psychologist in private practice, when making his recommendations, may not know the relationship between the child's classroom requirements and his emotional state. The private practitioner might with inadequate consideration request the school to relieve the child of his normal responsibility. We have known instances when the private practitioner has later corrected this kind of mistake when he discovers the limited view within which he has been working.

To be effective, he must know the full story of the child's plight at school. He cannot get this from the child or the child's parents alone. No matter how ill the child is, no matter how much the practitioner wants to help the child, he cannot treat him in a vacuum. The more the school and the private practitioner can work together, the greater is the likelihood of helping the child efficiently.

Sometimes the out-of-school specialist will not think well of the school and its impact on the child. Even professionals who ought to know better sometimes harbor stereotyped negative attitudes toward school. They may have negative attitudes toward their own schooling, leading to misunderstandings with the school in cases of children they both want to help. In such situations, if the child specialist does not take the initiative to get in touch with the school, the school must take the initiative or help the parents take the initiative with both the school and the outside professionals. This case of a high school youth who would not attend school illustrates the point.

> Fifteen-year-old Sam had missed a few days of school at the beginning of the fall term due to a mild respiratory illness. He did not want to return to school to face his incomplete work, so he feigned continuing illness, and his mother and father let him stay home. Since both parents worked, they did not have a chance to observe Sam's health during the day. The youth was skillful enough to present a good case of poor health in the early morning and again in the evening when the parents were at home. During the day, however, he would sometimes be seen in the yard or going to the store to buy comic books, hence his neighbors became suspicious.

Sam's parents seemed unable to cope with the boy's reluctance to go to school; they let matters slip to the point where school authorities had to step in legally and force the issue. They could not use the kind of informal approach that is often applied with youngsters because no one could see that Sam got to school and stayed there. The parents could not provide followup.

Sam's parents consulted a mental health clinician. At first he took the side of the parents, said that Sam was too emotionally ill to go to school and he should not be pressured. The clinician put himself between the school and the law, on the one hand, and the parents and the child on the other. The parents had consulted the clinician much as one would consult a lawyer; the clinician meant well, but working in the vacuum of his office, by accepting Sam's malingering, he really acted in the boy's worst interests, even though he did not intend to do so. After being confronted with the school's viewpoint and the legal reasons for the stand it had taken the clinician reversed his stand. Moreover, when he realized that Sam was spending many hours during the day in play and in visiting stores, his support for Sam's complaints diminished.

In recent years there have been many conflicts between schools and parents in regard to the dress and grooming of youth. Very long hair, fadish clothes, and a generally untidy appearance characterize many youngsters at school, particularly at the junior and senior high levels. One such child was simultaneously going to school and privately being seen by a mental health clinician. The school had adopted a requirement that hair not exceed a certain length, also certain clothing requirements were stipulated, and these measures were communicated to all parents at the beginning of the school year. This youth was supported in his individualistic dress style by his therapist. Unfortunately, the youngster quoted a disparaging remark the therapist had made about the school personnel. This in turn led to some heated exchanges and the eventual withdrawal of the child by the parents from that particular school.

Sometimes matters involving outside professionals and the school take on legal aspects, but most often they involve simple strategies in relationships among people. It is one thing to want to help a patient and quite a different matter to coordinate action among different professionals in various contexts.

In the case of Sam, with better communication between the school and the professional specialist, the entire episode could probably have been avoided. The youth was not too emotionally disturbed to play baseball and basketball on the school grounds after school hours and sometimes to attend movies at night with his friends. There was little to support the private clinician's viewpoint. There was no point in allowing Sam to go on in this way if he was not seriously ill, physically or psychologically.

In crucial tests the school, more so than private practitioners, must face its tasks within a practical social structure. It must be careful to see that—in its efforts to impose a realistic discipline on a youngster and his family—neither it nor the outside professionals are diverted from the vital issue of helping the child. The school is in a position to document and study specific cases and to make intelligent examples of them for its own use. This is an area for profitable research, which is too frequently overlooked. This is also a neglected aspect of school-community relations, and at the same time, it is an aspect which the school is forced to confront periodically. If the school accepts such a role, it can go a long way toward improving the disciplined educational effort and in educating and gaining help from the parents and the professional persons with whom it has to work.

SELECTED READINGS

Burton, W. H., "Get the Facts: Both ours and the other fellow's." *Progressive Educ.*, 1952, *29*, 89.

Combs, A. W., *The Professional Education of Teachers.* Boston: Allyn and Bacon, 1965.

DAVIS, A., and R. J. HAVINGHURST, *Father of the Man*. Boston: Houghton Mifflin, 1947.

DOWNEY, L. W., *The Task of Public Education*. Chicago: Midwest Administration Center, The University of Chicago, 1960.

FENTON, E., ed., *Teaching the New Social Studies in the Secondary Schools*. New York: Holt, Rinehart and Winston, 1966.

GAGE, N. L., ed., *Handbook of Research on Teaching*. Skokie, Ill.: Rand McNally, 1964.

HAND, HAROLD C., *What People Think About Their Schools*. New York: World Publishing, 1948.

HURLOCK, ELIZABETH B., *Child Development*. New York: McGraw-Hill, 1964.

KRUMBOLTZ, J. D., "Parable of the good counselor." *Personnel and Guidance, J.*, 1961, *43*, 118–24.

LEWIN, K., *The Relative Effectiveness of a Lecture Method and a Method of Group Decision for Changing Food Habits*. Washington, D.C.; Committee on Food Habits, National Research Council, 1942.

MIEL, A., et al., *Cooperative Procedures in Learning*. New York: Teachers College, Columbia University, 1952.

SASLOW, G., "Review of 'New Curricula.'" *Contemporary Psychol.*, 1965, *0*, 174.

SCOTT, C. W., C. M. HILL, and W. H. BURNS, eds., *The Great Debate*. Englewood Cliffs, N.J.: Prentice-Hall, 1959.

SIMPSON, RAY H., and K. L. CAMP, "Diagnosing community reading." *School Review*, 1953, *61*, 98–100.

SKINNER, B. F., *Science and Human Behavior*. New York: Macmillan, 1953.

WRIGHTSTONE, J. WAYNE, *Appraisal of Experimental High School Practices*. New York: Bureau of Publications, Teachers College, Columbia University, 1936.

12

PROBLEMS OF THE ELEMENTARY SCHOOL GRADES

Among the major events in the life of the child, entering school ranks high. School is often a wonderful experience for the youngster. He has seen his older brothers or sisters and friends trudge off to this mysterious place, and he wonders about it and often envies them. If he has no vicarious contact with school through older brothers or sisters, he has at least heard his parents and others talk about their experiences in school.

All of these observations fascinate but may also frighten the child. What about all the strange adults one has to deal with? And finding his way in foreign surroundings! There are so many children he will have to meet. The school may be a long way from where he lives, and the bus ride may be strenuous and disturbing. The school building is large and strange and vastly impersonal. Going to school is not all fun, he soon learns. In the abstract, the child may feel that going to school is a good thing, but the reality may create many problems for him. Most of these center around fears and reluctances about what happens in school.

Further along in the elementary school, problems generally smooth out or at least become more concentrated on achievement and less on social adjustment to teachers, students, and school procedures. Work habits that will carry over into the higher grades become set, and personal problems, too, originally exacerbated in the new freedom and pressures of school, may resolve over time.

THE VERY BEGINNING OF SCHOOL

A curious paradox arises with some children as they enter school. They want to go to school; they prepare for it each morning; they talk about it; they join hands with other children in going to school; they ride peacefully with mother or in the car pool until they actually arrive at the school door. Then they rebel. They fight, scream, cry, and act as if the world were coming to an end. Nor do preschoolers alone raise these objections to the actual facts of entering school, first graders and others do, too.

Frequently children are recalcitrant in this way even as late as the second or third grade and, in some instances, even in the junior and senior high school. Usually when, out of apprehension and uncertainty, children are strongly opposed to going to school, it shows itself early, then tends to subside, and only occasionally rearises in relation to specific, more or less temporary, pressing circumstances. But when children change schools, move to new communities, or are forced to be out of school for long periods of time, old tension may reappear.

Sometimes such problems are called *school phobia*. This terminology suggests that the child has an intense, irrational fear of going to school, a kind of, or symptom of "mental illness." How to overcome these apprehensions in the many children who cannot get to psychotherapy or do not really need it is another matter. Often the fear produces anxiety in the parents, or has an exaggerated effect on the child because of past failures in handling new situations. The very commonness of the problem, however, suggests that most remedies must be simple. It also requires us to differentiate between passing apprehensions, on the one hand, and the more formidable problems of emotional disturbance, on the other hand.

WHY DO SCHOOL PHOBIAS OCCUR?

The term "school phobia" is probably too formidable a diagnostic label for a common transitory problem. There may not be much "phobia" in the strict sense of the term which means irrational and disruptive fear. In all probability there is more a kind of immaturity that focuses now on one reluctance in relation to school and again on another reluctance in relation to play with companions, going on scout overnight hikes, engaging in extracurricular activities, or being away from school for periods of time.

Considering a school phobia or school reluctance an immaturity, one might expect that the child frequently does not like to do things on his own. At trying times he wants as much parental protection as he can get. If he is not sure he can get this, if he has to give up his dependence on others and navigate on his own, he becomes reluctant. An example of this was seen in a first grade child, Joanne.

> She had been going to school for about four months in a seemingly acceptable routine. She was liked by her peers and was doing satisfactorily at school. One morning, when her mother was away from home on a visit, her father was getting the children ready for school. All of a sudden Joanne announced that she was not going. Unprepared for this statement, her father looked at her with raised eyebrows and said, "The car for school will be here shortly." But it was apparent that Joanne meant business when she went upstairs and locked herself in her room. Her father was alert to this small bit of acting on the child's part, and, with a skeleton key, opened the door and gently brought her downstairs with a little force and will power. He helped her get on her coat and walked outside with her. He told the lady driving the car pool, that Joanne had a bit of an upset and was not sure that she wanted to go to school and asked that she keep an eye on Joanne. He then went inside and phoned Joanne's teacher, relating what he had just been through and soliciting the teacher's preparation for Joanne's reluctance. He let the matter rest there. Joanne came into the classroom, accepted the routine and nothing more was said about her reluctance to go to school that day.

The matter came up again about two days later when her mother returned home and heard about Joanne's behavior. She asked Joanne why she did not want to go to school; the child answered that since her mother was away she thought she might stay home with her daddy and maybe he would take her someplace. Joanne approached the matter, of course, in an awkward and backward fashion, but her behavior can be understood. The correct action and antidote to Joanne's behavior was the prompt action of her father. When Joanne was upset and stubborn, the time was not ripe to tell her that her father could not spend the day with her or take her places, particularly when she was supposed to be in school—getting her to school immediately had the highest priority.

Sometimes a child feels that going to school would be fun if some of the family members could be there all day, too, particularly the mother. This is not necessarily a special *school* fear on the child's part. It may be a general demand that he have with him, at all times, family members, pets, or articles toward which he feels affection. When mother and teacher, however, agree in advance to put the child on his own in the group, the problem usually can be worked out quickly. This is one situation where very strong cooperative effort between parent and school is vital.

Many times, like Joanne, the child will balk at going to school, then when actually left there will settle into the routine satisfactorily. On the other hand, if the mother or father is available and goes into the school, hoping to smooth the child's way into the daily routine, the child may continue to show his reluctance and increase pressure on the parent to stay, or to be allowed to go home with the parent. It aggravates the trauma of separation when the child's demands combine with the parent's anxiety.

Sometimes the child's adjustment may be accelerated if the teacher leaves the child to "cry it out" if necessary, in the context of play and activities with other children. The teacher can facilitate the child's adjustment if he does not try to "mother" the child or make up to him through profuse consolation, which encourages the child to cling to the teacher as a substitute mother. For many mothers, torn by their offspring's unhappiness and lamentations, leaving the child at school is anguishing; this conveys itself to the child and feeds the child's own reluctance. A clear-cut, matter-of-fact statement, such as "Goodbye, dear, I'll see you at noon," delivered kindly but firmly will often cut through the child's apprehension. It is often the conflict between choices—when the possibility of staying with mother appears as strong as that of going to school—which increases the child's hesitation to accept the new situation.

ANOTHER EXAMPLE OF
SCHOOL RELUCTANCE AND ITS HANDLING

Why do not parents and teachers try the more matter-of-fact approach more often with reluctant children? Probably because they consider the situation more serious than it really is. An example of such a case follows.

> Robert, a seven-year-old boy, an only child, just entering second grade went to school three or four days at the beginning of the term, then he began to feel sick in the morning while preparing for school. His mother became alarmed and let Robert stay home a few days without investigating whether he really was ill. Later when she reviewed the activities leading up to Robert's refusal to go to school, she realized that he was probably not ill at all during these first days of reluctance. She recalled that after a few minutes—when evidently he no longer had to struggle with his feelings of inadequacy about going to school on that day—he settled down, became cheerful, played normally, and showed no further signs of the stomach upset or headache he had so vigorously complained of earlier.

In Robert's case this problem rapidly grew to the point where no one could get him to attend school. Curiously enough he would arise in the morning, put on his school clothes, assemble his books, and proceed naturally up to the actual point of leaving for school. Then he would renege; he would begin to breathe heavily, become tense, then somewhat depressed, evidently because he was in intense conflict about going to school. He was ill not because of a stomach upset, from something he had eaten but because his stomach, along with other parts of his body, registered his emotional upset.

Various solutions were proposed for Robert. First, he was examined by a physician; then he was interviewed by a number of clinicians (psychologist, psychiatrist, social worker). His parents were interviewed; it was generally decided that they had given him the feeling that he would lose them if he went to school. Robert was diagnosed as a school phobia case. His excuses for staying home were considered his way of protecting himself from losing his parents. At this point he was brought to us for treatment.

With the view that Robert had *general anxiety* about facing many strange new situations, we strongly suspected that he did want to go to school, but like one experiencing stage fright, when he got to the actual point of performance (departure), his apprehension mounted to an extreme point. We do not think of the stage frightened person as not wanting to go on stage, but merely as being apprehensive about how well he is going to perform or about being in the public eye. Under what circumstances, then, should anxiety like that in school fright or stage fright be permitted to determine behavior, and when should it be struggled with directly? When should the child be treated like a sick person? And when should he be treated like a normal person who is better for trying to shake off a minor ache or pain or reluctance and proceed toward his objectives?

In interviews with Robert, he presented an essentially normal picture in most important ways, but he did show signs of tenseness and maladjustment. He bit his nails, he wet the bed almost every night and had done so all of his life; he was somewhat easily intimidated by other children his age or younger. With adults he was normal and very much in control of himself. In competition with other children he seemed to crumble easily. He found it very difficult to stand up to others when they directly confronted him in aggressive or assaultive ways, yet he could play satisfactorily in organized games and enjoy the usual childhood sports without any reluctance.

What did we do to help Robert? After deciding that he was not grossly disturbed, it was important to realize that he probably did not need psychotherapy for some repressed fear of school or some repressed apprehension about losing his parents. It is time for such consideration when more direct and efficient methods fail. We viewed Robert as a youngster who had not been sufficiently and firmly confronted with the responsibility appropriate for his age, who had grown accustomed to making excuses when he should have faced up to difficult situations, and who had learned to appeal to his parents or other adults to get him out of difficulty. It appeared that the adults concerned compounded his problem by accepting his excuses and failures too readily, by stepping in and doing things for him instead of requiring him to handle matters which were within his capacities.

By the time Robert came to our attention he had been out of school for nearly four months. Efforts to drag him to school had succeeded only in worsening his apprehension and increasing his resentment. After discussing the problem further with Robert and his parents, it was decided that, since the Christmas vacation was only a week away, no effort would be made to get him back to school before Christmas. Careful groundwork, however, would be laid to get him back to school immediately following the vacation. The reasons for not trying to get Robert to school before Christmas was the irregularity of the school routine those few days before the holiday, plus the fact that Robert had not been in on the Christmas preparations and would feel more left out than ever. A fresh start after Christmas appeared most desirable.

Robert's mother was asked not to discuss school with the boy, not to plead with him, not to give special attention to any of his preparations for school. She was encouraged to view Robert's problem as an expression of a combination of natural school reluctance, a tendency to give in completely to his feelings, and a more or less chronic lack of effective adult guidance in the right amounts and at the right times. She was, therefore, to give him some daily chores to do (such as making his bed, picking up his clothes, carrying out trash) so that gradually he might become more accustomed to routine activities, even though he did not want to do them. He was to be encouraged and reinforced for these achievements. A regular teaching period devoted to arithmetic, reading, and spelling was to be conducted by his mother daily so that Robert would make up, to some extent, the material he had lost during his absence from school. He could earn "credits" for this schoolwork—a TV program or a movie on weekends.

Robert was seen for weekly interviews between the middle of December and the end of the first week in January, after which school would reopen. The psychologist talked with him about his behavior and his activities at home and at school; he clarified problems and discussed better ways of handling them, and sounded Robert out—but only indirectly—about his willingness to try again to go to school following the holiday recess.

Additional evidence developed that Robert did want to go to school, but he had intense "stage fright" which we have referred to above. His frightened reaction alone made him ill, and the thought of carrying through on going to school and on studying, worsened his feelings. Since this feeling was not likely to go away by itself within a three- or four-week period, his mother was advised to take Robert to school on the first day after the holiday. She was told to expect that he might try to renege again, despite his resolution to try to stay. She was to help him follow through by going to his classroom door with him and then promptly turning him over to the teacher. The classroom teacher and principal were also approached with this tentative plan, which they wholeheartedly endorsed and were prepared to execute.

Finally the day arrived when Robert was to go to school. He got up and prepared as usual. He showed some reluctance when his mother said she was going to walk to school with him, a distance of five or six blocks. The walk to school was largely uneventful, the mother later reported. But Robert did begin to whimper and freeze up as he actually approached the school grounds. However, they went in a side door, directly up some steps to the second grade room, where the teacher was ready for Robert. His mother dropped him off, walked quickly out the door, and went directly home. Robert was a little upset for the first ten or fifteen minutes, but the children began to file in, and as the pace of activities began to overtake him, Robert fitted in and stayed at school all day. The children were glad to see Robert back and this was reinforcing. Precautionary deliveries of Robert to school by his mother were continued only three days, until it was evident that he was over his gross apprehension. Occasionally he voiced some concern about going to school and about school activities, but he never pushed them to a critical level.

Robert was seen for nine more interviews—dividing the interview time with his mother—spread over the rest of the school year. He continued to go to school without any acute problems arising. He made satisfactory progress academically and had pretty well caught up on all his deficiencies by the end of that school year. At home, the mother continued to work to get Robert to be more responsible and better disciplined. He overcame his bed-wetting within six months of his return to school. Periodic checks with his teacher revealed that Robert was adjusting well to the social, emotional, and academic demands made on him; he was also enjoying school and did not show the apprehensions and social immaturities of his first year of school, even before his school phobia became critical.

The case of Robert illustrates the importance of good discipline to mental health and school achievement. It further illustrates that fear of school leading to frantic efforts to stay away—as critical and upsetting as it is to parents and school authorities—is often simply the *culmination* of gradually progressing and general disorganization and immaturity.

The remedial efforts needed are often simple, but they need to be followed consistently, with home-school cooperation on similar aims and procedures. Without full home-school cooperation in Robert's case, he could not have been helped as quickly as he was. In many similar cases, children not severely disturbed have been allowed to drag on with school absences for many months, with no constructive action being taken. An appreciation of the immediately constructive and discipline-centered steps which can be taken with most children can lead to prompt and usually effective remedial measures.

EFFECTIVE APPROACHES
TO WORKING WITH THE HOME

Youngsters coming to school for the first time bring with them a reservoir of attitudes, habits, behaviors, and feelings learned at home. Sometimes their behavior at home, which has not caused any concern, may be of considerable concern in the school environment. And parents frequently fail to see the relationship between home behavior and school behavior. They become resentful of the school or teacher who proposes that Johnny is not as ideal at school as he is said to be at home.

How does the teacher communicate to the parent that their child needs some kind of help for special problems? There are no fixed answers to such a question. They depend upon the nature of the child's problem, the prejudices or stereotypes connected with such problems (for example, more emotional reaction is likely to arise from telling parents that their child has emotional problems than most other kinds), and the timing and skill with which the teacher deals with the parents.

Generally speaking, the sooner such problems are brought to the parent's attention, the better. It is important that during the first three grades the child's intellectual, emotional, and social status be understood as well as possible. This is necessary because it is desirable to make changes early and also because the parents are likely to be more cooperative earlier than later. If the school knows about or suspects a problem and does not get around to trying specific remedies until the child is in the fifth or sixth grade, the parents may be understandably surprised, disturbed, and resentful.

Going to school involves many adjustments. Children may, indeed, be happy and normal at home and not at school. A child disturbed at school is not necessarily disturbed at home. One has to ferret out the differences in expectations and roles in the two settings and in the kinds of behavior that are expected or rewarded in the two settings, and accept the fact that they can produce vastly different results in the same child, although this fact may appear inconsistent to the superficial observer.

How can the teacher best proceed with parents? He can accumulate a number of items on behavior or achievement at school that illustrate the point about the child's need for help. During the first three years of school, reading, arithmetic, and spelling are commonly learned at different rates by the same child; he may be advanced in reading and lag in arithmetic, or vice versa. He may need some extra help with particular subjects for a given time. The condition need not be considered to reflect inadequacy on the part of the teacher or the child. No one does all things equally well all of the time.

The teacher can accumulate the evidence of poor learning in spelling, reading, or arithmetic. He can call in the parent for a conference, papers, illustrating the quality of the work, can be sent home and also corrected, giving the child an appreciation of what is considered acceptable work. The teacher can keep open the lines of communication to the parents of a child who is not doing as well as he should be, providing for interim conferences or written reports between the regular six- or nine-week report card periods. If the teacher makes these reports systematically, final realization by the parents that the child needs help beyond what the school can regularly offer will not come as a surprise.

In the case of children with behavior or emotional problems, a daily or weekly itemization of the child's behavior will often help to make his record objective and serve as a useful guide to an interview with the parents. The teacher might write proceeding in this way:

> Mrs. Brown, I have noticed some things about Johnny's behavior and emotional development which I would like to talk over with you. Perhaps you have noticed similar things at home. I have written a log of events that have occurred over the past month. Johnny seems to want to go to the bathroom too many times. Last Wednesday, for example, he went five times between 9:15 and 11:30 a.m. On most days he needs to go to the bathroom two or three times in addition to the trip all children take in midmorning and again before lunch.

Rather than confronting the parent, especially an overanxious one, with too many items, the teacher can get the parent's reaction to each item in turn and then try to arrive at a general picture. The teacher should then be able to offer some step he believes the parents can take to remedy the situation. Too often, the parent is confronted with a circumstance at school which needs remedying, then when the school or the teacher has no solutions to offer, the parent is confused, perhaps angered, or less cooperative than he could be. The parent may be led up to a point of accepting the need for help, then be given no useful suggestions at the crucial time.

It is, of course, advisable to talk about the child's strong points first. The excerpt above is meant to illustrate that the teacher can proceed only after he has made some positive contact with the parent and has established good grounds for communication about the deficiencies.

SOME COMMON PROBLEMS
OF THE EARLY GRADES

Numerous problems arise requiring home-school cooperation for the student in the early grades. A small but representative sample follows:

1. Being chronically late in arriving for school.
2. Failing to leave school on time in the afternoon.
3. Failing to report home immediately after school.
4. Fighting en route to or from school or at school.
5. Teasing or bullying by older children at school or going to or from school.
6. Leaving schoolwork or supplies at home and having to return to get them.
7. Leaving needed work or supplies at school and having to return to get them.
8. Refusing to eat lunch at school or eating only desserts or having an otherwise unbalanced diet.
9. Continually teasing or calling names; taking advantage of shy or retiring children who do not or cannot stand up for themselves.
10. Getting too dirty by falling into puddles in the schoolyard, holding water fights in the washroom, and the like.
11. Stealing the possessions of other children and hiding these; stuffing handkerchiefs, caps, and such in toilets, putting them under water faucets, or hiding them.

An exhaustive list of such sources of problems is too long to consider here. Usually such matters require some better organization and direction of the behavior of youngsters at school and efforts to work out problems through home-school cooperation. An occasional disturbance of the type mentioned above is of no special concern, but when a given child is too often either on the giving or receiving end of such difficulties, some investigation should be conducted.

Very few kindergarten youngsters pose problems of an intractable nature. Most of these children are transported to and from school, and although they may cause some trouble in the car pool, they are usually easily managed within the confines of the school itself. But on occasion, one of them may develop habits that put him at odds with the teacher and with the other youngsters. If such problems are not caught early and corrected, they will often carry over to the first grade. An example of such a problem is Mike.

> A six-and-a-half-year-old first grader, had been a problem throughout his preschool years when it came to music or art work. He had stubbornly refused to sing or play with the rhythm band in nursery school and in kindergarten. He also refused to try to draw or paint at the normal times for these activities at school. Mike would be observed singing the same songs as the group or sneaking a few beats on the drum when the class was occupied with some other activity. At odd times he would also furtively get crayons and paper to do his drawings, even though he had refused to do the same kind of work at the appointed time in the class.

When Mike advanced to first grade and still persistently refused to engage in group activities related to music and art, his behavior could not be as easily overlooked as it had been in kindergarten. The kindergarten teacher had let him get by with too much; she had let him set precedents that later would have to be broken. After a few struggles, Mike did begin to participate in group music and art activities at school, but there had been many unnecessary complications.

The problem with Mike, initially, was not difficult. The preschool teacher first reacted to Mike's stubborn refusal to participate in art or music as "just a whim he has—he will soon get over it." But when he did not get over it, the teacher still felt it would have been pushing him too much to require that he conform to the group in these respects.

His kindergarten teacher, then, paid insufficient attention to three important considerations. First, Mike wanted to participate in art and music, which was shown by his furtive efforts in these activities. Secondly, the teacher overlooked the opportunity to test an alternative assumption about Mike, namely, that he could learn to conform to the group in simple, obvious ways and that such a requirement would not damage his self-respect or his liking for the activities. The teacher just assumed that Mike refused to take part in music and art periods because of some "basic psychological condition" which she had best leave alone. And thirdly, the teacher did not look ahead to see that Mike was setting a precedent for himself that would have to be changed by another teacher at another time. Unwittingly, this teacher was passing the problem on to others who might be in a less favorable position to solve it.

In general ways children bring their attitudes with them from home to the earliest years of school. Some of these attitudes are healthy, favorable to learning, and socially desirable, some are not. The new demands of the elementary school years, in comparison with the preschool years, often come as a shock to the child and even to his parents. "Why, you know, Robert did so well in kindergarten I felt he would have no problem with the first grade." Parents often make remarks like this about the kindergarten, first grade, third grade, fifth grade, and on up. Although preschool experience is often an excellent preparation for the formal elementary school years, it is not a totally sufficient preparation. New modes of behavior have to be learned as soon as the child enters first grade, and it is the teacher's and the school's responsibility to convey this to parents early in the school year. It is no criticism of the preschool and no particular shortcoming of the child when it is discovered that elementary school requirements are not being met; but it is a useful warning for those concerned with preschool education to project ahead to the child's elementary school years while observing his preschool behavior and attitudes.

SOME PROBLEMS OF THE
LATER ELEMENTARY YEARS

Most children progress quite smoothly through the intermediate school grades. After they have made the initial adjustment to school, they seem able to go about the business of learning without noticeable strain. The successful student is able to use the skills acquired in the first three grades, and he is able to mature and expand socially in accordance with his capacity and with environmental opportunities.

A few children falter when they enter the intermediate grades. If the child has not acquired some mastery in reading, writing, and arithmetic and has not gained some self-control and discipline in the social and emotional realm, he is in for continuous trouble. Beginning with the fourth grade, independence and self-direction are increasingly required. The child needs to have developed enough facility with reading to find his way through the pages of science and social studies books. He is expected to have developed some self-sustaining interest in reading for pleasure or knowledge. He is expected to have branched out in several directions, following his own interests and hunches, and not have to be guided at every turn in order to accomplish elementary detail. He should have a sufficient grasp of arithmetic fundamentals so that he can handle verbally stated problems requiring reasoning and interest.

Socially and emotionally, the child's maturity accelerates during the later elementary school years. By this time he has developed an often acute sense of humor; he appreciates jokes, plays on words, and humorous events in people's lives. He can bridge the gap between fact and fantasy much better than before. Storytelling on a more mature level, where the child becomes the leader in such social exchanges, is common. He is also sophisticated enough to appreciate the rules of games and their importance. Adults are often surprised at the social maturity shown by children in the ten to thirteen year age range. Studies suggest that children of this age closely approximate adults in their language skills also.

What is the picture then? The child in the fourth, fifth, sixth, or seventh grades, in the ten to thirteen age group, can act very maturely and take on many responsibilities. He can display important educational skills, reveal a considerable achievement of knowledge, and often surprise even himself with his social maturity. Much can be expected from him, but what if he cannot fit into such a picture?

TREATMENT OF A POOR ACHIEVER

Some children cannot match this normal development. This may then lead to major problems as it did with Betty.

Betty, an eleven-year-old, was the middle child of a family of five children. She was in sixth grade and had a tested IQ of 125; however, she was achieving on a fourth grade level. She made many careless errors in arithmetic, in spelling, and in her written work. She presented herself to the teacher in a way that suggested she simply could not do the work. In fact, for the previous three grades she had convinced each teacher that normal grade level work was too much for her. When she came to our attention, the school had decided not to promote her at the end of sixth grade because she seemed overtaxed in trying to do acceptable sixth grade work.

Testing made it evident that Betty could do acceptable and even superior work; however, she rose to this level only occasionally. On these occasions the teacher said she had been very firm with Betty. But the teacher thought that a steady policy of such firmness and follow-through was too much for the girl to tolerate. She therefore required acceptable work of Betty only about once a week. Betty's woebegone look and her show of extreme boredom when assigned such work as a spelling list or a dozen arithmetic problems, momentarily fended off the teacher. Betty appeared to be a helpless and incapable person. She had even begun to believe this about herself.

Within the course of a semester, a program of steady, daily homework and follow-through on seat work at school had begun to pay dividends. Betty was no longer permitted to avoid her work. She volunteered at times for extra work and began to accept her daily schoolwork with some positive feeling and effort.

Did Betty have the necessary basic educational skills at her command? Did she really know enough to do more than fourth grade work, even though she had been advanced to sixth grade? Was she unhappy? Had she been pressured too much? These and many other questions arose from conferences with her parents and her teachers past and present.

Betty's problems are typical of those of many faltering students in the upper elementary school years. She had adequate basic ability—an IQ of 125—but she lacked the skill to put her ability into operation. In the personality sphere, we saw her problem as feeling inadequate *because of her chronic failure* to achieve, to meet the demands of daily living at school. She displayed few problems at home except where schoolwork was involved; she got along well with her peers, played vigorously, and was enjoying herself in social activities not involving schoolwork. But she had acquired a defeatist attitude at school, which had become a habit in coping with daily demands.

The emotional attitude came, we believe, as a *secondary* but closely related problem. The primary problem was lack of application stemming from inadequate discipline and poor habits developed at home and at school. Accepting this point of view, the teacher made a persistent effort to structure Betty's daily work and develop self-discipline in the manner suggested in our earlier chapters.

As Betty gradually learned that she would be held to her educational responsibilities, she began to accept them as necessary. As she did so, she worked at them; as she worked harder, she achieved more. A new, positively reinforcing chain reaction was started, which moved in a positive direction; it replaced the old vicious circle of too little effort, failure, and discouragement, followed by still less effort.

MEETING DEMANDS AS THEY ARISE

By the later elementary school years, if the child has not progressed normally, the assumption is commonly made that the work is too difficult for him. This is more likely to be assumed here than earlier because the demarcation lines of what is expected of the child in grades four through seven are clearly drawn. And differences in starting points at the onset of schooling, aside from ability, should have been obliterated. It should be noted here that the label "lack of readiness" may be overemphasized as the cause of poor achievement at the intermediate school level. The same is true of "a poor emotional attitude toward school." If the child is permitted to get by and function on a bare subsistence level, educationally speaking, he will not easily take to the more demanding tasks of grades four through seven. This is one reason the importance of *daily tasks* at school needs to be emphasized and, equally, the importance of some homework in the early grades. They prepare the child for a steady diet of reasonably demanding work, geared to the level of complexity he can accomplish and accept. Not to tax the child at all is doing him a disfavor. Not to tax and challenge the child during the beginning years may lead to a state of educational doldrums at the intermediate level, as in the case of Betty.

If the child at the intermediate level has not learned to apply himself well, the junior high school years will find him woefully inadequate. Many children reach junior high school without adequate preparation in study habits and skills. To confront such junior high school students with a considerable amount of homework for the first time, with the preparation of term papers and reports extending over several days or weeks is to make educational demands they are simply not prepared to meet. As a result they may well fail. How much better it is to realize during the intermediate years, if not sooner, that the demands for more advanced skills relating to learning will be made, and made insistently, by the beginning of the seventh or eighth grade; students should be prepared to meet these demands.

The student's study skills should be examined directly. From there the teacher can turn attention to the emotional reactions that complicate the poor application of the youth's abilities to the tasks at hand or stem from them. Even among children who progress normally, there is usually room for improvement in the study skills, which are so essential for efficient learning.

Emotional complications may not be *fully* explained by the achievement problem nor by the manner in which the child generally applies himself. Although these complications may be extreme and critical, they can usually be alleviated by the solution of study and achievement problems where such exist. This is the most *direct and efficient route* and permits us to look for and apply practical methods to dissolve educational impasses. There is probably more undetected logjamming of educational achievement of this type at the intermediate level than at any other stage of education.

INTERMEDIATE GRADES
DO PRESENT BROAD PROBLEMS

We have not intended to give the impression that the upper elementary years are free from problems, there is a kind of exacerbation of some types of problems, and referrals based on them, that does not characterize the first three years of elementary school.

Behavior problem referrals show a considerable rise beginning with roughly the fourth grade, characterized by difficulties either better handled in the first three years or not recognized for referral. Boys more often than girls (in a ratio of three, four, or even five to one) present conduct problems in the classroom and on the playground; but, more than that, their problems tend to spill over into the community at large. There is stealing from local stores, damaging property, annoying or disturbing social behavior, smoking openly and boastfully, and in more recent years, attempting to use automobiles, motorbikes, and other power-driven vehicles carelessly, so that the attention of the police is invited. And there is even considerable evidence that serious drug problems have spread downward into the upper elementary grades in some cities and locales within large urban areas.

Sometimes these wider ranging behavior and social problems come in the wake of developing scholastic difficulties, but perhaps equally often they are simply generated out of the social milieu, the rapidly developing "sophistication" of the ten-to-thirteen-year-olds, and through the influence of older students who may occupy the same school premises as younger children or be housed nearby.

These problems, even at the upper elementary level, have posed serious community concerns. Communities have had, in some cases, to increase police surveillance, change the school hours, stop or greatly curtail night programs, and alter the availability of after-school recreation and play opportunities on the school grounds.

While many of these socially cancerous problems are more common in disadvantaged areas, they are beginning to occur in the more affluent neighborhoods as well. The issues, then, are not related wholly to age group (these problems become more common in the junior and senior high school levels), nor to economic and social conditions, but seem to reflect broad changes in our culture which are not as yet very well understood and surely not well controlled.

SELECTED READINGS

Baldwin, A. L., *Theories of Child Development*. New York: John Wiley, 1967.

Chamberlin, Leslie J., "Group behavior and discipline." *The Clearing House,* 1966, *41*, 92–95.

Cutts, Norma E., and Nicholas Moseley, "Four schools of school discipline— A Synthesis." *School and Society*, 1959, *87*, 87.

Greenberg, H., and D. Fare, "An investigation of several variables as determinants of authoritarianism." *J. Soc. Psychol.*, 1959, *49*, 105–11.

Jourard, S. M., and R. M. Remy, "Perceived parental attitude, the self, and security." *J. Consult. Psychol.*, 1955, *19*, 364–66.

Millard, Cecil V., and John W. M. Rothney, *The Elementary School Child*. New York: Dryden Press, 1957.

Schramm, W., J. Lyle, and E. B. Parker, *Television in the Lives of Our Children*. Stanford, Calif.: Stanford University Press, 1961.

Sears, R. R., E. E. Maccoby, and H. Levin, *Patterns of Child Rearing*. New York: Harper and Row, 1957.

Thomas, R. Murray, *Aiding the Maladjusted Pupil*. New York: McKay, 1967.

Verville, Eleanor, *Behavior Problems of Children*. Philadelphia: Saunders, 1967.

13

PROBLEMS AT THE JUNIOR AND SENIOR HIGH SCHOOL LEVELS

This chapter encompasses the problems that are the most acute, most intense, most fearsome to teachers and parents alike. Problems in discipline and achievement at the junior and senior high school levels have been intensifying particularly during the past ten years. This is partly because a larger number of students are being retained in school, partly because of an organizational looseness that seems to result when classes or schools are large, and partly because of the belief of many educators that the best organization of education is either a relatively permissive one or a repressive one, particularly in the face of rebellious students.

We recently heard a supervisor of instruction say to a group of teachers, "The most severe disciplinary problems in the whole school system either begin at or stem from the junior high school years." At least insofar as the overt appearance of problems is concerned, even though their origins may go back further, this supervisor appears to be correct. Passing the buck backwards, seeking origins or first causes is not, however, a remedial or therapeutic measure for high school students showing the problems. Taking preventive measures throughout school makes good sense, though.

As a simple check on the supervisor's statement, we traced back 21 random high school disciplinary cases and found that 17 of them first exhibited trouble during the junior high school years, with either no problem or only a minor problem showing up at the elementary school level. Why is this the case?

What is there about the junior high school level that gives rise to disciplinary problems? Or what is there in the junior high arrangement that exacerbates so many problems in discipline and achievement problems, too? Numerous answers have been proposed to these questions. In the following discussion some of the possible answers are surveyed.

SOURCES OF
JUNIOR HIGH SCHOOL PROBLEMS

First of all, students of this age group, roughly from thirteen to fifteen, are moving rapidly into adolescence, with its great emphasis on exploring new worlds of thought, feeling, and social activity. There is a strong drive to assert themselves, to begin to challenge adult authority more directly and powerfully than heretofor, and to shed the limitations of childhood. At the extreme, there are probably very few cases in every school of seemingly well behaved and able students who have "gone wild" upon arriving in junior high school. They often see themselves as grown-up, although their parents and they too know they lack the wisdom and experience to take full responsibility for their actions. They need discipline and guidance very badly.

A second reason that the junior high school is a period of great ferment is the change from one main teacher at elementary school to a situation of having four to eight teachers, all important—often very different in age, experience, attitudes, and understanding—requiring a sizable adjustment of the child. The fact that each teacher has a speciality that the youth is required to study, the conflicting demands from the various teachers, and the impression that each class has to be pursued for its own value are new concepts for the student to absorb and follow. At the elementary school level if a child was not very good in arithmetic but did exceptionally well in reading or other verbal subjects, the teacher might have overlooked the arithmetic deficiency and capitalized on the child's strengths. At the junior high level, this kind of accommodation is very nearly impossible.

A third reason for problems is that the junior high school youth does not spend all or most of the day in one room as he does in elementary school. He often moves about to as many as eight or nine rooms, besides which there may be a gymnasium, outdoor playground, and special music or art areas to find his way into and out of. Junior high school students are often confused at least initially by the maze of classrooms, teachers, hallways, gyms, shops, and other school areas they have to get used to if they are to move with the school routine.

Perhaps a fourth reason for ferment at the junior high school level is that when the seventh-grader enters it for his first class, he is the "low man on the totem pole," compared with his previous superior status in the elementary school. He now takes the brunt of the teasing of the upper-class students. He also sees boys and girls more openly expressing interest in each other and is introduced to close social communication between the sexes. The complexity and pace of social relationships can be dazzling to the elementary age child when he first sets foot in junior high school.

Perhaps age twelve is not the best time to expose children to this relatively mature and complex organization. With the age of adult-like responsibilities in church, home, and vocation being constantly pushed upward, perhaps the age of beginning junior high school should be raised a year or two. This, however, is a separate problem; this chapter will contend only with suggestions for handling problems as they now arise in existing schools and organizations.

The uneven sexual maturation paralleling the uneven social maturation also constitutes a problem in understanding the junior high school years. At seventh grade level some boys and girls are fully mature sexually, and may even have begun to have intimate sexual-social experiences. Others are still "little boys" and "little girls," immature physically and confused about relationships with the opposite sex, which they have not yet begun to perceive clearly nor know how to handle.

A sixth reason for junior high trouble lies in the fact that at this level particularly, the school appears to lack the structure, discipline, and definiteness of expectations put to the child at other periods. It seems to be a kind of no man's land in the eyes of some educators and psychologists. At times, it may even appear that the junior high school was almost designed to put an end to organization and guidance and similar matters painstakingly cultivated throughout the elementary years. At times the junior high school seems to flaunt all sensible organization of mental hygiene and educational practices. No one, of course, has intended that the junior high school be used this way, but in the vast reorganization of the child's behavior and the restructuring of his educational-social energies, poor structuring and near-anarchy often seem to prevail. However, the constructive challenges and the importance of this period should be emphasized, not blamed for the exacerbation of student troubles.

LIBERTY VERSUS CONSTRAINTS
AT THE JUNIOR HIGH LEVEL

The junior high school level does present challenges. It provides greater liberty to the child, but at the same time, it imposes greater constraints. It confronts him with a host of new educational experiences, which he is invited to sample, but simultaneously it demands more productivity from him on his own. It opens up social and intellectual worlds he is likely never to have thought of before, but it requires more precision and efficiency in his work.

With all the challenges and opportunities, a great deal of self-discipline and skill are required of youth. And if the challenges are not met well, the young people cannot get on well with their progression into high school. The greater the opportunities, the greater the personal organization needed to take advantage of them. The more stimulation the child has, the more he needs personal direction to be able to absorb the stimulation rather than to become confused and distracted.

Some school systems attempted to cope with these problems—not wisely, we think—by cutting out or never initiating the junior high program; instead students go directly into the high school at the eighth, ninth, or tenth grade. This merely passes the problem along one or two more years up the line. True, some stabilizing of social behavior, personal development, and educational skills may occur when the seventh, eighth, and ninth grades are kept within the framework of the elementary school (with its simpler approach and fewer elements). But sooner or later the same adjustments to the wider orbits of living must be made. To control the problem by eliminating the junior high school is like stopping the clock to control the passage of time. Junior high age level problems of social, emotional, and educational development will be present in some form regardless of whether the children are kept in an elementary school, passed on to junior high schools, or held back for a later but bigger jump to the senior high school.

The ever-present problems of education—related to good discipline, reasonable achievement, and adequate mental health—must, then, be faced. Basically those of the junior high school child are of the same nature, though far more intense than at the preschool and the elementary school levels. It is not so much that new features are added to these concerns, although there is a widening in all respects, it is that the breadth and complexity of the educational and social experiences make these matters harder to manage in continually constructive ways. For example, when the junior high school student has six different teachers with six different notions of conduct, achievement, and social maturity, he has very complex roles to follow. It is not surprising if he does not follow all of them well or if he is unable to handle some of the conflicts and inconsistencies inherent in this system.

SOME SPECIAL PROBLEMS
OF THE JUNIOR HIGH SCHOOL AGE

Through conversations with counselors about the achievement and conduct of students, one almost immediately realizes that intrastaff problems often arise in the junior high school. An English teacher may go along with practically all the suggestions offered by the counselor, but the math teacher will not. One teacher thinks only of training his students for advanced work in high school or college, another has standards that allow for terminal work at the junior high school level. One teacher stresses homework, another one ignores it entirely. One teacher tests every day, and another tests only once or twice each six-week or nine-week interval.

Counselors have a difficult task in gaining enough staff cooperation to give the child a feeling that a set of standards governs his schooling— standards in which all his teachers concur and on which he can base his progress. Each teacher usually wants to teach his course almost as if it were in a vacuum. Special interests and abilities in the teachers can enhance education, but they can also lead to confusion in the student if there is not some elementary degree of coordination about homework, amount of work, frequency, nature and time of examinations, grading, reporting to and consulting with parents. If such matters are not brought under some direction, disorganization will be accentuated in the junior high school student's educational life. With behavior already tending to become disorganized and with goals and means of attaining them tending to be unclear, it is all the more important that the usual complexities associated with junior high school years not be permitted to accelerate confusion and disorganization.

Also, the junior high school years are a period when young people seriously challenge the home as the source of knowledge, value, and conduct. Home and school are more likely to coincide in their social values and educational objectives during the elementary years than during the junior high school years.

As the child gets older and more choices are available to him, parents differ more widely on expectations of social behavior. Reporting home from school in the afternoon, the acceptance and control of part-time work, home responsibilities, freedom to go out during the evening, the time for coming home at night during the school week and on weekends—these and many sources of conflict affect the child's school and home behavior, his regard for school, his sense of responsibility toward authority, his investment in his own educational progress.

Usually it has been the parents of junior high school students who have developed codes of conduct to regulate the social and out-of-school behavior of their children. Various codes have encompassed such details as how to handle the homework problem at home, how much time is allowed for television viewing and when, how late students can stay up during the week, how late they can stay at parties, what kind of arrangements for supervision are important at social functions, and what arrangements should be made for dating and the use of automobiles.

Not only do parents have to grapple with these problems, but school personnel also must. Should the school be a social center during the evening and on weekends for parties, dances, and picnics? Is the school remiss in not offering more such social opportunities to students at a time when they would otherwise be out on the streets, congregating in drugstores, or going to clubs? Many parents blame the school for not doing more about regulating social activities. Many schools, on the other hand, feel an indirect impasse in that parents often do not work well together in groups, but if they are not effectively consulted about the social activities of their junior high children, the child's school routine may be impaired.

It is as if everything discussed earlier in this book about discipline and achievement and their integral relationships to mental health is intensified at the junior high school level. The execution of good solutions is also much more difficult. If a parent wants a report every week or two on how a faltering student is doing in one or more of his classes, the request usually has to come through the principal or the counselor, who, in turn, has to get the necessary information from the various teachers. Passing indirectly from teacher to parent, the necessary recommendations and messages may become garbled or delayed and misinterpreted. Many parents and teachers have given up in despair at trying to get direct information about a recalcitrant or underachieving student. Personal conferences are just as important as in earlier years, but they are much more difficult to arrange and integrate since so many more people are involved.

SOME PROBLEM-SOLVING SUGGESTIONS

At the top, the principal should certainly strive to bring reasonably uniform policies and structure to the administration of the school. He should, of course, encourage fresh thinking and new methods in his teachers, but steady attention should be given to the ready tendencies toward disorganization. The principal can transmit to the teachers the need for standards and common approaches that can, in turn, help bring structure to the student's life.

To let parents know how the student is progressing, some schools have used the home report form. The child picks up the blank form on say Thursday of each week, has it filled out by his teachers as he goes to the various classes, then returns the final product to the counselor or principal for initialing before bringing it home. This report form usually includes two or three items at least—how the child is doing in his daily work, whether his conduct and attention are satisfactory, and examination reports.

If this transmittal of information occurs expeditiously, there is time left for fence mending over the weekend if the child's report is not up to expectations. Parents cooperating with this kind of reporting can reward good reports with meaningful favors or hold up the child's weekend privileges (movies, Friday or Saturday night out, visits to friends etc.) if reports are poor, until corrective work is done—a form of managing the contingencies and the reinforcement factors which are very powerful in regulating behavior. On the following weekend privileges can be restored if the next report is better. Each week the child can start over again in his school efforts, rather than be penalized for long periods of time or slip by with deficiencies over a considerable period. For such a program to be most effective, however, the parents should insist on a regular, well-planned study program at home to correct deficiencies as they appear.

This type of home reporting can be highly effective if carried out properly by all parties concerned. Parents do not have to wait six to nine weeks to know how the youngster is progressing; they do not hear only at the last minute about their child's education or conduct disasters. Schools also can thus avoid the frequent criticism that they do not set standards and stick with them. The junior high school student is faced with daily responsibility for his work, and with reporting weekly to his parents. To know where he stands every week also should be most beneficial to him.

Not all teachers or school officials are willing or able to accept the reporting system we have described. One teacher told his class, "You just do your work, and I will take care of the exams and grades; you will get your report at the appointed time." In a sense this teacher is correct; he is following protocol, but protocol is often too slack to permit firm guidance of the educationally or behaviorally wayward student. Furthermore, any child or adult needs to know as soon and as fully as possible how well he has done on his work or an examination in order to profit most from the experience. Much greater attention to reporting on the youth's progress needs to be built into his *daily* educational experience. It should be emphasized as strongly as possible that teachers should not delay in reporting back to students on how they are progressing.

Firmness in setting expectations and promptness in reporting results of efforts go hand in hand. At the junior high level where there is so much looseness and uncoordination of structure inherent in the very nature of the child's psychological growth and his educational experiences, it behooves all concerned to be most careful in setting up and maintaining firm structure wherever possible.

In some instances problems associated with the present practices in the junior high school have prompted educators and psychologists to think more in terms of a "middle school," or a period of transition of a more gradual nature between the elementary and senior high school years. Perhaps this kind of thinking and planning is very constructive, but it will have to bring about more changes than simply what the school is called or easing up on the social requirements which now divide the elementary and junior high years, although these are important beginning points.

SPECIAL PROBLEMS OF THE SENIOR HIGH SCHOOL YEARS

Next to the junior high school years, the senior high school years are most fraught with difficulty. The dropout problem, the problem of delinquency, the problem of failure to progress with schoolwork, the problem of pitting long-range education against immediate financial and vocational aims all are especially intense at the senior high school level.

Senior high school students may as individuals show severe achievement problems, but as a group they are usually somewhat better adjusted to school than the junior high school students, for some of the reasons already cited. Also, some of the more recalcitrant and less able students have dropped out, and the remaining group has become somewhat more homogeneous in achievement and in amenability to good discipline. By the time they have reached high school, many youths are seriously intent on their studies and regard misbehavior as juvenile and unbefitting their more mature status. They tend also to censor others who misbehave unduly or who regard school as a joke.

This is not to say that senior high problems in discipline and achievement do not exist. Although crime, delinquency, and disruptive behavior have increased materially in the last decade, they still do not put a wholly new complexion on the high school years. Still there has been more time for problems to develop and to become more serious than in earlier grades, particularly if nothing constructive has been done about them. And opportunities for freedom and self-direction that have not been taken advantage of in constructive ways during junior high school years will continue to trouble the high school student. Here again, choices in the curriculum, the great variety of teachers and teaching standards, and the greater need to be a self-starter and self-director pose problems which many students will not have developed the resources to meet.

WORKING DIRECTLY WITH THE STUDENTS

The problems at this level are, then, of exactly the same nature as those we have already discussed, though different in form and intensity. All the combinations of disciplinary achievement and related mental health problems which the senior high school student may face will not be catalogued here. We will point to some of the issues which the school administration and the classroom teacher should especially consider, hoping in this way to sharpen the perceptions of school personnel and to facilitate more effective teacher-student relations.

> 1. The teacher may rely too much on appeals to the student's maturity in his efforts to motivate the student to work and behave better in the school environment. The teacher often says, "You're a high school student now, and you should know how to do this," or "You are a senior, and I expect you to act like a senior."

The teacher may be right in assuming that the status of the student in question should offer some guarantee of more mature behavior, but if this does not work, then such an appeal might as well be dropped as an inefficient way of motivating and guiding the student. It seems generally to be more effective to say in essence: "If you do your work or if you behave in an acceptable way, these good results will follow. If, on the other hand, you fail to do your work or to act as maturely as is expected of you, there will be these poor consequences. . . ."

Saying this kind of thing now and then—and always backing it up or proving it in concrete, meaningful terms—will save the teacher much indecision and conflict, will appeal to the students with what are actually the more mature and satisfying ways, and will demonstrate that the consequences of the students' actions are clear and unavoidable whether they are in the form of test or grade results or of special privileges.

> 2. By lowering a student's grades for misbehavior, the teacher may rely too heavily on grades to control student behavior in the classroom. This practice is often followed, even though a separate "attitude" or "deportment" rating may be given on the report card.

As indicated earlier, we believe that grades and conduct ought to be kept separate. If a student does good work but presents a disciplinary problem, it does harm to both areas of behavior to confuse the two. The poor conduct should draw its own consequences; the student's grades should be a matter of genuine academic achievement. Of course, if his conduct prevents his application or if behavior problems arise because he does not do his work, the loss of time and poor application will result in a poorer mark. This is a "natural consequence" of the youth's not having done his work, irrespective of the reason for the lack of work, but disciplinary problems should be handled as such in one of the many ways already discussed.

> 3. A student should have recourse to changing a class, a teacher, or a school when it becomes *objectively evident* that such action is in his best interests. Schools often refuse to let a student drop or replace a subject once

he has begun. They usually pivot their decisions more on administrative than on educational grounds.

One important reason for this recommendation, aside from the individual child's needs and school policy, is the compelling fact that teachers differ, too. Some teachers have a "style" that is particularly effective with a given age group or with slow or plodding students or with aggressive-interested-energetic students. Teacher-pupil "personality clashes" are common, and this fact should be taken into consideration when students are assigned teachers. We need to give as much attention here to the personality and effectiveness of teachers as we do to individual differences among students, and school policy.

It is, of course, possible for students and parents to misuse a flexible school policy in the matter of substituting courses or changing schools or teachers. But it is also possible for an objective assessment to be made when a seemingly legitimate request is made. Often students have had to stay in classes for which they had no talent or for which they were inadequately prepared simply because they were once assigned to the class. A too hasty registration policy makes many of these problems more common than they should be. In May students often sign up for courses for the following September without realizing or having had the opportunity to know what is really involved or being able to profit from changes of mind over the summer. It would seem more effective to require consideration and written approval from the parents at the time of registration, and an especially planned, realistic, and current consideration by the student, so that any doubts can be fully considered prior to the beginning of the school term.

If they have failed to make sufficient preliminary reconnaissance of the problem, the student and his parents should be given recourse to dropping or changing a subject perhaps up to two to four weeks following the beginning of the new term. This may be less efficient than having signed up correctly in the first place, but it is far better than staying put during the entire semester or the entire year for no productive reason except an administrative one.

Many poor school achievement and related disciplinary problems seem to be caused by the student's poor selection of classes. This is more true at the high school level than at any other. Many students take language courses for which they are poorly prepared. Such courses could either be subdivided into more or less demanding levels (as English often is) or be reserved for the more able students. Language courses and advanced math and science courses are too valuable and difficult to staff well to be wasted on incompetent or disinterested students, and the training of the less able student at the level useful to him and to society is more important than whether he takes advanced math or language courses. To mix indiscriminately the various levels and goals of students is wasteful, reduces achievement, and often triggers disciplinary problems. And to take the rigid attitude that once a student has registered for a course he must see it through, even though he will fail or will not profit from it, is enormously wasteful to everyone's time and energy.

4. Teachers and school officials should be alert to their wearing down and developing unduly pessimistic views of students. There is a strong tendency to pigeonhole youths by their ability levels or conduct patterns, with insufficient emphasis on how to improve both their learning and conduct.

We have often been told by teachers that "John belongs to the——— family; you know we have had three of his brothers, and none is any good." Even if the teacher is correct in this regard, such an attitude will impede solution of a difficulty with a given student. There are even occasional instances where a high school age youngster has been refused admission to a public school because of the bad reputation of older brothers or sisters, previously students in the school. Legally, under these circumstances the family has a right to require the child to be admitted if he meets the general standards, but from a psychological standpoint, they may question putting their youngster in a school prejudiced against him.

On the other hand, in spite of what a student's family record has been teachers have seen many instances where a recalcitrant student has developed well when firm, well-planned measures have been taken to help correct his behavior and study inadequacies. The teacher does reach the end of his rope with some students, but the percentage can be kept very small. And what is more important, school personnel generally can behave most positively if they maintain the policy of trying everything constructive up to its limit before dismissing a student.

Points three and four above are closely related. On the one hand, teachers and administrators may sometimes be too unbending about making *minor* adjustments, such as altering an individual's class, teacher, or curriculum schedule; and at other times they may overlook alternatives when "throwing the book" at the youth when they feel they have been pushed to the limits of their tolerance. Some schools (often reflecting community pressures or social trends) tend to oscillate between holding the student too rigidly to procedures, on the one hand, and too rigidly repudiating him for inadequacies on the other. Flexibility and resourcefulness characterize the most efficient administration and teaching.

5. The average high school student needs much help to learn how to study, how to concentrate, how to outline what he has read, and how to

prepare for examinations. He also needs help with the use of the library and other reference materials and, especially, with the problems of applying these resources over the long run when he has to write reports extending over days or weeks.

EFFECTIVE STRUCTURING OF TEACHING

The general problem of how to study is, of course, closely related to one of the main concerns of this book—the problem of achievement—but it deserves repeated emphasis in various contexts. It probably must rest with each teacher, especially at the junior and senior high levels, to give students some specific help in forming good study habits related to his course. The teacher must be as specific as possible about what is expected from the student. What constitutes a book report in English? Not merely how long it should be (a minor problem, but students often have no idea), but how it should be organized, and what the specific elements are which make up a good report. The teacher cannot afford to leave this to the student's discretion. Some structuring is necessary to achieve the goal— good future report writing.

The same can be said about examinations. Examinations should be frequently given enough so that the student has ample opportunities within a grade period to test his learning against the demands of the course. If only an occasional examination is given, then the student is seriously handicapped in his efforts to learn what is important and what is not. Students may be admonished to find out these things on their own, and some initiative is worthwhile, but it should be remembered that several instructors of the same course will probably differ about what is important and what should be learned and tested. The material itself does not come to the student tagged and evaluated; the teacher has to provide some structuring or teach less effectively than he might.

The teacher should organize his courses so that the student knows definitely and clearly what is expected of him—*how, when*, and *where*. Too little structuring, rather than too much, is the more common error. Good structuring is done by the teacher who presents a comprehensive outline. This outline would include measuring the child's efforts and requirements throughout the six- or nine-week period, perhaps, a semester or, perhaps, even the year. It would delineate what assignments were expected, what outside readings or reports were required, the dates these were due, and the times of the examinations. If possible, the teacher should indicate what kinds of examinations will be given—with examples—whether they will be objective, essay, or a combination of the two. The teacher who assumes the prerogative of when to test, how much to test, or what to test without sharing such information with his students, is wasting the effort and time of himself and the student, for this policy will lead to poorer results than need be.

Is the teacher who follows these strictures simply spoon feeding his students? The teacher wants to increase the student's initiative and thoughtfulness as well as his knowledge about the material. But how are such worthwhile objectives realized? We feel that simply to *present*, smorgasbord-like, a lot of facts, materials, and assignments, is not a useful or productive way to get students to be effectively self-regulating and self-disciplined. Left alone, some may, but many will not, learn in this way how to choose and direct themselves well. The amount of time students often spend on trying to find out what the teacher wants could be better spent on fulfilling more exactly stated requirements of systematic instruction.

In teaching students greater study skills, the emphasis should be placed on the importance of their reading material more than once. A once over lightly practice is common. (Students often think they have studied when they have merely passed their eyes absentmindedly over the material.) Also the use of index cards ("flash cards") to learn, for example, events in history (names, dates, movements, causes and effects) or to study vocabulary lists in foreign languages can be extremely useful.

If the average high school teacher would give the student specific help in how best to study to meet the demands of the particular course, he could probably help students raise their achievement levels appreciably. One way in which the teacher can be instrumental in helping students develop better study habits is to let them read a paragraph or two in class silently and then respond to "probes" which the teacher orally conducts. This helps the student know what issues in the reading material are important, how questions are formulated, and how brief but accurate answers can be given. Extending this from one or two paragraphs to a section or to an entire chapter will greatly enhance the student in learning and in preparing for examinations. Such procedures will help the student develop study skills that will ramify into other courses and other intellectual pursuits.

COPING WITH
MENTAL HEALTH PROBLEMS

Mental health problems of high school students are commonly related to their school achievement and to the uses to which they put themselves in their daily living. But perhaps the greater percentage of emotional problems are somewhat free floating, in that they do not reflect scholastic and achievement problems as directly as they did in the elementary school. Even so, the firming up of one's life in relation to schoolwork and achievement often assists in generally improving morale. This is just as true of the high school student and the adult as it is of any younger individual.

The classroom teacher, the school counselor, and the school psychologist can often help the ailing high school student by observing when the student is failing to live up to his own expectations. By recognizing how school achievement problems often impinge upon problems in social accomplishment or peer group acceptance, broadened scope and effect can be given to the teacher's efforts.

It is important for the classroom teacher and other school personnel to examine a student's daily routine for its close relationship to achievement and related problems. It often surprises the teacher or the beginning counselor to find that many student problems concerning feelings of inadequacy and inferiority, social acceptance, and peer relationships are closely related to the use the student makes of himself in the classroom on an everyday basis. The broader issues of self-regard and self-acceptance cannot be handled very effectively by the average school counselor or classroom teacher on an individual basis, but these people can help the student order his own life more sensibly and efficiently with regard to the limited subject matter the teacher is controlling and thereby, indirectly at least, assist his psychological growth.

Although teachers cannot become therapists, neither should they overlook their role in helping the senior high school student to come to grips with himself by bringing structure to his daily life and by helping him to develop more efficient methods of studying and achievement. This role is as useful at the high school level as at any other.

In short, emotional difficulties mirror one's dissatisfaction with one's self. One of several effective ways of handling such feelings consists of becoming more productive in daily living. The classroom teacher can be extremely helpful to most students in this respect.

MACHINES AS LEARNING AIDS

Reading and other learning or teaching machines are having an impact at the high school level at an increasing pace. Mechanical and electrical apparatus are already fairly common, especially in remedial reading programs. The use and value of these machines is potentially so great that their relevance for the main themes of this book should at least be touched on. Even though machines are still controversial and simply should not be substituted, on economy grounds, for good teachers, their supportive value has been clearly established.

The reading improvement machine, or the pacer, is important because it structures and programs the student's reading in a way that seems likely to increase his speed and comprehension if properly used. The reading improvement machine works with a select bit of material, presents it in a structured and organized way, and lets the student know immediately what his progress is. Thus, it incorporates the main elements of what we have described as an important aspect of the teacher's role in disciplined learning and what is integral in all learning. These factors are: clear presentation of materials, indication of objectives, immediate rendition of the results of the student's efforts (reinforcement), and self-pacing. The reading improvement machine does much more than merely present the material to be learned; it sets up the conditions necessary for learning and allows for the programming of the effort as well as the presentation of results. It also allows tailoring to each student's own level and rate of learning.

To some extent, a good teacher ought to teach as does a good machine. The teacher can learn from the machine to the degree that it has been properly developed along the lines of teaching methods of proven efficiency. Certainly, the good machine should duplicate as many methods as possible of the good teacher. The poor teacher is one who is disorganized in presentation, who only presents and does not follow through, or who does not acquaint his student with results of his work as soon as possible. Machine-programmed learning is systematic and structured; it is the disciplined approach. A good teacher follows the same procedures and, in addition, generates more intangible personal qualities which, at their best, are more likely than machines to attract and hold the attention of the student and to sustain and feed motivation. The teacher as a "reinforcing machine" can be a very powerful adjunct to the teaching or reading machine for presenting and following through on material.

Such machines will almost certainly be used increasingly. After extensive research, the armed forces—which since World War II have provided many other new teaching models for public education in the United States —are widely using programmed teaching. So are business organizations. The various programs against poverty have also stimulated the development of new and broader teaching aids.

Perhaps there are two reasons why the spread of machine-assisted learning is important. First, there are so many people capable of being educated further and needing to be that existing school resources are having to struggle hard to try to meet the need. Second, the machine will probably prove itself to be an exceptionally good teacher, often superior to the poor teacher, and at least judiciously and economically supplementing the good teacher. The machine will carry with it good object lessons. Systematic use and study of it is much easier than research with human teachers, and it can therefore teach us more about learning and educating than is likely to be grasped from present inherently hit-and-miss methods. In time, it can show us in clear ways how effective a disciplined presentation and follow-through can be.

SELECTED READINGS

Bijou, S. W., and D. M. Baer, *Child Development*. New York: Appleton-Century-Crofts, 1961.

Christensen, C. M., "Relationships between pupil achievement pupil affect-need, teacher warmth, and teacher permissiveness." *J. Educ. Psychol.*, 1960, *51*, 174–96.

Cunningham, Ruth, et al. *Understanding Group Behavior of Boys and Girls*. New York: Teachers College, Columbia University, 1951.

Davis, A., and R. J. Havinghurst, *Father of the Man*. Boston: Houghton Mifflin, 1947.

Donahue, George T., and Sol Nichtern, *Teaching the Troubled Child*. New York: The Free Press, 1965.

Holmes, Donald J., *The Adolescent in Psychotherapy*. Boston: Little, Brown, 1964.

Thomas, R. M., *Judging Student Progress*, 2nd ed. London: Longmans, Green 1960.

Ullmann, Leonard P., and Leonard Krasner, *Case Studies in Behavior Modification*. New York: Holt, Rinehart and Winston, 1965.

14

SPECIAL PROBLEMS
OF
DISCIPLINE

So far, we have dealt with four broad disciplinary relationships: general concepts and practices of good discipline; discipline in relation to achievement and social and emotional growth; the improvement of school effectiveness through the home and community; and the development aspects of discipline at different grade levels. Our concern in this chapter will be with some special problems of discipline in the school, particularly in handling delinquent or obstructive behavior.

ADOLESCENTS ON PROBATION

It is not likely that children under the age of twelve or thirteen will be placed on probation. When this does happen, the parents are often more directly involved than the child. Probationary cases under age twelve are most often the result of direct neglect or negligence on the part of the adults. The adolescent, on the other hand, is held responsible for himself in many ways. The fact that he has not always learned to exercise self-control effectively is no argument against training him to do so during the adolescent period. In fact, it is almost impossible to exercise the amount of control over the adolescent that one often can hold over the younger child. The adolescent has to be given a good deal of responsibility because he is exposed to so much freedom.

Probation, when it seems necessary, should be used as part of a retraining plan. It can be an excellent way of saying to the adolescent, "You are being given another chance, let's see what you can do with it. You will be held responsible for yourself, but you know what some of the stresses and strains are likely to be; you are on your own."

The probationary conditions may become complicated. If others know about it, the adolescent may experience much guilt; he may also have to adjust to social ostracism. Many youngsters, formerly accepted by their peers, after being placed on probation find themselves shunned. On the other hand, the adolescent may boast about his probationary status as proof of his prowess.

The school can reduce the adverse consequences of probation. School counselors and principals can coordinate the school and the court; they can interpret the adolescent's legal and social status to the teacher in an attempt to insure that the probationary status does as little harm as possible to the student's everyday life, and they can advise the court on tactful ways to handle its follow-up. The school can try to prevent a situation like the following from arising.

> David, a sixteen-year-old, was put on probation for stealing a car and driving without a license. He was adjusting well to his probationary period of eighteen, months, was visiting his probation officer every two weeks, and behaving in an improved manner at school. All went well for about three months when, during some minor disagreement in a classroom discussion, another youngster reacted personally to David's opinion, saying, "No wonder you're on probation, you're so stubborn and stupid." The teacher not knowing of the probation, was stunned, silent, and ineffectual.

Or a reaction like the following one.

> Fourteen-year-old Michael was caught with three other youngsters about 3 A.M. driving in a stolen taxicab. Looking for some excitement, the boys found the cab unattended with the key under the floor mat, and they had been driving around for two or three hours before; they were being observed by a patrol car at a heavily traveled, well-lighted intersection. Michael, who was driving the car, was the only one apprehended by the police; the others were able to get away in the darkness. Michael was forced to go to Juvenile Court and also Traffic Court. One day at school he was boasting to his friends when the principal overheard him say, "We were able to keep the car going for three or four hours before the 'fuzz' caught up with us. I may try it again and keep off the lighted streets next time."

Both the teacher in the first case and the principal in the second were confused and not sure what they should do. David's teacher had not been told of his probation; and Michael's principal, having no previous experience with juvenile courts, did not know whether he should take Michael seriously and report him to the court or not.

Had the teacher or principal been aware of the situation involving these youngsters each could at least have been prepared to control situations which might arise. Information like this can seldom be kept secret, and the teacher should be trusted to use it properly.

Secondary issues arose in the classroom and on the school grounds with both boys. David was shunned by many of his peers who had formerly liked him or who had at least been friendly toward him. He sensed the rejection of his fellow students and then of the staff. In the case of Michael, his boastfulness had turned the captain of the tennis team against him, and the principal who was basketball coach, too, also developed a distaste for him.

Sometimes students on probation have to leave school early in the afternoon, or they are forced to delay coming into school in the morning in order to make periodic reports to the court. When this situation is understood and planned for, complications may be prevented. If the school, however, does not know that the student must report to the court, excuses to get back into class may be delayed or confused, with the student suffering unnecessarily. On occasion the student who is on probation may use his trips to the court to get out of schoolwork also. Times and places of appearing at the court need to be known by the school in advance so that the student is not able to play one institution against the other.

Schools may need to provide information to the court about the delinquent student's adjustment, his conduct at school, and his previous school record. The court may be able to provide information, which the school has not had, relevant to the student's conduct in his home and in the community. Also, a good report from the school may give reassurance to the court—as it did both in David's and Michael's cases—about his adjustment.

It is common for the court to turn up instances of the probationed student's misconduct in connection with school property or school rules. It would be a misuse of such information if the school were to pile punishment for it upon the student who is already being punished, but it can be useful to the student's development to let him know that the school is aware of this other misconduct and that it expects different behavior from him in the future. For the student in such cases to admit his misbehavior to the school authorities is a useful mental hygiene practice as long as the school uses the information judiciously.

The ramifications of problems connected with handling adolescents on probation are endless. A few general guidelines for their handling may be useful here:

Dont's—Don't allow confidential information to become public. Don't allow other students to openly discuss in class the probationary status of any other youngster. Don't let the probationary status enter into the school's evaluation of the student; keep the disciplinary issue separate unless it is brought in by the student himself. Don't threaten the student with calls to the court about his conduct at school; rather, set up in a discussion with the student, the issues of his conduct as the school sees them if they are relevant to his school behavior and tell him of the school's responsibility to the court.

Do's—Do tell the student—the counselor or principal can do this—that school personnel know of his probationary status and that they are interested in helping him live up to its requirements. Do encourage him to call upon the school for counseling if he wishes it—not as a way for him to gain sympathy or to avoid the probationary requirements but to help him improve his standing. Do let the court know of improvements in the probationary student's conduct and schoolwork and of honors he may gain. Do try to regard the probationary student as otherwise normal; encourage him to regard himself as capable of maturing behavior in the school environment. Do attempt to treat him at all times without irrelevant regard to his disciplinary status; when his probation is over, try to let it drop from all consideration. Do assume that most students will adjust to their probationary period and get along normally thereafter and that they will not necessarily be branded for life nor emotionally scarred from it.

UNCOOPERATIVE PARENTS

Uncooperative parents of a youngster of any age present serious difficulties to school personnel. School staff often despair of trying to help the child of uncooperative parents. There is no easy road to the solution of this problem. Care must be taken, however, not to label the parents "hopeless" before making strenuous efforts to convince them of the importance of the child's problems and the need for their help.

Most often parents are uncooperative with the school because they disagree with the school as to the nature of the child's difficulties or how the difficulties should be managed. The school, on the other hand, knows its problems with the child very well and is trying to get the parent to share this concern. The school may feel that the parents are insensitive; the parents may feel that the school is making an issue where they see none.

Very frequently, these impasses require the help of an outsider, a professional third party, to mediate and interpret the problem to both the school and the parents. An example of such a logjam was the following situation:

> Stanley, a nine-year-old fourth grader, was a conduct problem at school as well as an underachiever. He had scored in the "bright-normal" intelligence range (IQ 116) but failed to work up to his capacity. The school talked with the parents about Stanley's misbehavior and his relatively poor achievement. The school felt that the parents simply acknowledged Stanley's problems but did nothing about them; they seemed to take the attitude that the school should solve its problems with Stanley at school, since they did

so at home. After several conferences matters grew worse, leading to tension between home and school, with Stanley caught in the middle. His parents insisted, for example, that he knew his spelling words when he wrote them at home; if he did not know them at school, well that was the school's problem. They asked what was going on at school that made Stanley's performance so precarious when he had shown evidence of knowledge at home. The school felt unfairly criticized and blamed. School and home each expressed its own feelings and intentions but failed to provide effective help for Stanley. Since an impasse had been reached, the school and parents agreed to seek outside professional consultation ot help solve their mutual problem.

A similar problem arose in the case of:

> Bill, a seven-year-old second grader, who had had difficulty playing with other children because they made fun of his awkward and uncoordinated movements. When the school consulted the parents about this, they dismissed it as simply an expression of Bill's lack of interest in physical activities. However, the principal and several teachers observed the boy at play and surmised there was a more serious problem. After a year of note writing and conferences between school and home, the parents finally scheduled Bill for a neurological and psychological examination. The result was a diagnosis of minimal brain damage, and special provisions for Bill's schooling followed. Here the school had acted in a way to alert the parents to a long-range problem, which they had formerly dismissed as not requiring special attention.

Sometimes parents feel that any school problem with the child is up to the school to settle. Even when they see problems at home, parents sometimes take this attitude, hoping the school will take care of the matter. And sometimes parents feel so offended by the school's attitude that any cooperation is precluded. Often parents simply take their child out of the school, and that ends the problem, temporarily.

Schools can, however, take several steps when they believe they have met thoroughly uncooperative parents. First, however, it should be clear that they tried to their limit to gain cooperation. Sometimes still further negotiations can resolve the problem. In the event of a seemingly intractable impasse, however, the school can do the following:

1. Call in school personnel from other schools and invite them to interview the parents, observe the child, or consult with the teacher and principal in the child's school.
2. Call in the juvenile court or other authorities if the difficulty with the child involves broad and serious disciplinary issues or other problems. It is important that the court be viewed as a moderator rather than as a policeman. The same is true for any medical or psychological agent outside the school.

3. Refer the parents to an outside specialist—for example, a child psychologist specializing in problems of the type in question or a physician or neurologist, where the problems appear to be largely medical. The school can give the parents the names of several specialists and let the parents choose one. An outside specialist can often be more objective and neutral than other school personnel would be. And a psychologist can use and interpret special tests as well.
4. Simply ask the parents in question to take the child out of the school system, since they seem unwilling to negotiate or take suggestions. We feel that this request should be only a last resort and that shifting the child to a different teacher or a different school within a school system might well be tried first.

Many problems with children can be fairly easily solved if one has the parents' cooperation. On the other hand, any problem becomes more difficult when parents will not or seem unable to cooperate. In these more refractory cases the problem with the child seems to recede into the background, and the issues begin to hinge on communication between school and parents. Children are generally much easier to deal with than adults—especially adults who bring to the controversy many negative attitudes toward the school.

School personnel must be careful not to blame the parents in general ways. They should keep to the issues at hand so that general stereotyped feelings are not called into play. The wider the stage of emotional conflict on which home-school controversies are played, the greater is the likelihood that no solution will be reached.

Keeping any discussion close to the questions at hand is important. One principal collected examples of a child's work for a whole semester, then called in the parents and showed them how the child had failed to progress at school. This principal also accumulated papers on the same topics and assignments of an average student, and a similar list of achievements of a student who was at the same intellectual level as the son of the parents called in for the conference. In this way, the principal made his point so clearly that the parents readily accepted the problem and agreed to seek help.

VALUE OF TEMPORARY EXPULSION FROM SCHOOL

Most schools hate to expel a student; they feel it is a reflection on the school and engenders more negative and damaging attitudes toward education in parents and the student. Most principals want to use expulsion only as a last resort. As the term is used here, "expulsion" refers to the act of sending the child away from school for periods ranging from a few hours to several months, or permanently. It might occasionally need to be permanent; however, this discussion will be concerned with the shorter, more strategic, less final measures which can have constructive features that are often overlooked.

In short, when a teacher has reached an impasse with a child despite the use of all ordinary classroom measures, it is sometimes of value to say, "Well, John, since you seem unwilling to behave, I think it is best for you to go home for the rest of the day." Or, "Since you will not work or behave here, I am going to call your mother and have her take you home so that you can do your work there for the rest of the day."

This tactic has worked very well with a wide variety of recalcitrant youngsters, particularly those at the elementary and junior high level. It has to be managed with considerably greater care at the high school level.

A teacher should contact a parent to let him know that such a procedure is contemplated. The principal's permission and support should also be obtained, preferably in writing. The parent can either come to school to get the child, have a taxi sent, or make some other appropriate arrangement. If the child lives within walking distance, the parent can simply watch for the child or go halfway to meet him. The exact implementation of the procedure will vary. Maximum value is obtained when all adults concerned are resolute about carrying out the temporary expulsion.

Some general safeguards need to be considered. Give the child a warning that says to him he will be sent home if he does not change his ways. Don't send him home without sufficient notice to the home. Let the child know that he is to remain home for the rest of the school day and that he will be expected to complete his unfinished work. He is not to go home to watch television, play outside, or go to local stores. He is to go home to work on the materials he was not working on at school. He is, of course, to return to the school at a specified time with the work finished. He should know that the same process will be repeated the following day if he does not rectify the behavior.

Some teachers and school personnel may feel that sending a child home is too traumatic, too abrupt, or too drastic. If properly handled, this need not be the case. However, it can be misused—like other corrective action. But in any case this measure should never be undertaken carelessly or thoughtlessly.

Most disciplinary techniques depend finally on how they are employed, by whom, and with what attitudes. The measure of sending the child home can be very salutary if properly executed. Other details of this approach have been discussed in earlier chapters. Why does this method of temporary expulsion work? What are its advantages? It works, it seems, for two main reasons. First, because it brings to a stop the behavior which is causing trouble for the child in the classroom. If he is "cutting up," it is a way of stopping this. Second, it provides a constructive recourse for the child to follow. In effect it says, "Here in this altered situation you can get your work done without any distractions; we will do what we can to see that you get the work done." Earlier chapters have been concerned with the importance of the corrective positive aspects of setting alternatives for children (as opposed to punishment). This is a good example of that course.

Parents will usually cooperate fully with a temporary expulsion plan if they know what is intended, what the value of the action is, and how it relates to them. It would not do to send a child home and then call the parents to inform them of the act. In fact it is doubtful that most state laws would allow the school to take such an action. The parents need to know that they should not punish the child when he comes home, that they should not play up the classroom misbehavior. They should see that the child begins work in an objective fashion, completes his unfinished business, and has no recourse to such forms of recreation as television.

In the case of older children, say, of junior or senior high school age, it is sometimes useful to set up a temporary expulsion plan which involves more than a few hours or one day. Thus a junior high school youth who is a difficult disciplinary problem may be expelled for several days—the period terminating upon his parents' application for his return to school. Such an application will often involve a full rehearsal of the issues with the youth and parental support in a way which might not have been elicited in earlier attempts. The pressures from the youth's peer group often are more powerful than one might suppose and often have a beneficial effect. The school can show a constructive strength in a temporary expulsion plan, provided it is carried out with planning and skill and provided the youth's grounds for reentry to school are explicitly spelled out.

WHEN IS A TEMPORARY EXPULSION PLAN INEXPEDIENT?

An expulsion plan is inexpedient when the youth (especially if of junior high age or older) does not want to attend school anyhow. Expulsion, in this case, plays into the youth's hands. Its ineffectiveness would stem from a lack of knowledge of the youth's values. A temporary expulsion is not advisable if school personnel are against it or if they cannot see its inherent advantages even if well executed. For the same reasons, if the parents do not approve of such a measure or do not wish to cooperate, it is not likely to succeed in its purpose.

Temporary school expulsion plans seem to work best when there is a combination of conduct and achievement problems; or where there is a

conduct problem which is at least indirectly related to ach'
the child misbehaves in lieu of doing his schoolwork. I
whether a child should be sent home to do unfinished work it n̄ɔ
a conduct problem. The reason school expulsion plans have not been u̇
more often or more constructively would seem to lie in the fact that their
constructive features have not been considered and that they have been
regarded entirely or primarily as negative and punitive or hostile. Also it
takes special efforts to get such a plan into operation in a constructive
fashion. With renewed interest in good discipline in the modern constructive sense of the term, such measures as temporary school expulsion can be
used more commonly with good effect.

SELECTED READINGS

AMSTERDAM, RUTH, *Constructive Classroom Discipline and Practice*. New York:
Comet Press Books, 1957.

BONNEY, MERL E., *Mental Health in Education*. Boston: Allyn and Bacon, 1960.

CHAMBERLIN, LESLIE J., "Group behavior and discipline." *The Clearing House*,
1966, *41*, 92–95.

EYSENCK, H. J., "Learning theory and behavior therapy." *J. Mental Science*,
1959, *105*, 61–75.

GNAGEY, WILLIAM J., *Controlling Classroom Misbehavior: What Research Says to
the Teacher*. Washington, D.C.: American Education Research Association of
the N.E.A., 1965.

HARING, NORRIS G., and E. LAKIN PHILLIPS, *Educating Emotionally Disturbed
Children*. New York: McGraw-Hill, 1962.

WAHLER, R. G., G. H. WINKEL, R. F. PETERSON, and D. C. MORRISON, "Mothers
as behavior therapists for their children." *Behavior Research and Therapy*, 1965,
3, 113–24.

WOODRUFF, ASAHEL D., "Discipline," in *Encyclopedia of Educational Research*,
3d ed. New York: Macmillan, 1960.

15

RECAPITULATION

This has been a book on a neglected and confused topic—good discipline and its relationships to achievement and mental health.

What is good discipline? It is not, we believe, a woodshed technique. It is not a matter of punishment nor a generally punitive attitude. It does involve setting up clear educational and behavioral standards and goals in advance, letting the child know how the goals can be achieved, and finding ways to implement the process.

We do not emphasize doing things *for* the child or *to* the child but, rather, the development of a *structure* which provides the best opportunities for the child to learn, achieve, and develop emotional and social maturity on his own. Structure is the crux of the matter. *Structure* is a definite concept; it is a way to come to grips with important problems. It is a kind of summary term synonymous with "order" and "planned learning," with effective feedback or reinforcement, and with consistency over time.

Good discipline is systematic, ordered learning. Ordered learning promotes achievement and performance. Good discipline in school helps to promote self-discipline, generally as a habitual way of behaving. Self-discipline contributes to self-assurance and thus affects one's outlook and confidence. Self-discipline becomes self-control.

We have tried to rethink with you some of the traditional problems in education and child development and of mental health in relation to them. We have proposed that you, as teachers or child counselors and trainers, try to become more active, more planful, more disciplined in handling average children in the classroom as well as problem children. Where problems in achievement or conduct or mental health exist and persist, those who are willing to try new approaches—when such activity is well considered—are the ones most likely to solve the problems. It is fruitless to continue with practices which are not working.

Children who do not concentrate, children who cannot remember, children who seem to learn but forget or misapply their knowledge, children who play all the time and do not work, children who will not cooperate or who continually stir up confusion and trouble, children who seem to try but do not achieve—what is wrong with all these? No one matter is wrong with all of them, but one theme does tend to run through all these cases and seems to play an important role in their plights. It is often a lack of good discipline in their environment and a lack of self-discipline in their own personal organization. Outer disorder leads to internal distress, outer disorder promotes insecurity.

Even unhappy children are included here. Often they are unhappy because they do not use themselves well. This is not usually because they have been misplaced in school (although this must be considered) but because they have drifted into misplacement through months or years of misapplication of their energies. Personal disorder, educational disorder, and other disorders result—vicious circles, dead-ends.

Should we let them be? Do we leave them alone and let them try to solve their problems on their own? In rare instances, perhaps Yes, at least for a time or when especially difficult circumstances are likely to pass. In the overwhelming majority of cases, No. Usually this will only allow them to perpetuate their poor use of themselves. Past behavior is the best predictor of future behavior unless something or somebody intervenes to promote change. Some order has to be brought out of their educational and personal chaos. Often the reason for delaying seems to be concern about the remedial measures; too often they are formidable, lengthy, threatening, intense, expensive, inconvenient, or isolated.

Too many teachers have often been too anxious or indifferent to develop or apply relatively simple, sensible, practical remedies. The term "emotional disorder" or "mental illness" has frightened too many people into inaction and into a feeling of futility about trying to solve problems. Trying new ways of helping the child through well-disciplined learning efforts, kindly and reasonably applied, will not injure the child; when injury is feared, good discipline is being confused with punishment or hostile attitudes. Increasing the meaning, value, and effectiveness of work and responsibility and the enjoyment of them will not harm the child, it will help him. And almost any teacher can help most children reach this goal.

We have emphasized the concept of good discipline because we think it has been neglected and misunderstood. We think it is essential to accomplishment and to mental health. It is also very practical to develop good discipline in the classroom.

Achievement is increased when the child can be directed to learn more effectively, or, in other words, to discriminate what is needed, relevant, useful, and important from what is not.

Motivation, readiness for learning, interest in work—all are important and are improved by a "set" to learn, which the classroom teacher can arrange and structure. Once the child begins to behave in the desired way, reinforcements are so available and so nourishing that behavior can readily be guided in desirable directions.

Mental health is also furthered by helping the child gain an objectively good opinion of himself.

Education has to be more than "served up" to the child. Learning situations cannot merely be presented. Ways must be provided for the child to be active with respect to the material. Too much has rested upon the techniques of presentation; too little has concerned developing an active role, leading to proper discriminations by the student himself.

Fads in discipline have come and gone, but there has remained a hard core of realistic practices which good teachers have always respected and followed. Efforts to understand children have too often led teachers and other adults working with children into a kind of passive contemplation, an often anxious and static posture. The child must be understood, to be sure, but his teachers and others also have to act upon this understanding; otherwise, it is not being tested to determine whether it is true and useful.

The child starts school; he passes through the middle grades; he goes on to high school and to eventual graduation; and he learns what the school program teaches. He goes to school at an appointed time each day; he goes to classes in a prescribed schedule; this is order. This does not mean that he has no choice nor flexibility, but it means that choice and flexibility are within predetermined bounds.

We are aware of the fact that this verbal rendition of well-ordered or structured learning and achievement is subject to attritional factors and to many distractions. Society itself, with its underprivileged and disadvantaged segments, makes orderly living difficult; and orderly learning in school is even more of a problem. Various handicapping conditions— sensory, motor, intellectual, or emotional—also make learning, achieving, and mental health difficult to come by. We know as teachers and parents that our well-laid plans can often fail to materialize because we do not pay enough attention to the individual and social realities with which a child lives while he learns. Calling attention to these attritional factors may make the teacher more wary, self-critical in a positive sense, and better able to help not only the average child but those presenting unusual problems of one type or another.

The child is not well ordered or disciplined at the start. He has to develop these ways of behaving, just as does a team, a factory, or a society. The child can be led to see in time as his experience accumulates, that an ordering of his life is important. So is an ordering of his educational day and program.

We have tried to develop practical ways of implementing these concepts: Know the child; set up the learning situation so that he will be active; set up consequences that he knows will be associated with his choices; keep the goals specific and clear; keep them proportionate to his intellectual capacity. Stay with him; be patient, firm, consistent. Keep the expectations clear and fair; have the rewards follow normally and inherently upon successful completion of the work; expect obstacles and learn to handle them as they arrive.

This is the way anyone achieves anything worthwhile. Self-disciplined work is vital to obtain one's satisfaction. The child has to learn, in many small and painstaking ways, how life (including school) realistically makes demands upon him.

No matter his age, no matter his ability and limitations, these concepts will apply to the child at his own level, properly individualized, and can enhance his achievement and his mental health. It is the perpetual good fortune and splendid responsibility of the teacher to be able to help the young to mature and to achieve.

INDEX